Crooked Paths to Allotment

C. JOSEPH GENETIN-PILAWA

Crooked Paths to Allotment

The Fight over Federal Indian Policy
after the Civil War

THE UNIVERSITY OF NORTH CAROLINA PRESS
CHAPEL HILL

FIRST PEOPLES

NEW DIRECTIONS IN INDIGENOUS STUDIES

*Publication of this book was made possible, in part, by
a grant from the Andrew W. Mellon Foundation.*

© 2012 The University of North Carolina Press
All rights reserved
Manufactured in the United States of America
Set in Minion
by codeMantra
The paper in this book meets the guidelines for permanence and
durability of the Committee on Production Guidelines for Book
Longevity of the Council on Library Resources.

The University of North Carolina Press has been a member
of the Green Press Initiative since 2003.

Library of Congress Cataloging-in-Publication Data
Genetin-Pilawa, C. Joseph.
Crooked paths to allotment :
the fight over federal Indian policy after the Civil war /
C. Joseph Genetin-Pilawa.
p. cm. — (First peoples : new directions in indigenous studies)
Includes bibliographical references and index.
ISBN 978-0-8078-3576-0 (cloth : alk. paper)
1. Indians of North America—Land tenure. 2. Indians of North America—Government
relations. 3. Indian allotments—United States—History. 4. Allotment of lands—
United States—History. 5. Self-determination, National—United States—History.
6. United States—Politics and government. 7. United States—Social policy.
8. United States—Race relations. I. Title.
E98.L3G46 2012
323.1197—dc23
2012010854
16 15 14 13 12   5 4 3 2 1

For Sara, Parker, and Onnalea
and in loving memory of my grandfather
Joseph Genetin (1927–2004)

Contents

Illustrations

Acknowledgments

Although I wouldn't understand it until much later, the ideas for this book began in discussions I had and short essays I had written many years ago at Bowling Green State University. Rachel Buff, Liette Gidlow, Donald Nieman, Robert Buffington, and Dave Haus pushed me to think critically about policy reform, and about history as a profession. Edmund Danziger, more than anyone else in my early education, encouraged me to understand how the telling of history is both demanding and vital, and perhaps even more importantly, he introduced me to Indigenous people in both the United States and Canada who drove that point home. He is a steadfast mentor and role model to this day.

I owe an immense debt of gratitude to scholars and teachers at Michigan State University. Susan Sleeper-Smith has provided gentle guidance and sharp scholarly critique through every stage of this project, and her influence is apparent throughout the entire book. She has been a most wonderful adviser, and I am a better scholar, professional, and person because of her. Though small in stature, Maureen Flanagan is an intellectual giant, and I want to thank her for her unflagging support and inspiration as she read and reread versions of this book. She is one of the sharpest critics I have ever had, and my work has benefitted greatly from her keen eye. Gordon Stewart's kind words and confidence in me has never failed to brighten my spirits and strengthen my resolve. I hope that forty-plus years into my own career I can maintain the enthusiastic intellectual curiosity and positive attitude that he demonstrates. Mindy Morgan's excitement about my research and Scott Michaelsen's deep theoretical insights pushed me to clarify my ideas and make them accessible to a larger audience. Many other faculty members at MSU gave generously of their time reading and discussing parts of these chapters. Thomas Summerhill encouraged me delve deeply into New York State history, David Bailey pushed me to remember the importance of the narrative, Mark Kornbluh and Lisa Fine urged me to connect the events I was studying to broader issues in U.S. history, and Laurent Dubois urged me to think about the evolution of U.S. settler colonialism in a global context.

The Committee on Institutional Cooperation-American Indian Studies Consortium played a profoundly important role in my education. Through it I had the opportunity to meet and work with some of the most amazingly talented and influential scholars. I would like to thank all of the members who listened to and commented on the various parts of these chapters at CIC-AIS meetings, including Frederick Hoxie, Brian Hosmer, Jeani O'Brien-Kehoe, Brenda Child, Dawn Marsh, Lucy Murphy, Ray Fogelson, Ray DeMallie, and Larry Nesper. Through the CIC-AIS, I also had the opportunity to exchange ideas and develop great friendships with Jennifer Giuliano, Michel Hogue, Jenny Tone-Pah-Hote, Jill Doerfler, and Chantal Norrgard. It was also through the consortium that I met Cathleen Cahill, and her generosity, support, and advice on everything from scholarship to parenting have meant very much to me. Our work overlaps in many ways, and at the end of dozens of conversations, one or the other of us has said, "You have to publish this already—I need to cite it!"

As this book developed, many scholars read parts of chapters or conference papers that would become chapters. Whether they were aware of it or not, Philip Deloria, Brian Balogh, Rebecca Kugel, Andrew Denson, and Deena Gonzalez all pushed me to clarify my arguments and develop my analysis in important ways. Kevin Bruyneel and Jean Dennison participated in an authors' workshop and read several chapters of the penultimate draft. Jean's suggestions for ways to consider political conflict and Kevin's advice about establishing my own voice in the text and leading the reader through the argument have made this a much clearer and stronger book. Greg Dowd read a version of the complete manuscript and offered critical feedback and encouragement at an early stage. Jacki Rand read and reread the manuscript as I revised it for publication. Her sharp critique helped me reshape its focus, and the image of her smiling while reading through my historiographical footnotes warms my heart. Jeffrey Ostler, who also read the complete manuscript through several rounds of revisions, encouraged me to clarify my theoretical foundation and sharpened my arguments by drawing my attention to the interconnectedness of Ely Parker's reform ideas as he articulated them following the Civil War. This is a much stronger book because of his generosity and insight.

I've had the pleasure of making this scholarly journey with two "intellectual siblings." We were undergraduate history majors together, though at different stages, and despite life's many twists and turns, they've remained pillars of support for me. My older "sibling," James Buss, has read and commented upon every single page of this book . . . many times. We've traveled to libraries, archives, and conferences together across the country, and although he beat me to the punch (a classic older brother move), and said it in his acknowledgments first, this book is largely a product of our long friendship. Our younger "sibling," Kristalyn Shefveland, has offered chapter comments, supportive sarcasm, and the occasional reality check. Although she jokes that she's always saying, "hey guys, c'mon, wait up," she is one of the strongest and most independent people I know.

I owe a huge debt to all of the librarians and archivists who assisted me in my research and the institutions that supported this project financially. For a scholar of American Indian history, the Newberry Library is one of the greatest and most welcoming places to work. I want to thank the friendly staff at the Newberry and especially at the D'Arcy McNickle Center for American Indian and Indigenous Studies. At the American Philosophical Society Library, J. J. Ahern's and Roy Goodman's enthusiasm for my work and knowledge of the collections helped immensely. I am also grateful to Daniel K. Richter, who opened his home to me and provided opportunities at the McNeil Center for Early American Studies on the campus of the University of Pennsylvania. The staff of the Rush Rhees Library at the University of Rochester introduced me to the papers of Lewis Henry Morgan and Arthur Parker. I want to thank Sarah DeSanctis and Mary Huth, in particular, for their hospitality. Paul Mercer, James Folts, and Chris Beauregard, as well as the rest of the staff at the New York State Archives, made my time there well spent. I want to thank Olga Tsapina at the Huntington Library for locating and shipping several materials that were crucial to the completion of this project. It was only at the very end of this process that I got the opportunity to visit the beautiful library itself. The librarians and archivists at the National Archives and Records Administration in Washington, D.C., and College Park, Maryland, kindly helped me navigate the complex and voluminous Record Group 75. Finally, I have the utmost respect for and gratitude to Laura Schiefer and the other staff members of the Buffalo and Erie County Historical Society Library. They do a wonderful job with minimal resources. The Schewe Library staff, especially Martin Gallas, Mike Westbrook, and Beth Bala offered expert support and brought exceptional research materials to our small, liberal arts campus for me to use. At a very late stage, Brittney Thomas offered her time and expertise in finding and securing images and permissions.

My research benefited from the financial support of the American Historical Association in the form of two Littleton-Griswold Grants for Research in United States Legal History and an Albert Beveridge Grant. I was also aided by a CIC-AIS/Newberry Library Fellowship and an American Philosophical Society Library Resident Research Fellowship (supported by the Phillips Fund for Native American Research). The History Department at Michigan State University funded initial research in the form of a Research Enhancement Fellowship, and Illinois College offered generous financial support during the revision stage, as did the First Peoples: New Directions in Indigenous Studies initiative.

I was welcomed into Illinois College with open arms. As I transitioned into professional life, colleagues and friends there provided guidance and good humor. I especially wish to thank Elizabeth Tobin, Karen Dean, Steve Hochstadt, Robert Kunath, Jenny Barker-Devine, and Winston Wells. It would be hard to imagine a kinder and more thoughtful faculty than the one in our small liberal arts community. For able research assistance, I'd also like to thank IC students Marlee Graser and Mitch Whightsil.

The editorial staff at UNC Press has been incredibly kind and helpful at every stage of this process. Mark Simpson-Vos, editor extraordaire, has been absolutely amazing as a mentor and guide to the world of academic publishing. I sincerely appreciate his willingness to read my rough manuscript, envision its potential, and then provide the direction and opportunities to make it happen. Tema Larter and Zachary Read have answered my naive questions with patience and wit, while Mary Caviness has clarified and improved the prose on almost every page of this book. At First Peoples, Natasha Varner has been enthusiastic, insightful, and motivating. Meeting her and sharing meals and conversations at conferences and workshops has been a lot of fun. Abby Mogollon is always available to offer advice and expertise, and I appreciate that greatly.

Graduate school friends fostered this project in many ways (and often provided much-needed distraction). I especially want to thank Heath Bowen, Carlos Alemán, Dan Dalrymple, and Ben Sawyer. I am also grateful for the wonderful conversations I had with the rest of the "room 8" folks and others at MSU, including Jaime McLean Dalrymple, Micalee Sullivan, Jason Friedman, Ted Mitchell, Andrea Vicente, Lindsey Gish, Brandon Miller, Thomas Henthorn, Ryan Pettengill, Sakina Hughes, and Megan McCullen. More recently, colleagues and friends from across North America have provided support, kind words, and advice, including Nancy Shoemaker, Katie Magee Labelle, Omeasoo Butt, Coll Thrush, Alyssa Mt. Pleasant, Audra Simpson, Mishuana Goeman, Meg McCune, and Justin Carroll.

I've been amazingly lucky to be surrounded by strong women my entire life. These members of my family have provided inspiration, and I am most grateful to them. My mom, Judee Genetin—a lifelong learner (and teacher)—demonstrated a love of reading to me at a very young age. Her love and confidence motivates me every minute. She's always encouraged me to pursue my own dreams, and I have taken her words and actions to heart. My grandma, Carol Genetin, inspired me to be creative and to think in new and colorful ways. If any part of this book paints a vivid picture, it's because of her influence. I am also blessed with amazing siblings.

Victoria's drive, convictions, and compassion; Elle's strength and willpower; and Jon-Michael's adventurous spirit and sharp wit are all inspiring in their own ways. My niece Isis's profound curiosity has inspired me as well. I am so thankful for their patience and love. My grandpa, Joe Genetin, did not live to see this project finished, but I know he would have been proud. This book is dedicated, in part, to his memory.

I also had the honor of being welcomed into another family as I worked on this book. I want to thank Jane and Dick Wright, Rich and Noah Wright, Christine Toma, and Amy and Justin Wainwright for their generosity and interest, as well as their support. Jane and Dick helped care for my newborn twins throughout the revision process and made my absences less disruptive.

My twin son and daughter, Parker and Onnalea, have been as patient and understanding as fetuses/infants/toddlers can be. They waited to be born until after I finished drafting a new first chapter, they sang and danced for me via Skype as I researched and presented at various conferences, and they put up with my daily absences as I wrote and revised. They've lived their entire lives with this book, but their presence reminds me what is truly important in this world and have changed my perceptions in both small and profound ways. Finally, I want to thank my partner, Sara. Without her, writing this book would have been far less rewarding. Years ago I asked if she would be willing to share this journey and these adventures. I am so thankful she said yes. To quote Ely Parker (in reference to his own spouse): "She is the one woman in all the world for me." Thank you, Sara, for putting up with the research trips and long hours, and for your love, patience, and support!

Crooked Paths to Allotment

Introduction

On April 9, 1865, General Ulysses S. Grant entered Wilmer McLean's parlor at Appomattox Court House and introduced his personal staff to Confederate general Robert E. Lee. Lee welcomed each man with a courteous, if condescending, handshake and greeting. That was until he saw Ely S. Parker, a Tonawanda Seneca man from New York State and Grant's personal military secretary. Witnesses in McLean's parlor reported that Lee became visibly angered at the presence of Parker, who he, at the sight of his darker complexion, mistook for African American. He thought Grant was insulting him by inviting such a person to the surrender negotiations. According to this oft-told tale, onlookers feared the negotiations were going to end immediately. Lee, realizing his mistake, composed himself and extended a hand, looked directly into Parker's eyes, and said, "I am glad to see one real American here." Parker grasped Lee's hand and replied, "We are all Americans."[1] Or, so the story goes.

It's impossible to know if this exchange actually occurred, but the story's message is significant regardless. At the very birth of the Reconstruction era, Parker's statement personified what many Americans believed would be the legacy of the Civil War—that in the end, the nation would overcome sectional differences and racial tensions. Even his presence—an Indian man—at this significant historical moment indicated the optimism that characterized the surrender. It also illustrates historian Hannah Rosen's recent characterization of the early post–Civil War period as "the beginning of a brief era in the United States of an imperfect but nonetheless far more inclusive political community and nation."[2] Possibility was the politics of the moment.

When we look back from the twenty-first century, however, Parker's response to Lee seems foreign, and perhaps a bit naive—his words and role at Appomattox fade into the recesses of an American collective memory that has come to emphasize a romanticized "lost cause" and political reunion over racial reconstruction. Clearly events in the mid- to late nineteenth century changed the ways Americans conceptualized notions of postwar reconciliation, reform, and the position of nonwhite thinkers and reformers within the processes of government—or as Heather Cox Richardson's influential book *West from Appomattox* recently revealed: "Postwar struggles over the role of government in society drove the transformation of Lincoln's midcentury vision of opportunity for all into the middle-class imperialism of [Theodore] Roosevelt's era."[3] In very real ways, the policies of dispossession and forced assimilation that won out in the late 1800s had profoundly disruptive and damaging results. But it could have gone differently.

In this book about the politics of Indian policy making, I dwell on several historical "moments"—moments that force us to stop and reconsider assumptions about the trajectory of American history and the Native experience, including paths not taken; moments that reveal the alternative possibilities that existed in the development of U.S. colonialism, or what might have been; moments in which power was questioned, policies debated, and uncontested "progress," well . . . contested. I argue that at several particular moments in the mid- to late nineteenth century, genuine reform alternatives emerged that destabilized—if only briefly—the status quo in federal Indian policy development. These constitutive moments—periods in which conflicts developed surrounding political issues that had previously seemed uncontested—revealed the fluidity and shiftiness of American colonialism as reformers pushed to roll back or modify policy directives.

Alternative reformers opposed forced land allotment, efforts to replace customary cultural and political practices within Indian communities with structures and values based on Euro-American models, mandatory Christian education for Indian youth, and compulsory participation in the market economy.[4] None of these policies could succeed, mainstream assimilationists believed, without the complete and total confinement of Indian people by the government.[5] Alternative reformers urged lawmakers to consider other approaches—pathways that would allow tribal nations and individuals time and opportunities to assimilate on their own terms and timelines, or perhaps not at all. They wanted to protect tribal landownership and sovereignty, to provide educational opportunities and capital, and to develop industry and agriculture.

These moments, though, also illuminate the strength and pervasiveness of American colonial thought as state actors consolidated or reconsolidated political power and repressed alternative pathways. While alternative efforts often failed to create lasting government reform, many of the reformers I focus upon in the following chapters introduced ideas and policy frameworks that cumulatively established a tradition of dissent against disruptive colonial governance.[6]

If the intellectual development of federal Indian policy in the nineteenth century was to be mapped out spatially, it would not resemble a singular, linear path leading directly toward allotment but rather a crooked path with curves and bends, or even a set of paths that dovetailed and separated at various points along the terrain. While it might be the case that mainstream reformers of the nineteenth century saw the development of land allotment and programs of coercive assimilation as the foregone conclusion of the "Indian problem," I think it is a mistake to allow their assumptions to guide our scholarly premises.[7]

By shifting the interpretive lens to focus on constitutive moments and viable alternatives, I re-center the discussion onto historical characters that often exist on the periphery of policy studies. Among the many reformers and activists who populate these pages, several stand out and require brief introduction here. Ely S. Parker and Thomas A. Bland were contested figures. In their careers they confronted powerful political opponents, and in the public discourse surrounding their policy reforms, their own characters came under fire. Since their deaths, both in popular memory and in the scholarly literature, their lives have been described as controversial, and their legacies themselves are contested.

Ely S. Parker—the Tonawanda Seneca leader who served with General Grant during the Civil War—became in its aftermath a military adviser on Indian affairs, then a peace commissioner in the West, and the first (and only in the nineteenth century) commissioner of the Office of Indian Affairs (OIA) who was himself Indigenous. Parker brought to his position a decade of experience working as an advocate for New York's Native nations and viewed Reconstruction as a moment of opportunity for a potential recasting of the relationship between Indian people and the United States, or at the very least, a moment to stop and question the prevailing framework of Indian confinement in federal policy.

Parker's alternative agenda differed from mainstream assimilationists in the high value he placed on enforcing existing treaties exactly as they were written, even if that meant adversely effecting non-Native settlement (or conversely, if it meant enforcing fraudulent or otherwise unjust treaties). Mainstream assimilationists, in certain circumstances, were willing to ignore treaty stipulations if they facilitated their larger goals. Parker would consider using the military to enforce treaties and to help implement social policy, but he did not want the military to engage Native people violently unless it was absolutely necessary and only as a last resort. Also distinctive to Parker was his effort to slow the pace of assimilation and provide opportunities for Indigenous nations to incorporate themselves how and when they chose. He sought to persuade Indigenous communities that incorporating within the United States could be positive and beneficial rather than forcing them to assimilate by whatever

Colonel Ely S. Parker, ca. 1860–1865. Courtesy of the
National Archives and Records Administration, College Park, Md.

means necessary, as quickly as possible. Finally, Parker, more so than most of his contemporaries, was fully convinced of the capabilities of Native people.

It is important to note, however, that Parker's moment on the federal level was short (his primary influence was strongest from 1867 to 1871). His alternative agenda was in the process of flux and had been only partially articulated when mainstream assimilationists swiftly and forcefully repressed it. That his opponents moved so quickly, though, reveals the very real fears they had concerning his ideas.

As a Native leader who chose to work within U.S. systems of governance, Parker was and remains a controversial character—a hero to some, a traitor to others. In the research for this book, I have read every bit of his writing available in libraries and archives across the country. Having done so, I would suggest that he was more complicated than that. To gloss over Parker's complexities is to fail to recognize the contradictions and inconsistencies of nineteenth-century federal Indian policy.

Thomas A. Bland—a second contested and often peripheral figure in the historical literature—was born in 1830 and spent most of his early life in Indiana. Trained as a physician, he served as a surgeon in the Civil War and later in the 1880s became a staunch opponent of the more often discussed "Friends of the Indian." His Midwestern upbringing and populist sympathies put him at odds with most of the eastern "sentimentalist" reformers who favored forced assimilation and continued dispossession as part of a protoprogressive campaign to use the government as tool to shape a proper polity according to their vision.

Parker, Bland, and their allies lost more political battles than they won, but studying their techniques, motivations, and struggles enriches and improves our interpretations, regardless of whether their reforms were implemented or not.[8] For example, Parker and Bland both displayed the characteristics of political entrepreneurs ("political entrepreneurship" is a concept drawn from the work of political scientists). Political entrepreneurs are strategic activists that seize moments of opportunity to shape political debates, frame issues, and influence agendas. They create and often transform policies and institutions. Although they might not experience immediate success, the ideas they introduce develop and evolve across time.[9] Parker and Bland's strategies, successes, and failures followed this model, and I draw attention to these moments in subsequent chapters.

Viable policy alternatives, which I define as ideas that challenged established and entrenched political combinations while still appealing to a comparatively large number of policy makers and reformers, emerged at several specific moments in the postwar United States. Political scientist Gerald Berk argues that in such constitutive politics, "fighting over what had once seemed routine issues inexorably opens conflict over the very grammar by which actors are made available to one another, identify allies and adversaries, and through which legitimate claims upon the state are recognized."[10] It was in these periods and in these ways that the larger trends and trajectories of federal Indian policy were questioned—that the politics of power, of the "fixed position," to use Berk's term, was under debate.

The late 1860s and early 1870s represented just such a moment as Americans emerged from the Civil War searching for meaning in their traumatic wartime sacrifices and willing to consider, at least initially, a drastically reconfigured nation that would be, at a fundamental level, more inclusive. The late 1870s and 1880s, with the rise of populist thought, labor strife, protoprogressive urban and political reform, and fears of unrestrained capitalism represented another. Finally, described only in my epilogue, the dire economic conditions of the Great Depression of the 1930s represented a third.

Crooked Paths to Allotment defines and charts the emergence of several viable Indian policy alternatives in the second half of the nineteenth century and then analyzes the repression of those alternatives by mainstream assimilationists within the context of nineteenth-century state development. As I describe each moment, I focus first on the individuals introduced above, those who play only marginal roles in other studies. Their stories are less familiar but no less deserving of historical scrutiny. Only after I have established their alternative frameworks and agendas do I widen the lens to incorporate the more commonly known individuals and organizations.

My methodology draws insight and inspiration from the field of American political development (APD) and postcolonial thought. It may seem odd at first to meld these two bodies of thought into a usable methodological foundation; APD studies think east to west, while postcolonial studies think west to east. The following paragraphs provide some justifications.

American political development seeks to understand the historical construction of politics, not simply to use American political history to test theories of politics. It starts from the premise that political institutions and governing structures are always in a state of flux. APD scholars Karen Orren and Stephen Skowronek note that "the insistence on treating every state of affairs as in transition, a state, as it were, in the process of becoming, sets APD's understanding of politics apart." Put simply, APD scholarship defines "politics as the current configuration of conflicts."[11] Although APD scholars have devoted few pages to American Indian history, I find their charge to view politics as historically constructed to be an ideal method for telling a more inclusive and dynamic story, reflective of the realities of the Native political experience.

APD scholarship views repressed alternatives in two different but related ways (Orren and Skowronek refer to a repressed alternative as "an idea stillborn, a movement crushed, a party abandoned"). First, it views them as evidence that policy-makers and reformers have long pursued plausible reforms that promised to push the nation in directions drastically different from those ultimately followed. Second, and more significantly for this study of nineteenth-century Indian policy development, it argues that the existence of viable alternatives "challenges the aura of inevitability and progress that history's winners tend to attribute to their own victories."[12]

I also follow the lead of postcolonial scholars whose work seems most useful in making sense of post–Civil War Indian policy reform, state development, and geographic expansion. Two elements of my methodology mirror the foundations of postcolonial scholarship and the ways it has been applied to the United States: I attempt to hear the voices of those often obscured, and I try to engage in a critical way the functioning of colonial culture. As for the latter point, Nicholas Thomas's *Colonialism's Culture* has been particularly influential. Thomas argues that colonialism was/is never monolithic—it is not always, in every way, a destructive force—it allows space for creative activity.[13] In her recent book, Jacki Rand—inspired by Thomas—provides a model for thinking more specifically about nineteenth-century American colonialism. She asserts that by widening our interpretative lens, we can move beyond a "limited and limiting study in domination." She reiterates that U.S. colonialism was both "destructive and productive" and, further, that both colonizer and victimized together created the conditions in which they both existed, "albeit in unequal relations."[14]

In both its methodology and its effort to draw connections between the development of federal Indian policy and broader trends in U.S. history, my approach is closely related to Kevin Bruyneel's in *The Third Space of Sovereignty*. Bruyneel draws from APD scholarship and postcolonial theory to demonstrate the significance of contestation and conflict in politics at the "boundaries." Post–Civil War U.S. colonial rule, he argues, has been characterized as an attempt to bind Indian political status in space and time. The geographical and temporal boundaries, though, are not barriers but "sites of co-constitutive interaction among groups, governments, nations, and states where competing notions of political time, political space, and political identity shape the U.S. indigenous relationship."[15] My effort to illuminate and interrogate constitutive moments in the subsequent chapters follows Bruyneel's model, and, like his book, I suggest that colonial rule and American democracy were not mutually exclusive.

My work is also connected to Andrew Denson's *Demanding the Cherokee Nation*, which charts the ways that Cherokee leaders and reformers attempted to demonstrate to federal policy makers that tribal sovereignty and U.S. expansion could coexist. He asserts persuasively that a possible resolution offered by the Cherokee reformers would have allowed the Cherokee Nation to maintain autonomy within the larger United States.[16] In important ways,

Denson's notion of "what might have been" is similar to my focus on viable policy alternatives advocated by post–Civil War reformers.

Finally, I build upon Heather Cox Richardson's persuasive arguments in *West from Appomattox*. She asserts that while questions about the role of the federal government and its relationship to its citizens were hardly new in the post–Civil War era, they took on new meaning and significance during Reconstruction and beyond as the power of the federal government expanded. Richardson's argument looks to the West in the late nineteenth century as a lens to view both the expansion of governmental activism and the emergence of a middle-class ideology based upon notions of inclusion and exclusion within the national polity. This emergent ideology proved very pervasive and appealed to a broad array of groups and individuals while simultaneously defining African Americans, Populists, labor activists, and others as potentially destructive to the United States. She concludes—and it is here where my findings reflect her suggestions most directly—that those who embraced this mainstream vision came to understand themselves as middle class and "deliberately repressed anyone who called for government action to level the American economic, social, or political playing field."[17]

Crooked Paths to Allotment presents evidence to refute the notion that late-nineteenth-century policies of dispossession and forced assimilation were inevitable. These stories reveal in powerful ways that at specific moments a significant opposition arose and suggested alternative policies, some of which were even partially implemented. These examples underscore how the development of federal Indian policy was contested and resisted, how it proceeded in fits and starts.

As a part of this approach, I reconsider how we critically engage the established narratives about Indigenous and non-Indigenous leaders whose lives defy simple categorization—whose legacies are contested. Ely Parker (like other prominent Indian leaders who worked within non-Native structures of governance) has been described as an Indigenous "sellout."[18] Thomas Bland, when mentioned at all in the literature, is portrayed as an eccentric outlier who enjoyed little support among mainstream reformers.

Instead of relying on these worn scholarly tropes, I suggest that Parker was an innovative policy maker—a political entrepreneur—who wedded an Indigenous worldview with a western intellectual framework. One of the most significant tragedies of his story, however, is that (influenced by a relatively unique political and social history in western New York State early in his life) Parker underestimated the extent to which agents within the federal government had invested in a system of disruptive expansion and coercive assimilation by the early 1870s. Viewed within the context of the evolving nineteenth-century state, his efforts to reform OIA corruption, to create policies, and to expand Indigenous educational opportunities can more appropriately be interpreted as a "path not taken," rather than an abandonment of Indigenous heritage.

Bland was most certainly a radical thinker whose education and experiences did not harmonize with those of other eastern reformers. A reexamination of the evidence, though, suggests that not only did his viable alternative policies carry significant support among other policy activists and legislators, but his successes in the mid-1880s scared his opponents enough to cause them to redouble their repressive efforts. In the end, it was Bland's inability to shape the terms of the policy debates in the press that led to the eventual repression of his reform agenda. The stories of both men's careers are also illustrative of the tensions and contestations that surrounded nineteenth-century leaders who sought to resist dispossession and cultural disruption by working within, rather than against, mainstream structures of governance.

Throughout *Crooked Paths to Allotment*, I reconsider some methodological trajectories in the study of American Indian history as well. Specifically I ask: How can scholars continue to honor the unique and important histories of individual tribal nations and Indian communities while simultaneously drawing attention to ways that the nineteenth-century Native experience shaped the United States in profound ways? In an effort to reject an older methodological approach that privileged the experiences of the U.S. government and government officials, Native and non-Native scholars have produced studies of the particular histories and unique circumstances of individual Indian communities.[19] On one hand, this trend has revealed the richness and depth of the Native experience within broader American history, but on the other, because it limits the ability to synthesize or demonstrate the connections Indigenous nations had to the United States, it has the potential to make the study of Indigenous history a marginalized, insular, or even ignorable field. In the chapters that follow, I suggest that one method to bridge this divide is to examine how a local issue had broader national implications. Along these lines, I analyze the connections between a unique controversy, namely the Ogden Land Company's attack on the Tonawanda reservation, and the reform agenda of the peace policy on the national level. Although separated by time and space, these developments indicate that it was Ely Parker's political experience during the removal effort in his homeland that provided the foundation upon which the peace policy was built. Approaching the study of Indigenous history this way demonstrates the interconnectedness of local events and national developments.

Ultimately, I complement the existing literature on the post–Civil War United States by connecting the development of federal Indian policy to broader national events. I do so by focusing on how and why so many reformers saw the Reconstruction era as a potential moment of optimism for the reconfiguration of racial politics as they pertained to American Indians. I also suggest that this moment, just as it was for African Americans, was brief and fleeting. This study spans the period between the Reconstruction and Progressive eras. Narratives of American state development generally focus on the significance of the Civil War and Reconstruction and then jump forward to urban social and political reforms and the bureaucratic innovations of the Progressive Era, surrendering the Gilded Age as a period of unimpeded corporate power, governmental passivity, corruption, and unrestrained inequity.[20] The mid- to late-nineteenth-century OIA, however, served as a crucial meeting ground for ideologies of governmental authority. Its development not only demonstrates the extent to which some actors in the federal government were willing to experiment in this period—policy makers allowed the state to take on increasingly interventionist functions—but also shows the evolution of social policy making from the hybrid public and private character of Reconstruction programs to the institutionalized federal compensatory programs of the early twentieth century.[21]

Highlighting the primacy of the OIA and recognizing how some state-centered social policy making was modeled first in Indian policy indicates the importance of the Native American experience in this era. It is also critical in developing an understanding of mid- to late-nineteenth-century U.S. history and further illuminates our problematic periodization of postwar nineteenth-century development.[22]

THE FIRST TWO CHAPTERS in the book provide a foundation and offer critical background information for understanding the development of viable policy alternatives in the post–Civil War era. In the first chapter, I present key concepts necessary to make sense of the experiences from which post–Civil War reformers drew. Rather than provide a simple chronological catalogue of congressional acts, Supreme Court decisions, and executive mandates, I attempt to group these developments thematically across time in an effort to demonstrate the confining nature of Indian-state relations in the nineteenth century (and to draw out connections between these policies and the broader yet fluid and fluctuating contours of American colonialism). Chapter 2 pursues two related goals. First, it presents a regional case study to provide insight into the national patterns described in the first chapter. Specifically, it illustrates how the Ogden

Land Company's assault on Tonawanda Seneca tribal sovereignty destabilized notions of governance and authority. Second, it suggests that this experience provided a foundation in political reform upon which Ely Parker could build. Throughout the campaign, he sought alternatives that might ease the pace of dispossession and colonialism and help the Seneca maintain their slowly deteriorating political position within the state. He, along with other Seneca and some non-Indian leaders, developed alternative theories of governance at the reservation, as well as federal, level based upon the protection of tribal sovereignty and Indian homelands combined with a belief in efficient and impartial bureaucracy.

The middle chapters form the core of the argument and examine the first of two major constitutive moments in post–Civil War Indian policy reform. In these chapters I describe the development of several components of the Grant administration's peace policy, and connect this development both to the presence of viable Indian policy reforms and to the repression of these ideas. Chapter 3 focuses on several events and individuals whose experiences are often exiled to the periphery of Indian policy development studies and suggests that the commissioners and participants in the Indian peace councils in the West and South in the late-1860s, especially Ely Parker, developed policy alternatives that broke with previous approaches in Indian affairs. Some of these alternatives evolved into critical elements of the peace policy, while mainstream assimilationists in Washington and elsewhere actively repressed others. Chapter 4 illustrates how policy makers began to implement reform alternatives developed in the late 1860s. The quick progress of these reforms within the context of the early Reconstruction era suggests that they constituted a viable program and perhaps provides some coherence to the historical literature on the peace policy. Chapter 5 argues that reformers opposed to the more far-reaching policy alternatives of the 1860s and early 1870s seized a moment to repress these reforms. Mainstream assimilationists sought to use federal programs to accelerate dispossession and coercive assimilation and to promote Indian confinement. At stake for these men was nothing short of their vision of a proper polity.

The final chapters examine the second major constitutive moment in the late 1800s, and seek to demonstrate how reformers in the 1880s built upon but expanded the terms of Indian policy conflicts and contestation. Chapter 6 examines the generation of reformers who emerged in the late 1870s and 1880s and debated legislative proposals to divide tribally held lands, dissolve tribal relations, and force Indigenous people to assimilate in as little time as possible. It focuses on Thomas Bland—editor of the *Council Fire* and founder of the often overlooked reform organization called the National Indian Defense Association (NIDA)—who supported a series of policy reforms that rejected forced assimilation and focused instead upon using mechanisms of the federal government to provide resources and opportunities for Indigenous nations protecting the integrity of communally-held land. His ideas confronted existing trends in Indian policy making that valued increasing confinement and diminishing tribal sovereignty. Chapter 7 illustrates the ways that Herbert Welsh and the Indian Rights Association (IRA), Bland's opponents, successfully repressed his reform program. It argues that they led a concentrated campaign in the newspapers and throughout Washington, D.C., to misrepresent and repress NIDA and Bland's alternative approach. It is due to IRA success, in fact, that NIDA and Bland have been ignored or overlooked in the literature. The chapter also asserts that, far from being a simple linear progression toward the Allotment Act of 1887, Indian policy reform was marked by significant contestation.

Finally, an epilogue focuses briefly on one constitutive moment in the early twentieth century and the development of John Collier's Indian New Deal during the Great Depression. The creation of this policy—in many ways a real and significant break from the larger and longer nineteenth-century trajectory of Indian confinement through federal policy—demonstrates both the uniqueness of the economic and political conditions of the 1930s and the ways that the tradition of dissent against policies of Indian confinement that were introduced in the 1860s culminated in the institutionalization of an alternative agenda seventy years later.

ONE

Confining Indians

Iroquois! departed people!—
Children of our living foliage—
Victims of successful warfare
In the viewless snare of Fate;
Not in servitude's oppression,
Not by power or subjugation,
Yielded thou thy lakes and rivers
And the rugged untilled borders
Of the confines of thy lands!
By thy haughty spirit fearless
In the domains of thy fathers,
In thy right of tributation,
Thou wert passive in submitting
To the light of peace that blighted,
In its withering embrace,

All the years of thy duration
In the thralldom and the shackles
Of the boundaries of man!

Iroquois! thou wasted people!
All thy council fires extinguished,
Waiting not, thy hapless nation
Knoweth not the hope expectant
Of their lights and kindling fires!
In the boundless limitation
Of Time's great eternal shadows
Thy sun behind the hills is rested
In its everlasting west!
—HARRIET MAXWELL CONVERSE,
"The Ho-De-No-Sau-Nee," 1885

On January 24, 1897, the *Buffalo Express* published an article by New York poet and Indian policy reformer Harriet Maxwell Converse. The article coincided with the reinterment of Ely S. Parker's body in the Forest Lawn Cemetery's Indian burial plot; he had initially been laid to rest near his final worldly home in Fairfield, Connecticut. Converse told a story about a prophetic dream that Ely's mother, Elizabeth Parker, had several months before his birth in 1828. An Iroquois dream interpreter found much significance in Elizabeth's vision, according to Converse. "A son will be born to you who will be distinguished among his nation as a peacemaker," he said. "He will become a white man as well as an Indian, with great learning." This son will "be a wise white man, but will never desert his Indian people nor lay down his horns (his title as Sachem) as a great 'Iroquois chief.'" The interpreter concluded that his "sun will rise on Indian land and set on the white man's land. Yet the ancient land of his ancestors will fold him in death."[1]

The veracity of this story is questionable. In fact, Ely Parker even doubted some of its elements. In a letter to Converse, he wrote that he had to "disclaim all knowledge" of his mother's dream.[2] The precise details of this prophetic dream are less important, though, than Converse's use of the story in her 1897 article. While her general tone was one of respect and reverence for Parker's life and for the Buffalo Historical Society, which funded the reinterment, she also lamented the position of the Iroquois at that time. Toward the end of the piece, Converse invoked Red Jacket's warning to the Iroquois that the "pale-faces will crowd you into nothing but a blanket at the last" and in her own words stated that New York's Indians had been "crowded into a few hundred acres of their once wide-spreading lands."[3]

While Converse's article might be read as a slight variation on the common nineteenth-century trope of the "vanishing Indian," it also reveals the powerful fact that by the late 1800s, the world into which Ely Parker and hundreds of thousands of other Native Americans had been born—one in which Indian nations negotiated with the United States as separate sovereigns—had changed profoundly.[4]

American Indian nations experienced a dizzying array of pressures and attacks from non-Native settlers, missionaries, private interests (merchants, traders, land companies, and mineral extraction corporations), state and local governments, state and federal courts, the Supreme Court, and the federal legislative and executive branches. While Parker rose to a position of power and respect through "great learning," by the late 1800s, the United States seemed less inclusive and less open, and, as Converse noted, many Indian communities had been "crowded" onto increasingly smaller plots of land. She acknowledged the reality that Indian nations as a whole were in a weak and beaten position. Confined.

By no means intended to be a comprehensive discussion, this chapter provides some critical background information and a brief introduction to selected, key concepts necessary to make sense of the experiences from which post–Civil War reform generations drew. I group these developments thematically across time to demonstrate the confining nature of Indian-state relations in the nineteenth century and to connect these policies to the fluid outlines of American settler colonialism. Although state- and local-level developments contributed significantly to the contour of Indian policy in the nineteenth century, I focus the following sections on federal policy and law.[5]

The nineteenth-century "Indian problem," as reformers understood it, referred to a fundamental contradiction. The United States acknowledged that Native American peoples existed as autonomous communities, sovereign or semisovereign collectivities—nations—that predated the United States itself. It did so through a complicated series of legal documents that included treaties, the Constitution, and court decisions. Simultaneously, it recognized Indians as dependent subjects who had exchanged land for economic assistance, educational opportunities, and legal protections within the purview of Congress. Put simply, the United States had a "trust responsibility" to the Indian nations with whom it negotiated.[6] One of the ways that nineteenth-century policy makers worked to resolve the contradictory position Indian nations occupied within United States law (while simultaneously opening Indian lands for settlement when not resorting to overt armed conquest) involved gradually chipping away at tribal sovereignty—the pre- and extraconstitutional legal status from which many believed the contradiction derived.

The Indian policy reformers who came of age in the mid-nineteenth century— the central figures of this book—were witnesses to and participants in profound shifts in the development of federal policy and American colonialism. Indian communities experienced an assault on external sovereignty, often driven by private interests, carried out through the treaty relationship, and justified by incomplete and sometimes myopic Supreme Court interpretations and decisions—ultimately confining Indian people on the land and limiting their movements. John Wunder has described this "Old Colonialism" as "the same colonialism that Europeans followed in Africa, North and South America, and Asia, [that] had as its primary goal the physical acquisition of valuable western and southern lands and the physical subjugation of its people." Gradually and simultaneously throughout the nineteenth century, this assault honed in on internal sovereignty as well, weakening tribal governance and increasingly subjecting Native communities to state and federal bureaucracies and legal systems—confining Indians in time, politics, and the law. "New Colonialism," according to Wunder, gathered "its strength and embellishment from legal argument and pronouncement . . . [and] attacked every aspect of Native American life—religion, speech, political freedoms, economic liberty, and cultural diversity."[7] These shifts corresponded with the development of the American colonial project. In the early part of this period, the state supported and benefitted from the settlers and private interests who invaded Indian country and drove colonial policy making. Between 1830 and 1871, though, the state itself became an increasingly active agent in this process. In important ways, Indian people participated in, resisted, created new opportunities within, and fell victim to this process.

Confining Indians on the Land

The United States' Indian treaty system, upon which post–Civil War reformers focused considerable attention, developed slowly, over time.[8] Indeed, the more than 350 treaties negotiated between the United States and different Indian nations were drafted in a piecemeal fashion contingent on the increasing economic and military dominance of the American state and often dictated by the immediate goals of non-Native settlers, private interests, and governmental representatives. This process had far-reaching consequences.

First, the treaties rested on a concept of Indian sovereignty. Even before the Commerce Clause in the U.S. Constitution (section 8, paragraph 3) acknowledged the relationship between Indian nations and the new American nation as one of separate sovereigns, representatives of the rebelling North American colonies treated with Indian diplomats.[9] At Fort Pitt in 1778, colonial leaders and Delaware representatives negotiated a formal alliance that referred to the Delaware as a "nation" and even provided a guarantee of territorial rights and representation in Congress.[10] Legal scholars and historians David E. Wilkins and Vine Deloria suggest that this notion of Indigenous nationhood was inherited from English colonial policy and that "the revolutionary and constitutional fathers accepted without question . . . the national status of an Indian tribe."[11] Although American leaders reneged on many of these promises (perhaps a foreboding omen for the future), this and subsequent treaties rested upon an underlying assumption of Indian independence and political autonomy. Although at times both settlers and federal officials ignored or disregarded Indian rights, the treaties provided theoretical and real protections for Indian people.[12]

The treaties negotiated in the aftermath of the Revolution recognized the weak position of the United States and the significance of stability along its borderlands. In fact, a strong argument could be made that, in terms of foreign affairs, relations with neighboring Indian nations presented more pressing importance than those with European nations. For example, when several early peace overtures to Creek leader Alexander McGillivray failed, President George Washington and Secretary of War Henry Knox invited him and several other Creeks to New York City for a treaty convention in 1790. The U.S. negotiators, led by Knox, spared no expense and lavished gifts upon the Creek emissaries, promising perpetual peace and friendship while seeking to regularize trade and military relations between the nations.[13] In fact, Knox drew from Enlightenment ideals, suggesting that the United States "be influenced by reason" in the development of an Indian policy that acknowledged Indigenous rights to the soil as a fundamental "law of nature."[14] Although many historians have overlooked this aspect of the treaty-making process, U.S. negotiators in the 1795 Treaty of Greenville recognized Native diplomatic practices as legitimate and participated in Indian cultural customs. Great Lakes Indian leaders,

especially among the Miami, Ojibwe, Delaware, and Wyandot, used this opportunity to seek the best terms for their own communities, as well as their
neighbors.[15]

Following the War of 1812, however, the significance of Indian military
prowess and trade relations diminished significantly in the eyes of U.S. politicians, and the treaties written in this period reflected that shift. The majority of the negotiations between federal officials and Indian groups in the
Northeast, Southeast, the Old Northwest and trans-Mississippi West in the
period 1813–20s involved cessions of land, the establishment of geographic
boundaries and reservations, and the regulation of commerce. Rather than
reflecting a unified policy direction, though, these treaties were based primarily upon local interests. An important insight from postcolonial scholarship
demonstrates that within the context of colonialism, metropolitan ideologies
rarely translated accurately into local-level action. Instead, local practices,
local knowledge, and local interests drove policy making.

The treaties negotiated in the aftermath of the War of 1812 also increasingly included stipulations that the United States would provide opportunities
and protections in exchange for land.[16] Among other things, the treaties from
this period obliged the colonial state to provide onetime gifts in the form of
goods, as the negotiators of 1826 treaty with the Potawatomi Nation did. These
treaties also often included ongoing annuity payments, which Indian leaders
preferred to be paid in the form of silver, as well as livestock and other agricultural equipment, as in the 1825 treaty with the Osage Nation, negotiated by
William Clark, that provided hundreds of heads of cattle, hogs, oxen, and fowl.
Others provided funding for educating Indian youth and reserved hunting,
fishing, harvesting, and other resource rights.[17] The federal government's "trust
responsibility" to Indian groups, though not constitutionally based, became
firmly ensconced as a political and legal concept in these treaties.[18]

As the nineteenth century unfolded, it became increasingly difficult for
some of the central reformers discussed later in this book, such as Ely Parker
and Thomas Bland, to countenance the treaty system because Indian nations seemed to be negotiating from an ever-weakening military, political,
and geographic position, yet they saw the perpetuation of the trust responsibility, though inextricably interwoven with the treaties themselves, to be of
paramount importance and necessary for the survival of marginalized Indian communities. Mainstream assimilationists, such as William and Herbert
Welsh, members of the Board of Indian Commissioners and the Indian Rights
Association, frequently saw the trust relationship as a hindrance to forced
assimilation.

The removal treaties of the 1830s and 1840s demonstrated dramatically the assault on external tribal sovereignty. In important ways, they also demonstrated the significance of incomplete, myopic Supreme Court decisions, and the role of local-level interests in driving federal policy. In 1823, John Marshall, chief justice of the Supreme Court, penned a thirty-three-page justification, well beyond that which was necessary to reason a recent Court decision, in *Johnson v. M'Intosh*. In the process, he formalized the "discovery doctrine" in the U.S. legal system that led to a political catastrophe for Native Americans.

In *Johnson v. M'Intosh*, a case in which land speculators sought to exploit legal loopholes in the developing federal judicial system to validate their claim to millions of acres, the Court ruled that Native people (in this case the Piankeshaw Nation) held a "right of occupancy" but not the ultimate title to their homelands and therefore could not sell land to private citizens. In his lengthy opinion, John Marshall wrote that as "discoverers," European nations assumed free title to the land, while the Native occupants they encountered were never really considered "land owners," but tenants. Further, he declared that tribes could relinquish their "occupancy right" only by selling it to the "discovering sovereign" (a status the United States inherited in the aftermath of the Revolution).[19]

This case reveals several important insights into early-nineteenth-century American settler colonialism. While many scholars have interpreted the discovery doctrine as Marshall's effort to develop a clear and rational framework for colonial land acquisition, the circumstances of the case suggest that he was just as likely attempting to provide a mechanism by which the veterans of Virginia's Revolutionary War militia—his friends and former colleagues—could receive the bounty lands promised to the them. In addition, the land speculators in the case bribed and colluded with powerful politicians and leading members of the early republic. They also fabricated evidence and manipulated embryonic federal judicial rules. The legacy of the decision and the establishment of the doctrine of discovery cannot be understated. Marshall's shortsighted ruling provided the legal basis upon which the state of Georgia attempted to impose its law on the Cherokee Nation; it also provided the basis for Congress to pass the Indian Removal Act of 1830. Although Marshall attempted to repudiate it in his 1832 *Worcester* decision, subsequent cases ignored it in favor of the earlier ruling, thereby institutionalizing a legal regime based on a wrongly decided case.[20]

By the end of the 1820s, Georgia officials intensified their attacks on Cherokee sovereignty and asserted absolute jurisdiction over Georgia state law.

Following the election of Andrew Jackson, Congress built on the foundation of the discovery doctrine and moved to pass the Indian Removal Act, perhaps providing a more intentional and rational, though no more just, framework for land acquisition. Cherokee appeals reached the Supreme Court, first in the case of *Cherokee Nation v. Georgia* (1831) and then in *Worcester v. Georgia* (1832). Chief Justice Marshall, though acknowledging that from the moment of settlement Indian communities had been "treated as a State," could not define them as foreign nations, entitled to sue U.S. states. Instead he asserted that they were "domestic dependent nations," maintaining a relationship with the United States that "resembles that of a ward to his guardian." In the latter case, though, Marshall seemed to back away from this perspective and acknowledged that Indian nations had always been "distinct, independent political communities . . . [and] the undisputed possessors of the soil."[21] Marshall's effort to repudiate his earlier decisions and vindicate Indian nations failed in the short term since the Jackson administration ignored the *Worcester* opinion and, when Marshall died in 1835, Jackson's pro-removal appointees fully restored the *Johnson* discovery ruling.[22] In the long term, the *Worcester* ruling would provide a strong, though not impenetrable legal barrier protecting tribes from state jurisdiction.

The events that followed comprise one of America's greatest tragedies. The removal process of the 1830s and 1840s that was forced upon northern and southern Indians east of the Mississippi River resulted in a shocking loss of life. Though an accurate count is difficult to calculate, most scholars estimate the number of lives lost among the Cherokee alone to be between four and eight thousand.[23] Those who survived faced the physically and psychologically devastating prospect of establishing themselves in new and foreign territories far from their homelands and ancestors. The Cherokee removal story has been firmly established in the historical literature[24] and the next chapter examines an alternate removal case study, so I will not dwell on it here, but it is difficult to find a starker demonstration of the American colonial assault on external sovereignty and how drastically the relative economic and military positions of the United States and Indian nations had shifted since the 1790s.

In the 1850s, escalating U.S. western settlement brought larger numbers of non-Native settlers into contact with Indian communities in the Plains, California, and Oregon Territory. While these encounters created new and drastically different interactions, the federal government continued older policies, asserting the prerogative of a "discovering sovereign," establishing permanent or temporary reservations, and negotiating a high volume of formal treaties. In fact, the number of treaties negotiated in the 1850s rivaled that of the 1830s and would have surpassed it had the Senate ratified them all. Significantly, although the context in which treaties were negotiated changed dramatically, the purpose and function of the treaties themselves remained remarkably the same.

In the 1850s, Commissioner of Indian Affairs George Manypenny worked tirelessly to consolidate American territorial acquisitions and colonial control in the West, (but later recognized the damage his actions had caused to Indian people and communities and worked to protect Indian rights). In 1856 he summarized the goals and nature of midcentury Indian policy: "first, treaties of peace and friendship; second, treaties of acquisition, with a view of colonizing the Indians on reservations; and third, treaties of acquisition, and providing for the permanent settlement of the individuals of the tribes, at once or in the future, on separate tracts of land or homesteads, and for the gradual abolition of the tribal character."[25] In the 1850s, federal administrators sought to extend an overextended colonial framework by substituting "simple administrative measures" for formal treaties and by frequently ignoring or otherwise failing to honor the state's trust responsibility to Indian nations.[26]

The 1860s represented the final decade of the formal treaty-making period. During these years, Indian leaders struggled, especially in the South and Southwest, to persuade the Union government to continue making good on its preexisting treaty obligations. They then sought to take advantage of the complex and paradoxical postwar moment that seemed to provide new political and economic opportunities for some, while pressures from non-Native western settlement increased exponentially. Leaders of the southern Indian nations, notably the Five Civilized Tribes who had faced the full force of American colonialism during the removal era only a generation before, found themselves again in a difficult position at the outbreak of war. The Union government failed to provide protection for these communities, and in an effort to carve out a more equitable position, or under outright military duress, many of them signed treaties with the Confederate States of America. In the aftermath of the war, in the councils held at Fort Smith in September 1865, U.S. negotiators asserted that the Cherokee, Chickasaw, Creek, Choctaw, and other Indian nations voided their previous agreements by signing treaties with the Confederacy, and by allying themselves with the losing side, they existed at the mercy of the federal government. Ely Parker served as a representative of the United States at these negotiations. On one hand, this period would represent the ultimate moment of Indians' confinement on the land. The colonial state operated from a position of unprecedented strength, and following the new negotiations with southern Indian nations, federal agents launched into a flurry of new treaties with Great Plains Indian nations and those in the West.[27] On the other hand, the immediate post–Civil War moment was one of the key turning points of the nineteenth century: in the context of Reconstruction, if only briefly, there were new opportunities available for Native individuals and communities.[28] Many sought to take advantage of them.

The net result of more than seventy years of treaties and judicial decisions cannot be understated. Indian communities had been confined on an increasingly smaller land base. When Harriet Maxwell Converse invoked Red Jacket's prophetic words, she acknowledged this reality. Confinement on the land carried far-reaching consequences for the continuing development of American colonialism in the nineteenth century. It was through this critical process that federal administrators imagined transforming Indians from victims of conquest into colonized subjects. Their ability to locate specific individuals in space and time facilitated other technologies of colonial statecraft, including the distribution of benefits, as well as the disbursement of punishment. To locate a population in space and time made it "legible" to colonial administrators.[29] While the treaties of the early nineteenth century contained provisions that firmly established the trust responsibility and obligated the American colonial state to Native nations, the military and economic positions from which the United States negotiated had shifted so dramatically that it had become clear to many reformers that Indian people would experience ever-increasing difficulty impelling it to honor its obligations. Importantly, in ways that overlapped and surpassed geographic confinement through American settler colonialism, Indian nations faced an equally confining assault on internal sovereignty.

Confining Indians in Time, Politics, and the Law

"Indian sovereignty is not simply a legal concept," wrote Vine Deloria Jr. in 1979.[30] Though the meaning of the term "sovereignty" has varied through history, it has come to refer to the capability that a group of people has to make its own choices and manage its own affairs in relation to its homeland.[31] As the nineteenth century unfolded, post–Civil War reformers, while not always employing the modern political language of sovereignty, nonetheless recognized the ways in which Indian nations experienced not only confinement on an increasingly smaller land base but also a weakening of tribal systems of governance and concurrent solidification of state and federal bureaucracies and legal structures in Indian Country. These shifts can be defined broadly as confinement in time, politics, and the law.

Article 1 of the U.S. Constitution refers specifically to American Indians in two places. In the first instance (section 2, paragraph 3), "Indians not taxed" are excluded from the formula for apportioning representatives to Congress, implying that individual Indian people may or may not be considered citizens subject to taxation. The second instance, known as the "commerce clause," is more significant. Congress, in section 8, paragraph 3, is given the power "to regulate Commerce with foreign Nations, and among the several States, and with the Indian Tribes."[32] While it seems clear here that the Constitution deemed tribes preexisting sovereigns, it did not clearly define tribal sovereignty.[33] David E. Wilkins has argued that tribal sovereignty is not only preconstitutional; it is also extraconstitutional, "on the one hand, [making possible] the imposition of federal authority over tribal lands and Indian citizens and, on the other, creating a set of legal (some say moral, e.g., 'trust doctrine') barriers designed to protect tribes from federal agencies, states, and private parties."[34]

The imprecise position of Indian nations within nineteenth-century political and legal thought helps to reveal the ways in which the American state acted energetically, becoming an increasingly active agent in the colonial project. Although this idea conflicts with standard historiographic notions that portray the national government as playing a very limited role in nineteenth-century society, recent reinterpretations suggest that while it did not do so "visibly," the federal state acted powerfully and intervened in the lives of Americans in many important ways, including through the law, economic development, and western expansion.[35]

An example of the energetic state in the nineteenth century was the U.S. Congress's increasingly overt assertion of "plenary power" over Indian nations. Understood as "unfettered authority," plenary power is an often ignored but persistent element of state power.[36] The federal government's assertion of plenary power pervaded the assault on internal tribal sovereignty and is illustrated by the ways Indian treaty negotiations significantly weakened tribal governance.

There was considerable confusion among U.S. agents concerning political units within tribal nations and the coercive power wielded by individual leaders. In 1829, Lewis Cass and William Clark described assembling councils that operated as "pure democracies, in which every one claims an equal right to speak and vote."[37] But Cass and Clark worked from specific experiences among certain northern nations and lacked insight into the behind-the-scenes influence of tribal politicians, clan matrons, and others. At times federal officials consciously selected leaders who favored federal policies over those who were less amenable, especially in their dealings with the Cherokee and Great Lakes nations in the 1830s and 1840s, and the Plains nations in the 1850s and 1860s.[38] In the process of negotiating treaties in this manner, representatives of the colonial state destabilized ideologies and structures of tribal governance. Within

Indian nations, factionalism, jealousy, scorn, frustration, and fear resulted, allowing settler colonial policies to become more solidly entrenched and reifying the long-established notions that Euro-American governing structures were superior to all others. The removal crisis at the New York State Tonawanda Seneca reservation in the 1840s and 1850s illustrates all of these elements (and chapter 2 focuses on this event in greater detail).

Political relations between the United States and Indian nations not governed by treaties or the Constitution were determined by the Indian trade and intercourse acts passed between 1790 and 1834. These acts sought to regularize Indian trade, restrict liquor sales, and systematize the disposition of Indian lands. Demonstrating another facet of the assault on internal sovereignty, the final Indian trade and intercourse act of 1834 stated that "so much of the laws of the United States as provides for the punishment of crimes committed within any place within the sole and exclusive jurisdiction of the United States, shall be in force in the Indian country" and thereby "gave the federal government broad criminal jurisdiction over the tribes and over whites on tribal lands."[39] Although the 1834 act did not apply to Indian-on-Indian crime, its passage began a trend that would, over the course of the 1800s, widen the colonial state's jurisdiction over crimes committed by Native people within their communities. In the 1840s, for example, President James K. Polk and Congress sought to extend U.S. criminal law to Indian country, but the Cherokee Nation protested to the Senate, citing treaty rights and warning that such an action would set a dangerous precedent.[40]

In 1846, the Supreme Court, under Chief Justice Roger Taney and acting on behalf of the energetic, colonial state, took a critical step in establishing the plenary power notion (the final and most definitive legal step would occur in the 1880s). In his brief opinion (only three pages in length), Taney rendered a decision in the *United States v. Rogers* case that was based on historically inaccurate information and erroneous ideas and had a general lack of case law for support.[41] William Rogers was a white man who had married a Cherokee woman, been adopted by the tribe, and lived exclusively in the Cherokee Nation after 1836. In 1845, he killed another white man who had married a Cherokee woman and became a citizen of the Cherokee Nation. Taney—ignoring decades of case and treaty law—asserted, "Native tribes who were found on this continent at the time of its discovery have never been acknowledged or treated as independent nations." Therefore, according to the chief justice's logic, the murder took place on lands within the jurisdiction of the United States. He went further, arguing that Rogers, though adopted by the Cherokee and considered a member of the nation, could not be considered an Indian because that was a racial, not a political designation.[42] As was true with *Johnson* in 1823, Taney's decision would have profound consequences for Indian nations.

In 1851, Congress extended U.S. law by establishing the Western District Court with full federal jurisdiction over Indian Territory, though at this point, it still covered only non-Natives living on Indian lands. While few cases pushed the issue of federal jurisdiction over internal Indian affairs forward during or immediately after the Civil War, as the western expansion of non-Native settlement increasingly surrounded Indian nations, the idea gradually gained momentum.

In the landmark case *ex parte Crow Dog* (1883), the Supreme Court reiterated that the United States did not have jurisdiction over crimes committed by one Indian upon another.[43] Crow Dog, a Sioux leader, had been convicted of killing Spotted Tail, and although the Sioux had already exacted justice according to their own legal doctrines, the First District Court of South Dakota sentenced Crow Dog to death. The Supreme Court overturned the ruling, upholding Sioux tribal legal doctrine, but, almost immediately, the finding motivated legal reformers and American colonial officials to act, and in doing so, they usurped tribal law and struck a major blow to internal tribal sovereignty. In 1885, Congress passed the Major Crimes Act as a rider attached to a general appropriations bill. This act defined seven "major crimes," including murder, rape, arson, assault with intent to kill, manslaughter, larceny, and burglary and extended federal criminal jurisdiction over all Indian nations (although the Five Civilized Tribes and several others were excluded).[44] Historian Sidney Harring notes that, while this was a departure from existing Indian policy, "it was consistent with the [increasingly overt] move away from a policy based on treaty rights recognizing Indian sovereignty and toward one of dependency and forced assimilation."[45] Opponents initially questioned the act's constitutionality and challenged it in the Supreme Court.

In *United States v. Kagama* (1886), the Supreme Court upheld the Major Crimes Act and denied nearly a century of constitutional and legal precedents. In the *Kagama* case, two Indian men from the Hoopa Valley Reservation in California were indicted for the murder of a third Indian man. Justice Samuel Miller, speaking for the Court, drew from ideas established in *Johnson*, *Cherokee Nation*, and *Rogers* to assert that "tribes are the wards of the nation. They are communities dependent on the United States."[46] He concluded further that the "power of the General Government over these remnants of a race once powerful, now weak and diminished in numbers, is necessary to their protection. . . . It must exist in that government, because it never has existed anywhere else."[47] The result of this fifty-year-long assault on Indian internal sovereignty was that, by the late nineteenth century, Indian nations had been confined legally, largely within the framework of U.S. law. Federal district courts could define who was to be considered Indian before the law and by what metrics justice would be meted out—completely undercutting tribal notions of criminality and retribution.

There is another important component to the nineteenth-century assault on internal tribal sovereignty that needs to be addressed as part of this discussion. In 1871, as a rider to an appropriations bill, the House of Representatives, acting on behalf of the colonial state, unilaterally ended the treaty-making system as the defining feature of the political relations between Indian nations and the United States. The rider stated: "That hereafter no Indian nation or tribe within the territory of the United States shall be acknowledged or recognized as an independent nation, tribe, or power with whom the United States may contract by treaty: *Provided further*, That nothing herein contained shall be construed to invalidate or impair the obligation of any treaty heretofore lawfully made and ratified with any such Indian nation or tribe."[48]

The treaty "substitutes" that the colonial state employed after 1871 continued to use treaty language, and many federal government officials still believed they were making treaties. Vine Deloria Jr. and anthropologist Raymond De-Mallie suggest that the "appropriations rider in 1871 might therefore be regarded as only a minor and temporary conflict between the Senate and the House of Representatives." The roots of this prohibition did stem, at least in part, from an increasing frustration on the part of the House that treaties negotiated by the executive branch and ratified by the Senate committed them to budgetary constraints well into the future.[49] However, the 1871 rider can also be seen as the culmination of the groundswell shift away from policy based on treaty rights and Indian sovereignty, and it provided additional support for later Court decisions, such as *Kagama*.[50]

The end of the treaty-making system in 1871 symbolized the confinement of Indians in time. Emerging late-nineteenth-century conceptions of progress and modernity could not include a place for Indigenous political identities because, to the federal government and the American nation, such identities directly opposed progress, rationality, and the state. Kevin Bruyneel asserts that because federal policy makers recognized that certain Indian nations were independent and powerful enough to make treaties with the United States, the end of the treaty-making system was not a recognition of the actual political development of diverse tribes and nations; instead, "it was about how indigenous political development was imagined and constructed in relation to the 'progress' of American political development."[51] In other words, the 1871 rider confined Indian nations and individuals in time—as existing in different political time—in relation to the United States. The importance of state-building, western expansion, and the stability of U.S. sovereignty in the wake of a traumatic war facilitated this process of temporal confinement.

The confinement of Indian nations in time, politics, and the law shaped post–Civil War reform efforts in important ways. Reformers who rose to national-level significance did so at the same time that Native people faced these increasing pressures. Some, like William Welsh and the Board of Indian Commissioners, saw in Indian confinement a pathway to Native survival. From this perspective, they existed in such a weakened and corrupted condition that their only hope was through the moral obligations of non-Native philanthropists whose work was aided by systems of confinement. Other reformers—Thomas Bland comes to mind here—also recognizing the weakening position of Indian nations in relation to the United States, sought to soften systems of confinement by slowing the pace, providing time and opportunities for individual Indian people to compete more actively within a changing economic, political, and social environment.

The Limits of Confinement

As powerful as the nineteenth-century confinement of Indian nations was, it was a *limited* as well as *limiting* process. Native notions of peace, law, and governance existed prior to American state development and U.S. colonialism, and they have continued to exist.[52] During the invasive and intense nineteenth-century process of American expansion, many Native communities fought to hold onto homelands, claimed rights guaranteed through treaties, continued practicing cultural traditions, and made decisions that they believed would be in the best interests of their descendants.

Nineteenth-century Indian leaders, as well as Native and non-Native reformers, consistently drew attention to the existence of inherent tribal sovereignty and used it to create or maintain political space. Tribal rights were, they asserted, "affirmed in hundreds of ratified treaties, acknowledged in the commerce clause of the U.S. Constitution, and recognized in ample federal legislation and case law."[53] Cherokee leaders who opposed the extension of federal criminal jurisdiction over Indian country in the 1840s successfully employed this argument, first against President Polk, and then against Congress for a lengthy period of time. Later, in the post–Civil War context, they used similar arguments to shift and change elements of federal policy they found disruptive, in particular arguing that receiving annuity payments for land cessions did not make them "wards" of the paternalistic, colonial government but made them equal sovereigns who entered into a contractual relationship symbolized by the treaties.[54]

Native nations that seemed to have succumbed to removal, such as the Potawatomis, Wyandots, Delawares, and Shawnees, were forced to become exiles from their homelands and to recast themselves as pioneers on the prairies of Kansas. There they cultivated the soil, built new structures, and adapted to a foreign environment. As residents of a critically important region in the 1850s and 1860s, these nations participated fully in land rushes, regional trade, slavery, and the Civil War. Although the four nations continued to face dispossession into the 1860s and 1870s, their leaders made decisions related to tribal status and landownership that allowed their descendants to survive, persist, and once again begin to thrive in the late twentieth and twenty-first centuries.[55]

In another example, although the Kiowa Nation confronted an invasion by the colonial state, especially through the 1867 Treaty of Medicine Creek, members were able to maintain their lifeways, illustrating "the importance of life-sustaining habits of mind and practice and self-imagining under a colonial regime."[56] Ration distributions and annuity payments were insufficient to create dependence on the colonial state, although much of the existing literature suggests this is exactly what happened during the mid-nineteenth century. Instead, Kiowa men and women continued to produce food and goods in ways that had structured their lives for generations. When the annuity goods failed to provide sufficient sustenance, Kiowa young men raided surrounding settlements to procure food, stock animals, and supplies, despite the fact that the federal government had criminalized this customary practice and defined it as warfare. They also created cooperative relationships with off-reservation Kiowa groups, challenging notions of "traditional" versus "progressive" Indians.[57] Young Kiowa women sought to continue customary cultural production and social values, but in the process fought Kiowa destitution by creating a new relationship with the capitalist marketplace. They did so through the development of commercial beadwork and the creation of tourist goods, such as jewelry, sashes, moccasins, and cradleboards.[58] Historian Jacki Rand, rejecting the notion of a monolithic interpretation of colonialism, describes the nineteenth-century American colonial confinement of Indian nations as a process in which the colonizers "and the victimized do the work of creating a new set of conditions in which they both exist, albeit in unequal relations, heavily weighted to the Americans' advantage."[59]

In considering the origins of the trust responsibility, it might make sense to consider how Indian diplomats understood "trust" and the ways in which the process of treaty making itself created the trust relationship within the context of the colonial confinement of Indians on the land. Interestingly, John Marshall, first in *Cherokee Nation*, then in *Worcester*, acknowledged Indian visions of law and peace, if only in the paternalistic language of the 1830s. He wrote that in the treaties they negotiated, Indian nations "look to our government for protection; rely upon its kindness and power." He later noted that in the eighteenth-century treaties, Indian nations did not cede all sovereignty but, as nations, claimed and received protection from the United States.[60] These decisions, as noted above, were then confirmed by many subsequent court cases and treaties, and provided the foundation for a significant portion of federal colonial policy. Out of creative space generated by U.S. confinement, Indian visions of law and peace influenced the development of the trust relationship.[61]

REFORMER HARRIET MAXWELL CONVERSE'S 1897 article that lamented the "pitiful" Seneca who were confined upon a few hundred acres of their "once wide-spreading lands" bore witness to a potent reality. By the end of the nineteenth century, Indian nations existed in a weak and beaten position. Elizabeth Parker's dream, interpreted as a metaphor for her own son's life, might also be understood as a representation of the political and legal power of all Indian nations in the United States. While their "sun" had risen over their own homelands, by the end of the nineteenth century, at least, it appeared that it was setting on "the white man's land."

The reformers who sought to advocate for Indian rights in the post–Civil War era had witnessed a sea change in U.S.-Indian relations that encompassed an assault on both external and internal tribal sovereignty. They would have to work within, as well as against, the contradictions constructed by the confinement process. Converse's article did not reveal the entire story, though. The nineteenth-century confinement of Indian nations on the land, in time, politics, and the law, was a *limited* process. As with all facets of colonialism, confinement allowed for creation and provided space for the continuation of tribal practices.

The next chapter provides a focused case study to illuminate many of the broader developments outlined above. It examines the nineteenth-century history of the Tonawanda Seneca within the context of a removal crisis and an assault on tribal sovereignty. In some ways, the Tonawanda experience illustrates a common story of the power and pervasiveness of confinement; in other important ways, though, it was unique. Within this context, Ely Parker was born and came to understand the pressures Native people faced. Out of this context, Parker emerged as an important advocate for Indian nations and a political entrepreneur at the national level during one of the key constitutive moments of the nineteenth century.

TWO

Tonawanda Seneca and the Assault on Tribal Sovereignty, 1838–1861

[T]he simple laws that governed your fathers 50 or 100 years
ago, are not adapted to your present condition.
—ELY S. PARKER, letter to the chiefs and people
of the Tonawanda Band of Seneca Indians, 1861

After "raising" Ely Parker to the position of "condoled chief", Tonawanda Seneca leaders in 1852 appointed George Cooper, Parker's maternal uncle, to serve as his "sub Sachem." Cooper immediately wrote to Parker asking for advice. He wanted to know "exactly my duty, or the duty of my office under you." He also wanted an assurance that, if he spoke during a council, Parker would support him.[1] Parker likely found this request awkward, for in the Seneca kinship system, a young man's uncle held an important position as a role model and adviser, often even more significant than his father. In this case, however, a removal crisis, entering its fourteenth year, had destabilized notions of authority and inverted these roles.[2] Parker replied deferentially, perhaps hoping to maintain some appearance of customary kinship status. He wrote to his brother Newton, "I cannot dictate to Geo. Cooper what he shall say or do in council . . . [nor can I] dictate what his opinions shall be. Our positions are not now what was assumed by Chiefs 50 or 75 years ago . . . now we have to act the moment we think, or else our affairs must frequently suffer."[3]

Rocked by a removal crisis that carried on through the 1840s and 1850s, the Tonawanda Seneca followed a path very common for eastern Indian nations. Representatives of a private company with a tenuous land claim, the Ogden Land Company, attempted to manipulate Indian leaders, as well as state and federal officials, in an effort to dispossess an Indigenous nation from its homeland. Within the Tonawanda community, leaders resisted these efforts but often fought bitter battles over how to best respond to removal pressures. Parker's comments in 1852 suggested an awareness of this context but also reflected the growing number of Indigenous leaders who sought alternative pathways to Indian policy reform in a moment of increased American settler colonialism. More importantly, Parker's early experiences instructed his notions of proper Indian policy later in life, when he served as commissioner of Indian Affairs and helped draft federal Indian legislation. In this way, Parker's personal history helps inform a much broader picture and connects this local story to a larger national narrative.

This chapter pursues two related goals. The first is to illustrate how the Ogden Land Company's assault on Tonawanda tribal sovereignty destabilized Seneca notions of governance and authority. This regional case study provides insight into the national patterns described in chapter 1, but it also highlights unique political strategies employed by the Seneca. The second goal is to demonstrate that this experience provided Ely Parker with a foundation in political reform upon which he could later build. Throughout the campaign, he sought alternatives that might ease the pace of dispossession and colonialism and help the Seneca maintain their slowly deteriorating political position within the state, while dividing his time between the halls of government in Albany and Washington, D.C., and the councils at Tonawanda. He, along with other Seneca and non-Indian leaders, offered alternative theories of governance at the reservation and at the federal level based upon a recognition that tribal sovereignty and Indian homelands should be protected and a belief in the effectiveness of an efficient and impartial bureaucracy. In some important ways, Parker's work at Tonawanda proved successful. The band held on to a significant portion of its homelands. In other ways, though, the Tonawanda experience typified the increasingly powerful and pervasive national assault on tribal sovereignty.

Parker's alternative approach to reform—reflective of ideas presented by other Native leaders in similar situations—proved particularly significant due to his eventual position as commissioner of Indian Affairs. In that position, he embraced the role of political entrepreneur and created a vision for the relationship between the federal government and Indian people in which the Office of Indian Affairs would provide educational, employment, and economic opportunities to Native communities to counterbalance dispossession and colonialism. While his ideas took shape during the Tonawanda Seneca campaign against the Ogden Company, in the Reconstruction era they provided the basis for his federal reform efforts.

The Ogden Land Company and the Buffalo Creek Treaty Period

Any discussion of national Indian policy reform must begin with a primer on Iroquois history. Due largely to the Iroquois' historically powerful confederacy and their geographic location, Iroquois affairs in the late eighteenth and early nineteenth centuries shaped federal Indian policy in important ways. For these reasons, too, from the perspective of many late-eighteenth-century Americans, the Iroquois represented one of the most significant Indigenous groups with whom the United States had to negotiate.[4] In the aftermath of the American Revolution, western New York was contested territory. By 1790, the eastern nations of the Iroquois confederacy (the Oneida, Onondaga, and Cayuga) had ceded significant portions of their land to New York State through a series of fraudulent and deceitful negotiations. The Seneca (the westernmost Iroquois nation), though dispossessed of their homelands in the Treaty of Fort Stanwix (1784) as punishment for their allegiance to Great Britain during the war, recovered considerable western tracts in the Treaty of Canandaigua (1794).

In the intervening decade, New York State ignored federal prohibitions on land purchases, and in an effort to avoid a general war with Indian nations and regularize Indian affairs, Congress passed the first two Indian Trade and Intercourse Acts (1790 and 1793), requiring national approval for any Indian land purchases by states or individuals. In 1794, Timothy Pickering, George Washington's negotiator, met with the Seneca over a period of two months in an effort to accomplish two goals. First, he sought to keep them from allying with western nations such as the Shawnee, who were engaged in warfare against the United States over lands in the Ohio Valley. Second, and more importantly, he also sought to clear federal title to those lands. In a significant break from tradition, the resulting treaty dealt separately with each Iroquois nation, rather than as a whole confederacy. While the Treaty of Canandaigua can be seen as a victory for the Seneca—they received back, at least momentarily, the lands they had lost—historian Jack Campisi notes that "the treaty also marked a shift in the relationship between the Iroquois and the United States . . . a transition from independent Indigenous nations, to what Justice Marshall was to call, some forty years later, domestic dependent nations."[5] In other words, in the eyes of U.S. policy makers, the once powerful confederacy had become a group of disparate and increasingly politically insignificant communities.

Massachusetts and New York also claimed Seneca land, the former through the charter of the Massachusetts Bay Company and the latter through a royal grant to the Duke of York. When these two states met in Hartford, Connecticut, in 1786, Massachusetts transferred their claim to political rights within the disputed ground to New York in exchange for the preemptive rights to the soil. Thus the Seneca homeland fell within New York's political/geographic boundaries. If the Seneca chose to sell their lands, however, Massachusetts would profit financially. This preemptive right changed hands several times during the subsequent decades. Individual land speculators Oliver Phelps, Nathaniel Gorham, and Robert Morris first purchased the land rights from Massachusetts, and, in 1797, members of the Morris family negotiated the federal Treaty of Big Tree, under which the Seneca sold all of their western New York territory except large reservations on the Buffalo Creek, Allegany River, Tonawanda Creek, Cattaraugus Creek, and Genesee River. Morris subsequently sold the preemptive right to the Holland Land Company. In 1810, this company transferred these rights to David Ogden and the Ogden Land Company.[6]

Throughout the late 1700s and the early 1800s, New York State and the United States both attempted to diminish tribal sovereignty and establish political and legal jurisdiction over the Seneca. For example, Albany legislators tried to extend New York criminal law over reservation inhabitants, especially after Soonongise (commonly known as Tommy Jemmy), a Seneca chief and follower of the Seneca prophet Handsome Lake, ritually executed Kuaquatau for allegedly practicing witchcraft, in 1821.[7] Local non-Natives, outraged by the act, pressured the state legislature to impose state legal codes on the Indians.[8] These efforts reflected the movement to confine the Seneca on the land and in time, politics, and the law.

In the early nineteenth century, Quakers—both Hicksite and Orthodox—established missions and schools on the western New York reservations while the Ogden Company struggled to profit from their land speculation by encouraging the Seneca to part with their remaining lands.[9] Thomas L. Ogden suggested to Quaker missionaries that all of the New York Seneca move onto the Allegany Reservation.[10] The missionaries, though, believed that Allegany land could not sustain the entire Seneca population and opposed the land speculators. Still trying to profit from their investment in 1819, the Ogden Company drafted a proposal to consolidate all the Seneca to Allegany, but the Indians, supported by Quaker missionaries, resisted their efforts.

Cities along the Erie Canal expanded in the 1820s, and by the early 1830s, land values had increased dramatically, especially those on the Buffalo Creek Reservation bordering the city of Buffalo.[11] The Ogden Company hoped to capitalize on the population growth in Buffalo and appealed to legislators who supported emerging national Indian removal policies. Red Jacket, Cornplanter, Handsome Lake, and Governor Blacksnake, as well as other prominent Seneca leaders, rejected many offers to sell their remaining lands in New York; however, individual interests, political disputes, and confusion instigated by Ogden and the state commissioners resulted in an important land cession treaty in 1826.[12] In it, the Seneca ceded all of their remaining lands in the Genesee Valley and agreed to a reduction of the Tonawanda, Cattaraugus, and Buffalo Creek

Reservations.[13] Indian leaders, most notably Red Jacket, later argued that they never truly supported the treaty and that without Senate ratification, it held no power. Prominent Seneca men charged that U.S. commissioners, influenced by Ogden officials, coerced them to sign by threatening that federal legislation would remove them from their homes without compensation. Nevertheless, the 1826 treaty and its land cessions stood.[14]

The 1828 election of Andrew Jackson and his vice president, New Yorker Martin Van Buren, both champions of Indian removal, empowered the Ogden Company to pursue the Seneca more intensely. By the early 1830s, Buffalo continued to flourish and became a center for both lake and canal shipping. Ogden Company trustees Thomas L. Ogden and Joseph Fellows planned to make additional Indian lands available for non-Native development. Historian Laurence Hauptman has called the 1838 Buffalo Creek Treaty "one of the major frauds in American Indian history," comparing it to the Walking Purchase of 1737 (Delaware), the Treaty of Dancing Rabbit Creek of 1830 (Choctaw), and the Treaty of New Echota of 1835 (Cherokee).[15] In the treaty negotiations, the three men hired by the Ogden Company, James W. Stryker, Ransom H. Gillet, and John F. Schermerhorn, used alcohol, bribery, forgery, threats, misinformation, and a contempt for customary Seneca governmental practices to dispossess the Indians of all their remaining New York lands except the unoccupied, one square mile Oil Spring Reservation, as well as their rights to Wisconsin lands purchased for them by the United States. In return, the Ogden Company paid them $202,000, and the federal government provided a large reservation on lands west of Missouri to be settled by all of the Iroquois nations.[16] While all three of the men the Ogden Company hired to negotiate the Buffalo Creek Treaty were Democratic Party loyalists and eastern New Yorkers, Schermerhorn had a particularly interesting resume. He arrived in Buffalo after successfully negotiating the Treaty of New Echota in Georgia and brought his skill at creating internal chaos among Indian communities to bear on the Seneca. Quakers in New York, Baltimore, and Philadelphia (almost immediately) filed charges of fraud against the Ogden Land Company. Seneca groups claimed that most Iroquois did not support the treaty and that only a minority actually signed it.[17]

In 1842, after four years of intense protest, federal, state, and Ogden Company representatives once again met with the Seneca at Buffalo Creek. This time they drafted a compromise treaty that returned the Allegany and Cattaraugus reservations to the Indians but did not return either Buffalo Creek or Tonawanda.[18] While the Ogden Company profited financially from the second treaty, New York Whigs and Hicksite Quakers, as the primary architects of the negotiations, created an alliance and reshaped state-level Indian policy. In the treaty, they established themselves as the political, educational, and spiritual "fathers" of the Seneca. (In fact, Laurence Hauptman has suggested that the treaty be called "the New York Whig–Hicksite Friend Compromise of 1842.")[19] As they had with the previous treaty, the Tonawanda Seneca refused to sign the compromise. At critical moments during the negotiations, prominent Tonawanda leaders spoke out against the proceedings and the Seneca who signed the document. In so doing, they split from the communities at Allegany and Cattaraugus, a political move that proved significant later in the 1840s and throughout the 1850s.[20]

Tonawanda Resistance

As part of the evolving confinement of Indians on the land in the 1830s, state, federal, and private interests in the eastern United States banded together in a lethal alliance that built upon the discovery doctrine to skillfully dispossess and remove many Indian groups to reserved lands in the West. By the time of the Buffalo Creek Treaty, however, Andrew Jackson no longer held the presidency, and his successor, Martin Van Buren, struggled to control the Democratic Party in the face of the Panic of 1837—especially in New York State.[21] In fact, the 1842 compromise treaty demonstrated New York Whigs' willingness to abandon the Democrats' policy of removal and replace it with a cost-effective "civilization" campaign led by Quaker missionaries.[22] As an interpreter and a leader in the Tonawanda resistance campaign, Ely Parker recognized that it was the Ogden Company itself that posed the most immediate danger to his community.[23] Simultaneously, imprecise state and federal legal doctrines that were complicated by states' rights concerns provided a space within which Seneca leaders could act politically and appeal to sympathetic politicians for at least some safeguards. Parker also began to realize the potential utility that state and federal bureaucratic agencies held for Indian communities, provided the agencies presented them with viable alternative policies and political motivation.

Early in their resistance campaign, Tonawanda leaders, such as Two Guns and Jimmy Johnson, urged prominent national statesmen, especially Whigs, to support the Seneca. In a letter to Henry Clay, Two Guns acknowledged Clay's sympathies for the Indians and asked that the senator exert himself "powerfully" on their behalf so that they would not be "driven to the painful alternative of accepting the western country."[24] When Parker began to serve as an interpreter in 1844, he immediately investigated whether the Ogden treaties could be enforced. He learned from Thomas Hartley Crawford, the commissioner of Indian Affairs, that neither the War Department nor the Office of Indian Affairs had the power to do so. Parker elatedly wrote to his father, "The United States say they have no power whatever to enforce this treaty."[25] Soon after, both New York governor William Bouck and Massachusetts governor George Briggs assured Tonawanda leaders that they had neither the power nor the interest to implement the treaty stipulations.[26] By the mid-1840s it was clear that government officials would not forcibly remove the Seneca, as they had the Cherokee several years earlier. The Ogden Company, though, exploited legal loopholes in ways reminiscent of the land speculators in the 1823 *Johnson v. M'Intosh* case. It moved non-Native settlers onto the reservation lands, confiscated improvements such as sawmills, fenced lots, and fields, and continually sent or threatened to send appraisers to judge the value of the various lands, structures, and resources according to the treaty provisions.

In 1845 Tonawanda leaders sent an appeal to Silas Wright, the new governor of New York, alleging that the company sold their lands at a public auction and that settlers were moving onto the reserve en masse. Unfortunately for the Seneca, Wright was a loyal Democrat, a personal ally of Martin Van Buren, and a supporter of Indian removal.[27] The governor warned them to refrain from attacking the settlers and to wait until the validity of the treaties had been determined before taking other actions. Simultaneously, though, Joseph Fellows, the Ogden trustee, wrote to Parker that "a great deal of money and much vexation will be saved by avoiding litigation in the Courts which must eventually result in disappointment to the Tonawandas."[28] Despite this warning, Seneca leaders again petitioned Governor Wright, this time asserting that the Ogden settlers "dispossess us of large quantities of our forest lands . . . [and] of improvements actually made by our own hands." And, citing the New York Constitution of 1821 and an act passed that same year that forbade non-Indians from "settling or residing on Indian land," they asked that the Genesee County district attorney enter formal complaints against the intruders.[29] Based on these developments, the Tonawanda Seneca, with Parker's guidance, created a three-pronged resistance strategy that involved physically blocking additional attempts at settlement and appraisal, applying for judicial action to remove trespassers at the state level, and continuing to file appeals to national politicians to invalidate officially the treaties through the Senate Committee on Indian Affairs.

Articles 4 and 5 of the 1842 compromise treaty stated that prior to removal, two arbitrators had to survey and assign monetary values to all unsettled and improved lands on the Buffalo Creek and Tonawanda reserves.[30] Parker reasoned that if this process could not be carried out, provided that neither the state nor the federal government forced the Indians to assent, then the treaties could not be honored. He therefore counseled community members to resist the arbitrators, refuse any improvement moneys, defend against non-Native settlement, and repel "every individual who should attempt by fraud and deceit to remove them."[31] Allowing any of these things to take place, Parker recognized, could be construed as an assent to the treaties.

Following this advice, Nicholson Parker and several other Tonawanda members planted crops in a field cleared by a non-Native settler. The Genesee County sheriff arrested the Seneca men for trespassing and transported them to Batavia.[32] The settler eventually withdrew the charge. In 1849, Judge Thomas C. Love, one of the Ogden arbitrators, vacated his position, and the company applied to replace him with J. S. Wadsworth. The new arbitrator proposed a different appraisal method. Rather than surveying the lands and improvements in person, he would rely on informants familiar with the reservation to describe and estimate the values, thus circumventing Seneca efforts to block his surveys. The Tonawanda chiefs presented a united front against this move and drafted an appeal to the War Department. In it they argued that, because the Indians had made many "very valuable and important improvements" since the 1842 treaty, it would be impossible to make an accurate appraisal of the reservation as it existed then, thus invalidating the treaty.[33] In this way, the landscape itself and the ways that Seneca people changed it became a weapon in the resistance effort. The Tonawanda community guarded its homeland throughout the 1840s and 1850s, inviting only trusted non-Native advisers and friends onto the reservation for fear that other whites might attempt to defraud them.

While the Tonawanda Seneca waited for the Senate Committee on Indian Affairs to review their case, they pursued legal recourse against non-Native invaders in an effort to stem the tide of dispossession. In 1846, Nicholson Parker traveled to Albany with John Martindale, a non-Native lawyer who played an increasingly significant role in the Tonawanda resistance campaign throughout this period. There he requested a state supreme court warrant of removal for the settlers claiming titles under the Ogden treaties.[34] Although the judge refused their request, the Seneca did file several notable trespassing cases, the most significant of which was *Blacksmith v. Fellows*. In it, Seneca sachem John Blacksmith charged that Ogden officials Joseph Fellows and Robert Kendle trespassed upon his land, assaulted him, and claimed possession of his sawmill. Blacksmith won the initial trial, and Fellows appealed the case all the way to the U.S. Supreme Court. In 1857, the Court found in favor of Blacksmith on the grounds that the treaty of 1842 never authorized any sort of forced removal.[35] The ruling validated the long-held Seneca belief that the treaties were unjust and fraudulent.

Dispossession and confinement on the land were among the most visible and practical dangers that unscrupulous speculators and business interests such as the Ogden Company posed to Indian communities, but, as the Tonawanda experience demonstrated, threats of removal also disrupted notions of governance and authority. In their petitions and memorials to state and federal policy makers, the Seneca community presented itself as "unitedly and unanimously" in agreement. However, the whirlwind of court cases, appraisal attempts, conflicted messages from government officials, and company threats clearly unsettled the reservation inhabitants.[36]

In 1851, after the death of John Blacksmith, the Grand Council of the Iroquois condoled Ely Parker to Blacksmith's leadership position and bestowed upon him the hereditary name Do-ne-ho-ga-wa, or "Open Door."[37] It was unusual for an Iroquois man in his early twenties to be raised to such a revered position, but because Parker was a member of the powerful Wolf Clan (other members included Red Jacket and Jimmy Johnson, Handsome Lake's successor) and because of his leadership in the resistance campaign, it appears that clan matrons made an exception. That he was chosen for this position was also reflective of the shifting notions of governance and authority taking place in the face of the removal crisis.[38]

Correspondence between Ely Parker and his family in the 1840s and 1850s paint a picture of a community struggling to come to terms with an emerging younger generation of leaders. These men claimed their positions because of their abilities to negotiate both Native and non-Native legal and political concepts. In an 1846 letter to his brother Nicholson, Ely Parker acknowledged that divergent political groups had begun developing among their people and struggled against one another for control and authority. "If ever the Tonawandas were required to be united in their plans and purposes," he asserted, "it is now. . . . The interests of future generations hang upon the course we pursue." Ely's comments to his brother after a Tonawanda man named Stephen threatened the legitimacy of his position, however, indicate just how difficult it would be to stay united. "You say Stephen talks much about my being too young to attend to matters of such great importance," Parker wrote. "I do not envy his misery. . . . Nothing else troubles him more than the mere knowledge of the fact that a little boy has superseded him in wisdom and power, although he [Stephen] is old enough to be his [Parker's] grandfather."[39]

Parker expressed regret over the political battles at Tonawanda, but he reminded Nicholson, "No matter what . . . let us try and be united and hang on to our land as the fox hangs on to its prey."[40] Perhaps Tonawanda leaders heard Parker's concerns, because they immediately drafted a letter reminding him of the confidence they held in their young spokesman, and to demonstrate this, they sent him some additional funds for living expenses. "You may think toward us that we are not united, but we tell you that [we] are," they assured him. "The evidence is clearly shown in sending that sum of money to you for it passed through the Nation."[41] Parker's youth, though, would continue to be an issue of contention and concern.

The majority of the Tonawanda Seneca chose to remain in their homeland and fight against the company's efforts to dispossess them, but, like the Cherokee a few years earlier, some believed that moving to the West would provide opportunities otherwise unavailable. These personal choices not only disrupted community solidarity, which was significant enough on its own due to the value Seneca history placed on unanimity, but they also caused rifts within families. The case of Spencer Cone and the Parker family illustrates these issues quite effectively.

Thirteen years older than Ely, Spencer Houghton Cone was the only member of the Parker family to support the Treaty of 1838. Cone had taken the name of the Baptist clergyman who helped facilitate his education, but it has also been suggested that because of his support for the treaty, William Parker, his father, forbade him from using the family surname. Cone may have even acted as an agent for the Ogden Company and for a time lived in Enterprise, Missouri.[42] Arthur C. Parker compared Cone to Nathaniel Thayer Strong, a young removal advocate from the Cattaraugus Reservation, and described him as restless and temperamental.[43] Cone argued that the Tonawanda Seneca were being led by ignorant chiefs and should move west. Interestingly, though, in a letter to his father—one of the chiefs he criticized—Cone simultaneously defended the choice to move west and his love of their Tonawanda homeland, stating, "I respect my rights and love my lands." Ely Parker, perhaps suggesting that his brother should reconsider his position on the issue, told Cone that he supported the resistance campaign because the Seneca had been unjustly treated by the "rascally white race." Later, Cone even threatened that he had knowledge of a document in which Tonawanda leaders agreed to the 1842 compromise treaty, a fact that would have been devastating to their resistance campaign.[44]

Cone was not simply the black sheep of the family, though; it was his involvement with the Ogden Company that caused the division. In fact, he later ended his association with Ogden, returned to the reservation, and seemingly rectified his family relations. He began to use the Parker name around 1850 and was raised to the position of war chief. He died in 1851 at the age of thirty-six.[45]

During the removal campaign in Georgia, local citizens and state and federal policy makers banded together in a strong political alliance against the Cherokee. The national political culture of the Jacksonian era, land settlement patterns, development, and mining prospects, as well as the history of Georgia's aggression toward its Native residents, created an insurmountable obstacle that Cherokee leaders such as John Ross could not overcome.[46] The situation was quite different in New York State in the years immediately following Andrew Jackson's presidency. There, the Democratic Party struggled to maintain control as local citizens—farmers and laborers in the central and western parts of New York—joined with middle-class Whigs to oppose large landholders and pressure for land policy reform through a new state constitution. It was within this context that Parker and the Tonawanda Seneca established unlikely alliances with and found political support from public intellectuals, fraternal organizations, local non-Native farmers and laborers, and middle-class professionals.

Tonawanda leaders and their non-Native neighbors understood that population growth, transportation innovations, and market development had created a situation in western New York in which Native communities could not or would not continue to exist as they had in the past. In Parker's words, "the circumstances and influences" surrounding Tonawanda homelands would require some significant changes.[47] Local farmers and citizens, however, viewed eastern New York land speculators with skepticism at best, but more often with disgust. Local politicians, particularly Whigs, sought to challenge the Democratic Party and its costly removal policies, while local public intellectuals, many of whom were familiar with regional Indian history and culture, hoped to sustain these nearby communities to aid their own pursuits. The Seneca at Tonawanda, under Blacksmith's leadership and later under Parker's, actively pursued these alliances.

In 1844, Lewis Henry Morgan, the lawyer and founder of the Grand Order of the Iroquois, met sixteen-year-old Ely Parker in an Albany bookstore. Morgan later stated, "To sound the war whoop and seize the youth might have been dangerous," so he instead chose to speak to the young man.[48] Morgan saw Parker as a potential informant, a source of knowledge on Iroquois history and society. In Morgan, Parker found an ally, a legal expert, and a conduit to larger networks of politicians, lawyers, and professionals. The relationship was symbiotic. Parker provided Morgan with the insight and knowledge necessary to complete his first ethnographic work, *The League of the Ho-de-no-sau-nee or Iroquois* in 1851.[49] Morgan, for his part, lent his increasingly national reputation to the Tonawanda resistance campaign and helped to shape and direct non-Native support for the Tonawanda throughout the land dispute period.

Early in 1846, Morgan and other members of the Grand Order mobilized the non-Native allies that the Seneca had amassed in several New York counties. While in Washington, D.C., with other Tonawanda leaders, Parker wrote to Morgan saying that this encouragement gave him and the delegates "additional strength" and that it made "a very strong impression upon the feelings of many of the citizens [in Washington] in favor of the poor Indians." He also reminded Morgan that if the Grand Order continued in their support, they would "not be sorry for it."[50] To show their appreciation, the Tonawanda Seneca, in the fall of 1846, formally adopted Morgan and two other Grand Order brothers into their community. They bestowed the honorary name Tah-yad-da-o-wo-kuh, or "Lying Across," upon Morgan, perhaps recognizing his ability to build support between Native and non-Native people.[51]

Lewis Henry Morgan was not the only nationally known public intellectual to support the Tonawanda. Henry Rowe Schoolcraft, who had previously served as an Indian agent and federal negotiator in Michigan Territory, first visited the reservation in 1845 to complete his census of New York Indians.[52] In a letter written shortly after his visit, Schoolcraft thanked the Seneca for their "friendly disposition."[53] Playing the role of political entrepreneur, Parker used this opportunity to develop a friendship with the ethnographer, and a year later asked if Schoolcraft would be willing to supply some information for the Tonawanda to present to the Senate Committee on Indian Affairs in their fight against the Ogden Company.

Although Schoolcraft had served as an agent of dispossession in Michigan, he willingly provided information based on his research that the Seneca knew would command the respect of the committee. Community leaders wanted to demonstrate that the Allegany and Cattaraugus Reservation land could not support all the New York Seneca and that, in the history of the Seneca people, chiefs made all political decisions using the principle of unanimity, not a system of majority rule. Schoolcraft replied immediately with useful responses. He stated that based on his "observation on those reservations [Allegany and Cattaraugus,] . . . they are insufficient in extent to accommodate, permanently, the entire Seneca population." He also asserted, as Parker knew he would, that "in former times, the majority-principle was not known . . . Unanimity, appears to have been necessary, in the result of all important national questions."[54] Tonawanda leaders used this information from a "recognized" Indian expert to add credence to the petition Parker drafted and delivered to President Polk and the Senate.[55]

Schoolcraft continued to support the Seneca resistance campaign into the late 1840s. Congress paid him to conduct a lengthy study of Indian people and compile the information into a usable format.[56] During his time in Washington, Schoolcraft monitored developments in the land dispute and, at a critical moment in 1849, informed Parker that the Ogden Company would employ a new appraiser.[57] This information provided Tonawanda leaders with time to react accordingly and to develop a successful petition to counter the Ogden maneuver. Schoolcraft and Morgan gave credence to the Seneca resistance movement that other non-Native policy makers recognized and respected.

Other non-Native New Yorkers played key roles in these events. In early 1847, Parker wrote to Lewis Henry Morgan from Washington, "Petitions from western and central New York are almost daily presented in our behalf, and I have no doubt [these petitions] will have a great bearing in the final issue of the matter [the land dispute]."[58] The signatories to these petitions held and worked the land in Genesee and the surrounding counties; they were farmers, laborers, and regular citizens. If these men had lived in Georgia a decade earlier, they would have supported Cherokee removal, and one might have expected them to support the removal of the Tonawanda Seneca in the 1840s. That they did not can perhaps best be understood as a function of the history of landownership and land policy in New York State.

In a holdover from the colonial period, large landowners in New York, such as Stephen Van Rensselaer III, established their political and social status through paternalistic influence and a manor system of land distribution that included inheritable life leases. The Revolutionary generation of landholders and tenants saw this system, as mutually beneficial because it insulated both groups against market forces, but in the nineteenth century, their sons, swept up in the tensions of an emerging capitalist economy, fought bitter political battles over land policy reform and governmental representation. Tenant farmers viewed themselves as the offspring of the Revolution and therefore deserved the right to own the land they worked. Furthermore, as small producers, they saw themselves as the most trustworthy and responsible candidates for political office. In the antirent wars of the 1830s and 1840s, they wore Indian costumes when they protested or committed violence against the landholders. During the concurrent Ogden removal crisis, local citizens saw their interests as parallel to those of the sedentary agriculturalist Seneca and opposed the private company of elite eastern businessmen who held vast tracts of land but did not work the soil.[59]

In petitions they submitted to the U.S. Senate, non-Native farmers and laborers employed language that revealed their connection to and appreciation and support for the Tonawanda community. One petition stated that the treaties gave Indians "for their lands but one-tenth of their value, and nothing for one of the finest water privileges in the State." The signers asserted that the Tonawanda were "moral, industrious, honest people, rapidly improving in their condition, possessing good farms," and, like the farmers themselves, they were "strongly attached to the homes of their fathers." Finally, petitioners assured the Senate that the "people of the State of New York do not desire their removal, and have no sympathies with their spoilers."[60] In another petition, the residents of western New York argued that the treaties of 1838 and 1842 were "contrary to every principle of justice and humanity" and that "these Indians have been unmercifully defrauded."[61] Their support gave Tonawanda leaders strength and added weight to the arguments they presented in front of state and national policy makers.

Nathanial Thayer Strong, a young removal advocate at the Cattaraugus Reservation, offered another explanation for non-Natives' support, charging that non-Natives who opposed removal did so out of personal greed. In his *Appeal to the Christian Community on the Condition and Prospects of the New York Indians*, he argued that these men sold liquor to the Indians, leased them water rights, bought lumber from them, and held licenses to live on their lands.[62] They stood to profit in many ways from the Indians' continued presence in the state.[63] Strong's *Appeal*, however, can be read as a defense of his own actions—he not only signed the Treaty of 1838 but also served as an interpreter and assistant to the New York agent at Buffalo and "encouraged" Seneca leaders to sign the treaty and move west with cash payments and other bribes. It can also be read as a defense of the other pro-removal chiefs among the Indians. Strong's vociferous support for removal hints once again at the divergent political strategies among the Seneca, but his argument was less than persuasive. It is perhaps true that cash annuities owed to the Seneca through previous treaties may have provided western New Yorkers with much-needed specie, especially in the wake of the Panic of 1837. The language local farmers used in their petitions, however, drew upon the history of land policy and the relationships between large landholders and tenants and therefore suggests that their support for the Indians emerged from philosophical and political beliefs rather than from simple greed or self-preservation.[64]

While non-Native farmers and small producers conducted their petition drive, other citizens in western and central New York—lawyers, merchants, and businessmen—met and drafted lengthy memorials to the president and

Senate to express their support for the Indians and outrage at the conduct of the land company. Some of these individuals, such as Frederick Follett, a well-known politician and newspaper owner in Batavia, and Batavia and Rochester lawyers Isaac Verplanck and John H. Martindale, offered continuous support to the resistance campaign.

In 1846, a "large convention of the citizens of Genesee county" assembled in Batavia to discuss the land dispute at the behest of the Genesee grand jury. Once there, the men organized committees and drafted resolutions and memorials to be delivered to Washington, D.C. They wanted to make it known that "the public feeling of the people . . . is greatly shocked at the threatened perpetration of this wrong [Seneca removal]." In their memorials they outlined various "revolting, reprehensible, and barbarous" Ogden Company practices, including the use of liquor and bribes to obtain signatures.[65] Because the treaties did not honestly represent the free and voluntary assent of the Tonawanda people—none of their leaders actually signed either treaty—convention delegates argued that it was the responsibility of the federal government to ensure that they would not be removed. They also argued that if there was no other solution, the federal government should purchase the lands from the Ogden Company and transfer title to the Tonawanda people.[66]

Later, when a rumor circulated that the federal government would appoint a commissioner, dispense treaty payments, and hasten the removal process, several notable western New York citizens, many of whom had been involved in the earlier convention, voiced their support for the Tonawanda people. Marcus H. Johnson, an Indian agent from Randolph, N. E. Paine from Rochester, Isaac Verplanck, and Frederick Follett wrote letters to President Pierce, Secretary of State William L. Marcy, and Secretary of the Interior Robert McClelland protesting the rumored action.[67] Paine stated that his words of protest represented "the almost universal opinion of this community." Follett, one of the most outspoken of the Tonawanda supporters, did not mince words: "We all know in this region that the Treaty in question is a *fraud*," he wrote. He also estimated that "99 out of every 100 of the inhabitants of this region" agreed with his protest. The rumor proved to be false and was probably started by the Ogden Company to confuse and frustrate the Indians.[68] Local, non-Native citizens' support, though, strengthened the Seneca's resolve and encouraged them to continue their resistance.

As was the case with Lewis H. Morgan, some local, non-Native citizens provided support beyond drafting memorials and letters. Batavia lawyer and Seneca ally John H. Martindale took a leading role as legal council, and his efforts proved crucial to the Tonawanda fight against the Ogden Company.[69]

Martindale graduated from West Point Academy and would later serve as a brigadier general for the Union army in the Civil War, but from the early 1840s through the conclusion of the removal crisis in 1857, he provided critical legal counsel for the Indians. Following Martindale's advice, the Tonawanda leaders pursued reservation trespassers using the law established in the New York Constitution in 1821.[70] It was Martindale who argued the successful *Blacksmith* case, both in New York State and in the U.S. Supreme Court.[71] Along with Frederick Follett, he also visited Washington, D.C., at a crucial moment in 1857, helping to bring the removal crisis to its ultimate conclusion by persuading President Buchanan and others to allow the Tonawanda to use removal funds to purchase their land title from the Ogden Company.[72] When Tonawanda leaders sought to reform reservation governance in the aftermath of the removal crisis, it was Martindale who provided significant guidance and helped lobby for necessary legislation in New York State.[73] Experiences such as these demonstrated to the Seneca that they were not alone in their fight.

When Seneca delegates traveled to Washington, they met often and interacted with prominent national politicians who believed that Ogden officials committed great frauds and pledged support for the Tonawanda. During one trip to the capital, Parker remarked, "Calhoun and Crittenden are with us, as well as other able and heavy men."[74] Later the young Seneca described in his diary a Sunday evening meeting with Henry Clay. During their discussion Clay stated that he supported the Tonawanda case, and even considered submitting an application to try their claim before the Supreme Court.[75] These national politicians did little but sympathize with Parker and his community, though, and the lack of legislative action led Parker to refer to his efforts as "a miserable work."[76] Nevertheless, their support indicated to Parker that if viable alternatives could be created, bureaucratic structures, legal doctrines, and perhaps even federal policy makers could serve as a buffer for Indian people against unscrupulous land speculators and state legislators.

Reforming Reservation Governance

After almost two decades of struggle, the Tonawanda removal crisis ended in 1857. In June and July of that year, Ely Parker, John Martindale, Frederick Follett, and William G. Bryan met with federal officials and President Buchanan to challenge what they heard was the executive's plan to immediately remove the Tonawanda Seneca from New York State. The rumor was unsubstantiated, and instead the men negotiated a new program in which the Indians would relinquish their rights to federal lands in the Kansas Territory and use federal funds to purchase title to all or part of their reservation from the Ogden Land Company.

In late 1857, Indian and Ogden leaders met with Office of Indian Affairs representative Charles E. Mix and signed a new treaty based on the recently negotiated program.[77] Under this plan, the Seneca purchased from the company about three-fifths of the land they had held prior to the Treaty of 1838.[78] Though they point out the land loss, most scholars assert that the Tonawanda Seneca fared as well or better than any of the other Seneca communities in New York State. The Buffalo Creek Reservation no longer existed, and its people were scattered across lands to the west and in the Allegany and Cattaraugus communities. In 1848, social instability followed political revolution at these two reservations. Chaos ensued and continued through the 1850s. "[T]he Tonawandas' government remained unchanged," scholar Mary Conable has asserted; they "maintained an identity based on their geographic location and their adherence to traditional forms of government."[79] Historian Mark A. Nicholas suggests, too, that the Tonawanda Seneca maintained a public image of their community as the last true embodiment of traditional Seneca culture.[80] With the Tonawanda Seneca's customary chiefs still in power in the late 1850s, these statements adequately describe the situation immediately following the land dispute; however, events in the early 1860s demonstrate that the crisis had fundamentally altered Tonawanda society and governance.[81]

After ratifying the new treaty in 1857, leaders of the Tonawanda community hoped to encourage land improvements and agricultural development among their residents. These two activities had not received particular attention during the land dispute, despite Parker's assertion that they had, because people feared that they would lose their lands and their work would be for naught. Eager to make a profit, though, many Indians cut timber and extracted other resources from newly secured common lands—against the wishes of the chiefs—and sold them cheaply to non-Natives. In the postdispute political environment, chiefs struggled against one another to influence events within the community. Seneca residents, witnesses to the struggles of the resistance campaign, came to view their leaders as weak. William Parker wrote to his son in 1860, "The Chiefs in a great measure have lost their power, for in their annals, whatever they may pass, has no affect in the least." He asked Ely "to take some course of legal proceedings to clothe the Chiefs with an additional power with which to rule the band."[82] For Tonawanda leaders, these problems proved embarrassing.[83]

At Allegany and Cattaraugus, the removal crisis left more extreme political instability. In many ways the developments there set the stage for Parker's 1861 alternative political reforms at Tonawanda. In 1848, frustrated by the proceed-ings of the Buffalo Creek Treaty of 1838 and the compromise treaty of 1842, and suspicious of the process in which customary chiefs distributed treaty an-nuities to individual families, a revolutionary alliance emerged calling for a convention and a reconstruction of reservation governance. The New Gov-ernment Party, as they became known, created a pact with Hicksite Quakers and successfully instituted a system of government based on annual elections rather than hereditary and lifelong leadership positions. The Old Chiefs Party, as the defenders of the status quo were known, allied itself with Orthodox Quakers, but was unable to stem the revolutionary tide. Young Seneca men and Hicksite Quakers appealed to federal officials—men much more likely to support a system of government based on the democratic principles of the United States over one adhering to ancient Seneca traditions—arguing that a firm majority of the Seneca supported the changes. Tonawanda, as it had done since the 1842 treaty, maintained its autonomy from the other two Seneca reservations.[84]

When the Allegany and Cattaraugus Reservations declared themselves the Seneca Nation and drafted an official constitution in 1848, they modeled their government very closely on that of the United States.[85] They likened the traditional powers of chiefs to that held by the British aristocracy at the time of the American Revolution and replaced the older system with a three-branch government. It was comprised of a legislative council chosen annually, a president, treasurer, and clerk as executive officers, and a group of peace-makers serving as a judiciary. Any adult in the general population could be elected to these positions. When Parker returned at the behest of his father and other Tonawanda leaders, he carefully distinguished his own alternative governmental reform plan from the sweeping changes at the Allegany and Cattaraugus Reservations.

Like William Parker, Ely recognized that the removal crisis had upset Tonawanda notions of governance and authority, and the plan for reform he developed with John Martindale demonstrated a certain political acumen. In fact, Parker's actions here demonstrated most clearly at this stage in his life how he had become a political entrepreneur. With Martindale's help, he sought to "consolidate innovations into lasting change." As political scientist Adam Sheingate has argued, "It is during times of crisis and uncertainty when politi-cal entrepreneurs can offer alternative or competing narratives that redefine political interests in a manner that opens up new coalitional possibilities."[86]

The Parker/Martindale government plan designated six elective offices: three peacemakers, a treasurer, a clerk, and a marshal. These officers would be elected exclusively from the ranks of the customary chiefs and warriors of the Seneca, and all male residents over the age of twenty would be eligible to vote. The peacemakers would hold powers and responsibilities similar to justices of the peace in non-Native society. They could pass judgment on any civil suit or property case up to one hundred dollars. The clerk would be responsible for keeping records of all elections as well as the proceedings of councils held by chiefs and peacemakers. The treasurer would keep and disburse band monies, and the marshal would serve as a constable.

In addition to these elective offices, the plan outlined several legislative mandates. The first would prohibit residents from selling timber and other natural resources held in common by the Tonawanda to non-Native people. The second would allow residents to select and occupy specific tracts of reservation land provided they obtained the consent of the chiefs. The third would give chiefs the power to plot and build roads and fences throughout the reservation. The final mandate would prohibit residents from leasing their lands to non-Native people or allowing non-Natives to work Indian lands in shares.[87] In early 1861, Parker and Martindale traveled to Albany, where the state legislature officially ratified by the plan.

As a customary chief himself, it was not Parker's goal to usurp power and authority from the traditional leadership of the community; rather, he sought to provide a legal framework through which customary leaders could validate their policies in the face of a changing social and political landscape on the reservation. "There were times in the history of the [land] struggle," he wrote, "when we seemed to be enveloped in utter darkness, and our wise men were lost in doubt what to do." The government at Tonawanda had "no power to enforce or execute its will." He reassured the community that the new system did not abolish traditional Seneca governing structures but that it simply added vitality, efficiency, and impartiality so that the community could continue to "exist and prosper."[88] Although Parker's goals involved ending political squabbles on the reservation, his new system of governance was based on non-Native governmental ideals. He claimed that this system did not take away the power of customary chiefs, but it called for a series of elections that would empower a small number of chiefs over the other leaders, an idea that ran counter to the customary notions of Seneca authority under which all leaders held an equal position within a system based on unanimity.

Though Parker did not describe it as such, the reform that he helped institute on the Tonawanda Reservation represented an important political transformation. While one of the primary goals of this reform was to strengthen the executive power of customary leaders to enforce their policies on the reservation, it also "provided that the District Attorney of Genesee County shall be the attorney and counselor of the Tonawanda Band . . . paid by the State . . . to prosecute all white persons who violate the wise provisions of the law . . . and to settle all difficulties between Indians when in his power."[89] Requiring state-level ratification of Tonawanda reforms and employing a county-level district attorney reflected the larger national assault on internal sovereignty between the 1840s and 1880s that resulted in the confinement of Indian communities within the framework of U.S. law. In addition, the fact that Seneca leaders felt it necessary to have this reform structure ratified by the New York State legislature suggests how significantly Tonawanda Seneca sovereignty had become destabilized by 1861. The band did not fully surrender plenary power to the state, but by midcentury, it appears that Tonawanda's ability to craft its own policies was in question.

The Parker/Martindale alternative differed from the earlier political revolution at Allegany and Cattaraugus in several important ways, too. First, Parker, as a customary chief, reformed rather than replaced the structures of Tonawanda governance. He stated, "We have only asked for some new rules to give new vitality and efficiency to your government and materially enhance your prosperity."[90] Aided by Quakers, the Allegany and Cattaraugus revolutionaries existed outside customary roles of power and authority. Peter Wilson, for example, was not even a Seneca but a Cayuga living in the Seneca community.[91] These men removed customary leaders or at least created the legal and political means by which they could be removed. More importantly, Parker's reforms sought to end factionalism on the Tonawanda reservation, while the revolution at Allegany and Cattaraugus intensified factional struggles. Throughout the 1850s, the New Government and Old Chiefs Parties staged political battles, protested to state and federal officials about reservation events, and traded electoral victories and defeats. It was a complex and chaotic period, during which the political future of the newly formed "Seneca Nation" was uncertain. The Old Chiefs won elections in 1851, 1852, and 1854, and after each victory, they attempted to abolish the new constitution but were never successful.[92]

Parker recognized the immense emotional consequences of this political revolution. In 1858 he wrote to the Seneca president that the Indians' land claims in the West were in jeopardy, but if the Indians could "unite and agree upon some course," Congress would assist them in receiving proper compensation.[93] In an earlier letter to Henry Rowe Schoolcraft, Parker stated his concerns more directly. "[T]he old system should be restored [at Allegheny and Cattaraugus]," he wrote. The "new has made so much trouble, caused so much bitter and hard feeling among our leading men . . . that by all measures the old should be restored and sustained." A drastic political revolution was not necessary for the future of the Seneca people. "When the masses shall be properly educated," he argued, "the transposition of one state of Gov[ernment] to another would hardly be noticed."[94] Between this political revolution and his own reform efforts at Tonawanda, Parker attempted to develop a viable alternative that would minimize internal strife and allow the Seneca people to retain as much autonomous control as possible in the face of the evolving assault on tribal sovereignty in the state and nation. "[I did] not contemplate that you will ever become citizens of the United States, or that you will ever want to be such," he assured Seneca leaders. "And therefore we have guarded your lands in such a manner that you and your children may always enjoy the fruits and benefits of it."[95]

THE TONAWANDA SENECA emerged from the removal crisis and resistance campaign weak and bruised, but not entirely defeated. The state and national assaults on tribal sovereignty had certainly destabilized notions of governance and authority within this Indian nation, but it was within this context that Ely Parker and other young leaders rose to prominence and shaped a resistance campaign that eventually led to a permanent title to their homeland on the Tonawanda Creek.

On many levels this outcome can be considered a success; however, it came at a severe cost. Parker's actions ultimately confined the Tonawanda to a significantly smaller land base. He acknowledged that the Indians' "happiness, security, and probably their continued existence [were] powerful motives to them to cling to their present homes," but in order to do so, they paid $165,000 for 7,540 acres of an original 12,800-acre tract, a significant price to pay for one's own land.[96] At the beginning of the Buffalo Creek Treaty period, the New York Seneca had occupied roughly 110,000 acres; by the controversy's conclusion, they were confined to 60,547 acres.[97] They expended a significant amount of political and actual capital to conclude the land dispute, and they would not play a significant political, economic, or social role again in New York State until the twentieth century.

This experience was profoundly important for Parker. It provided him a foundation in political reform upon which he could build and presented opportunities for him to display, early in life, the characteristics of a political entrepreneur. During the crisis, he established a pattern of seeking alternative paths that might help the Seneca maintain their slowly deteriorating political position within the state. His program of reform revealed a hybrid framework, one that drew from non-Native governmental ideals and structures but also maintained a focus on Indian sovereignty and an awareness of Indian communities' customary social and cultural practices. The realities of dispossession and removal threats in early-nineteenth-century New York, especially at the hands of unscrupulous land speculators, made some customary Seneca leadership practices, such as the principle of unanimity, impractical or, worse, dangerous. Political disunity, coupled with divergent individual interests, and an incomplete knowledge of non-Native contract and treaty law slowed the pace of decision-making and, according to Parker, threatened the Seneca's future in the state. By instituting structures that more closely resembled county government, while at the same time maintaining some elements of customary Seneca practices, Parker acted in ways that reflected the work of other Indian leaders faced with similar crises, but, as the next chapter suggests, his experience is of particular significance because it foreshadowed developments on the national level.

THREE

Peace Policy Precursors, 1861–1868

This project, at first blush, may seem to be devised on too extensive a scale,
and involving too much expense for an experiment. I cannot regard it so.
—ELY S. PARKER, report on Indian affairs, 1867

Acknowledging the gradual but persistent confinement of Indian people in
the conclusion to their investigation of the Fort Philip Kearney (Fetterman)
fight in 1867, General Alfred Sully and Colonel Ely S. Parker wrote, "The Indian Territory is every year becoming more and more contracted. . . . [Y]early
Indians are dying from *actual* starvation. Is it to be wondered at that they are
sometimes hostile?" Urging Congress to take an immediate measure to ease
their suffering, they warned, "You cannot talk to a starving man about patience."[1] In their impassioned call for a reconsideration of Indian policy, Sully
and Parker sought to harness the federal government's postwar reformist spirit
and direct it toward Indian affairs. Both men had devoted significant portions
of their careers working among (or fighting, in Sully's case) Indian people, and
both viewed the early Reconstruction period as a moment of opportunity for
a potential recasting of the relationship between Indian people and the United
States, or at the very least, a moment to stop and question Indian confinement.

This chapter focuses on several individuals whose experiences and roles in
important events are often exiled to the periphery of Indian policy development studies. It suggests that the commissioners and participants in the Indian
peace councils in the West and South in the late 1860s, especially Ely Parker,
developed viable policy alternatives that broke with previous approaches in
Indian affairs. Some of these alternatives evolved into critical elements of the
peace policy, while opposing reformers in Washington and elsewhere actively
repressed others.

Parker's alternative approach to Indian policy reform during the early Reconstruction era focused on several related ideas and proposals, some of which
were distinctive to him. Among the most important ways Parker differed from
mainstream assimilationists was the high value he placed on enforcing existing

treaties to the exact letter in which they were written, even if that meant adversely affecting non-Native settlement (or conversely, if it meant enforcing unfair treaties signed under suspected fraudulent or coercive circumstances). He was willing to use the military to enforce treaty stipulations and to help implement social policy, much as it was being used to direct reconstruction efforts in the South simultaneously. He did not want the military to engage Native people violently unless it was absolutely necessary and a last resort. Also distinctive to Parker was his effort to slow the pace of assimilation and to provide opportunities for Indigenous nations to incorporate themselves how and when they chose. He sought to persuade Indigenous communities that incorporating themselves within the United States could be positive and beneficial as opposed to forcing them to assimilate by whatever means necessary, as quickly as possible. Finally, Parker, more so than most of his contemporaries, was fully convinced of the capabilities of Native people. If they were given the right tools, incentives, and opportunities, he believed not only that they would choose to assimilate into mainstream culture and society on their own terms and according to their own time frame, but also that they could be productive contributors and rational citizens of the expanding United States.

Other elements of Parker's alternative dovetailed with ideas advanced by the larger body of reformers. However, Parker's advocacy of these common ideas predated that of most of his contemporaries. For example, Parker and Sully's final report of the Fort Philip Kearney investigation likely influenced the recommendations of the better-known Peace Commission of 1868. Some of the common ideas Parker advocated included making the administration of Indian policy more efficient by consolidating power within the Office of Indian Affairs (OIA); streamlining the bureaucracy of that office; providing oversight in the procurement and distribution of Indian treaty rations, supplies, and annuities; compensating Indian communities for land loss; and continuing U.S. colonialism.

Many of these ideas stemmed from Parker's earlier experiences as a political leader in New York State during the Tonawanda Seneca resistance campaign against the Ogden Land Company and as a reservation government reformer in its aftermath, as well as his experiences with federal bureaucracy before, during, and after the Civil War. Like many other reformers and activists who lived through the war, Parker found his worldview profoundly shaken. He and his allies presented a policy agenda that, while not rejecting Indian confinement and U.S. expansion outright, at least questioned the methods through which these were being achieved. They posed less disruptive alternatives that might provide Indian people with multiple paths toward a healthy and productive existence in the postwar nation. Some scholars have characterized this period in Indian affairs as "a mere hodge-podge," but examining Parker's role in the early development of the peace policy suggests that there was a consistent, though contested, movement toward an increasingly efficient and impartial bureaucracy, and an effort to treat Indigenous people more justly than had been the case in the past.[2]

Public Debates and Indian Policies

The Civil War represented the complete and total breakdown of civil society. It exposed the inability of the federal government to solve fundamental issues of racial equality and regional differences, but it also allowed antislavery and abolitionist humanitarians to gain a foothold in federal policy making. While Indian affairs seemingly received little attention during Abraham Lincoln's presidency, Lincoln himself and several other individuals considered reform in the Indian Office to be an important priority; of course, sectional conflict and the administration of the war effort often superseded any other actions.[3]

Two of the most prominent individuals who sought reform in Indian affairs in the late 1850s and early 1860s were John Beeson and Bishop Henry B. Whipple. Beeson was a British immigrant who settled first in Illinois and later in the Red River Valley of the Oregon Territory, where he would eventually be run out of town as an enemy of the people because of his support for Indian rights during the Rogue River War. Though he was not a member of any particular church, Beeson found motivation in Christian philosophy and argued in his book *A Plea for the Indians* that it was not "civilization" that was destroying Indian communities but "the more highly energized Savagism that creeps under its mantle, usurps its prerogative, and does unspeakable wrongs and mischiefs in its name."[4] Beeson later wrote several letters to Abraham Lincoln and visited the president in Washington, spending part of seven different winters there advocating for Indian rights. As the Civil War began, he suggested that it was not slavery but Indian dispossession and U.S. colonialism that was the true cause of sectional conflict. According to historian Henry Fritz, Lincoln once replied to Beeson in a letter that he heard many of his pleas, and though he had not responded sooner, he had given Indian affairs much thought. He said that when "the pressing matters of this war is [sic] settled the Indian shall have my first care and I will not rest untill Justice is done to their and to your satisfaction."[5]

Episcopal bishop Henry B. Whipple devoted his life to advocating for Indians as well. His work in Minnesota would ultimately put him into contact with many important national leaders and reformers, including the Welsh family in the 1870s, but even before that, he predicted the 1862 United States–Dakota War, arguing that dispossession would make the Indians desperate. In the aftermath of the war, Whipple cared for Indian victims, wrote in local newspapers that white settlers needed to remain calm, and traveled to Washington to plead with President Lincoln for leniency in dealing with the captured Dakota warriors.[6] Both Whipple and Beeson helped to draw public attention to Indian issues and suggested that the recent history of Indian confinement had created a volatile and unstable situation and that violence between Native and non-Native communities would likely intensify. Several bloody clashes between the U.S. military and Indians during the Civil War, including the United States–Dakota War, caused reformers and humanitarians to focus on Indian affairs more directly.

During a six-week period, between August 18 and September 26, 1862, starving Dakota community members, particularly Mdewakanton and Wahpekute Band members, attacked local white settlers around the Lower Sioux Agency near St. Paul, Minnesota, and their actions thrust Indian affairs into the public eye already focused on the Civil War.[7] While the cause of the attack remains an issue of interpretation, most agree that the failure of the federal government to provide annuities stipulated by a series of treaties in 1851 intensified a situation already made volatile by dispossession, non-Native settlement, and continuing colonialism.[8] The Dakota warriors moved south toward New Ulm and north along the Missouri River destroying farms and homesteads, killing settlers, and capturing immigrants and mixed-race men, women, and children. Estimates place the death toll at approximately 500 whites and an unknown number of Native people, while roughly 269 white and mixed-race men, women, and children were taken captive by Dakota warriors. The U.S. military, led by Major General John Pope, commander of the newly created Department of the Northwest, with the help of the Minnesota volunteer militia, gained control of the situation by the end of September. Brigadier General Henry Hastings Sibley established a military tribunal at Fort Release (which was later moved to nearby Fort Snelling) and in a gross violation of due process rights, tried and convicted 303 of 393 of the Dakota "hostiles." The tribunal condemned all 303 men to execution, but Abraham Lincoln pardoned 264 of them. On December 26, 1862, only a few days before Lincoln signed the Emancipation Proclamation, the U.S. military hanged 38 Dakotas in the largest mass execution in its history.[9]

The events of the United States–Dakota War received widespread public attention. Most commentators, especially those in Minnesota, supported the actions of the military and militia, some even criticizing Lincoln's leniency. Other outspoken critics, though, took this opportunity to argue for the need to reform Indian policy and the Bureau of Indian Affairs. Bishop Whipple asserted in a letter to Lincoln that the president needed to find honest Indian agents, reform treaty-making practices, provide legal representation for Sioux peoples, and control the liquor trade. Commissioner of Indian Affairs William Dole argued that the problems in Minnesota emerged from an inability to control non-Native settlers and that this problem would likely be seen elsewhere as Native peoples came into increasingly close contact with non-Natives. One of the women who had been held captive by the Dakota, Sarah Wakefield, even published a short book titled *Six Weeks in the Sioux Tepees*, in which she criticized the government's policies. She argued that the Dakota had only fought for what was rightfully theirs and that her "heart bled" as she "listened to their tales of suffering and distress." Wakefield concluded: "I pray God they may for the future be more mercifully dealt with by those that are in authority over them."[10] As the Civil War raged on, Indian affairs remained on the periphery of the national consciousness, but less than two years later, dramatic events would again thrust Native issues forward.

On November 29, 1864, Colonel John M. Chivington led more than 700 volunteer U.S. soldiers into a village of peaceful Cheyenne and Arapaho Indians in southeastern Colorado. The Indians, led by Black Kettle and Left Hand, had assembled along Sand Creek to distinguish themselves from the other Indians in the region who were actively pursuing military engagements with the United States. Attacking at dawn, Chivington and his volunteers flushed the Indians from their village. Even though Black Kettle—a proponent of peace—raised a U.S. flag and white surrender flag above his lodge, the soldiers relentlessly pursued the fleeing Cheyenne and Arapaho. They pinned the Indians in the dry streambed, an area several hundred yards wide containing sandy soil. It was there that the noncombatant women, children, elderly, and weak struggled but could not escape the soldiers' small arms and howitzer fire. More than 150 Indian people and nine non-Natives lost their lives.[11]

This massacre brought the ineffectiveness of federal Indian policy into the public view. Coupled with the earlier events in Minnesota, it inspired reformers and journalists across the nation to protest. As Francis Prucha wrote, the massacre "became a cause célèbre, a never-to-be-forgotten symbol of what was wrong with U.S. treatment of the Indians, which reformers would never let fade from view."[12] In 1865, the *New York Times* argued that "hostile" Natives needed to be punished severely, but "the history of the Chivington massacre is too fresh in the public mind, and will forever be too atrocious in history" for the nation to support current Indian policy.[13] *Frank Leslie's Illustrated Newspaper* asserted that the massacre was the government's fault, particularly the Department of the Interior and the OIA. Military actions against Indians meant lucrative contracts for the private companies that supplied war materials, and agents and officials grew rich from bribes for preferential treatment.[14] The *Times* also argued that "Indian matters . . . have been horribly bungled, and they will be in a mess until they turn over the Indian affairs to the army, as it was years ago."[15] Throughout 1867, the *Times* ran editorials supporting the notion that not only was Indian policy in its current form incredibly costly to the government, but it also resulted in "frightful wrongs to the Indians."[16] These articles and the public discourse that surrounded the Minnesota and Colorado events led to increasing pressure for reform. In response, the federal government formed two separate commissions to examine Indian policy making, the Doolittle Commission, led by Senator James Doolittle of Wisconsin, which found Chivington and his volunteers guilty of conducting a massacre, and the Peace Commission of 1867, which worked to ease tensions along the Bozeman Trail (discussed below).[17]

The Civil War experience itself helped motivate postwar reform initiatives. Government officials, military leaders, and civilians alike sought peace and a return to normalcy after four long years of war. And many of them, reflecting on the idealism that had developed during the war, hoped their sacrifices would not have been made in vain. Indeed, the *New York Tribune* exclaimed, "The new era has begun! . . . A new world is born."[18] For many reform-minded individuals, historian Mark Summers has asserted, "it *was* a new world . . . the Civil War left them with a sense of purpose renewed . . . a new commitment to make America better, if only to requite the lives lost."[19]

Many, as General Sully and Colonel Parker expressed in their 1867 report, believed the postwar years signaled a moment of opportunity for profound changes in the handling of Indian affairs. In fact, the hybrid, public and private framework of the Freedmen's Bureau, the perceived successes of the War Department during military occupation of the South, and the general optimism of the Radical Republicans in the immediate postwar years all provided models for reform, as well as inspiration.[20]

Parker likely looked to other military leaders and saw reflections of his own beliefs about the importance of postwar reform. General Oliver O. Howard, the newly appointed head of the Freedmen's Bureau, for example, viewed the war as a "calamitous" event but believed the mid- to late 1860s were a key moment that could bring former slaves "toward their rightful freedom." One of Howard's primary subordinates in the Freedmen's Bureau, Brigadier

General John W. Sprague, was chosen to help institute bureau programs in Arkansas. Sprague grew up in New York State, like Parker, and parlayed his training at Rensselaer Polytechnic Institute into service for the War Department. He argued that the Freedmen's Bureau needed to emphasize self-sufficiency and allow former slaves a certain amount of self-determination. There were others, of course, who were less optimistic at this moment, and William Tecumseh Sherman was certainly one of them. He told Howard that he would likely be able to fulfill less than 10 percent of the expectations set out for the Freedmen's Bureau.[21]

As public and governmental attention began to focus more intensely on western expansion and settlement (especially in terms of safeguarding against the rebirth of North-South sectional tensions), peaceful interaction with, or at least the peaceful removal of, Native American groups became a driving goal.[22] The expansion of federal power and the general reformist orientation of the government during the Reconstruction Era also were major factors in the development of reform in Indian affairs. As historian Andrew Denson has noted, wartime victory was followed by a surge of nationalism, especially in the Republican North. The destruction of slavery suggested that, if used properly, the federal government could be a tool for progress, a positive and active influence in the lives of Americans.[23] During and after the war, the federal bureaucracy grew and the functions of local and national governments became more integrated.[24] These developments combined to provide the mechanisms and the motivations for individuals to focus on Indian reform.

Ely Parker's career trajectory and previous experiences dovetailed nicely with these broader developments within the federal government. He led a distinguished career as a statesman on the local level in the 1840s and 1850s on behalf of his Tonawanda community in western New York, spent his youth and early adulthood traveling to Albany and Washington D.C., and helped negotiate an agreement with the federal government in 1857 that allowed the Tonawanda Seneca to buy the permanent title to some of their reservation lands from the Ogden Land Company.[25] In the aftermath of the removal crisis, Parker oversaw the construction of customhouses for the federal government as an employee of the Treasury Department first in Detroit and later in Galena, Illinois.[26] In Galena, Parker met and befriended a store clerk and Mexican War veteran named Ulysses S. Grant. Although he returned to Tonawanda in 1861 to reform reservation governance, when the Civil War broke out, he petitioned the Department of War for a commission in the Union army, citing his militia experience. He even appealed to Secretary of State William Seward for assistance. His request was denied.

General Ulysses S. Grant and staff. Known as the "Grand Photograph," this picture was taken by Matthew Brady after Grant and his men returned to City Point, Virginia, from Appomattox Court House on April 12, 1865. Courtesy of the National Archives and Records Administration, College Park, Md.

With Grant's help in 1863, Parker was finally granted a commission at the rank of captain, and he joined the Illinois general at the Battle of Vicksburg. He served first as an assistant adjutant general (an administrative position) and then quickly became Grant's military secretary, as well as a cherished member of his inner circle. At the war's end, Parker stayed in Washington as Grant's aide-de-camp and took the opportunity to work for the OIA, a longtime career aspiration.[27] Like Beeson and Whipple, Parker also approached President Lincoln with his concerns about Indian policy. While the Union army bogged down at City Point in 1864, Lincoln visited the encampment and spoke to Parker about Indian affairs. Also like Beeson and Whipple, Parker found the president to be "sympathetic to the Indians' plight and hopeful that the nation would someday make amends for the injustices done to them."[28] In June 1865, he went with Grant to the Cooper Union in New York City, a center for higher learning and a bastion of Indian reform sentiment, where, within a few years, the U.S. Indian Commission (a precursor to the Board of Indian Commissioners) would be founded.[29] In the late 1860s then, Parker was in an ideal position to play a key role in the development of Indian policy.

While many factors shaped postwar Indian policy reform, Parker seems to have been one of the most influential. As an Indian man educated both among Seneca people in the eastern Great Lakes region and within a western intellectual tradition via several New York State academies, he brought a unique view of the history of Indian/white contact to the reform discussion. His focus on protecting the integrity of Indian communities and providing compensation for dispossession and continuing colonialism and his experience working on behalf of Indian communities on the local and state levels also played a major role in his approach to reform. During the Tonawanda resistance campaign, he witnessed cooperation between communities in western New York, as local non-Natives, outraged by the land company's treatment of the Seneca, signed petitions and advocated on the Indians' behalf. He knew that when private corporations outside the jurisdiction of government regulations, such as land companies or transportation agencies, appealed to state policy makers and influenced colonial action, Native people faced injustice, dishonesty, greed, and dispossession. As a civil engineer working for the Treasury Department and having received praise and acclaim for the customhouses he built, he also came to understand the importance of an efficient and impartial bureaucratic structure.

Perhaps more importantly, Parker participated in and witnessed the work of a series of significant peace commissions that engaged Native nations in the 1860s. The commissions, created at the behest of the Interior Department with the support of the president, brought together unique individuals, including military, civilian, and religious officials, with varied perspectives and experiences living or working among Indian people. Several scholars view these commissions as having established the tenants of peace policy reforms; however, we can complicate and broaden our understanding of policy development by focusing on some of Parker's alternate justifications for reform mandates. Examining Parker's role also reveals some of the underlying tensions between reformers.[30]

In September 1865, Grant sent Ely Parker as a representative of the army in the commission established to meet with southern Indian nations, some of whom had signed treaties and fought alongside Confederates during the Civil War. Dennis Cooley, the recently appointed commissioner of Indian affairs, led the commission. Other members included Elijah Sells, the head of the southern Indian superintendency; Thomas Wistar, a Quaker leader from Philadelphia; and General William S. Harney, who had fought against the Lakota in the 1850s and was known to them by the name "Woman Killer." For most of September, the commissioners met with representatives from the Creek, Choctaw, Chickasaw, Cherokee, Seminole, Osage, Seneca, Shawnee, Quapaw, Wyandotte, Wichita, and Comanche Nations assembled at Fort Smith, Arkansas.[31]

The Fort Smith commission was charged with several important tasks. First, they were to explain to the Indian representatives that according to a clause in a congressional appropriations bill passed in July 1862, any Indian nations that had allied with the Confederacy nullified preexisting treaties between themselves and the United States. In practice, though, even those who remained loyal to the United States would be forced into new treaty relationships. Second, the commissioners were to explain that as a result of Union victory and the passage of the Thirteenth Amendment to the Constitution, southern Indian nations would be required to abolish slavery within Indian Territory. Finally, they were to negotiate new treaties that took as their model recently approved Senate Bill No. 459 (commonly known as the Harlan Bill after James Harlan, the Iowa senator who authored the bill).

Harlan had been a prominent member of the Senate Committee on Indian Affairs and in 1865–66 served in President Johnson's cabinet as secretary of the interior. The Harlan Bill sought to organize Indian Territory (as a federal territory) with the ultimate goal of voiding Indian land rights and opening the territory to white settlement and economic exploitation (especially from railroad companies). Political theorist Kevin Bruyneel has argued persuasively that the Harlan Bill was "an effort to impose the boundaries of American colonial rule on indigenous political life."[32] Indeed, although the bill made it no further than the Senate, it provides clear insight into one direction of federal Indian policy at this moment: increasing the political, social, geographic, and economic confinement of Indian people. Even though he was a member of the commission and ultimately signed his name to the final reports and agreements, it is unclear how strongly Parker supported its overall aims.

In her description of the Fort Smith peace council, historian Annie Abel, who penned a trilogy about southern Indians during and after the Civil War, makes a provocative statement. "Of Parker, little can be said," she wrote, "though much was then expected. He was a Seneca and might be thought to have possessed some inherent sympathy for his own race." She concluded, though, "Frankly-speaking . . . it must be admitted he gave little evidence of it. Was his appointment somewhat of a blind?"[33] Abel provides no evidence to support this statement, and unfortunately there is little in the historical record that captures Parker's own thoughts and words at Fort Smith. We do know that he took an active role in the proceedings, presiding over the council at one point, addressing the Indians on behalf of the commissioners at another, and negotiating directly with Choctaw and Chickasaw delegates throughout.[34] In fact, when the other commissioners decided to send Parker to Colorado Territory before the conclusion of the Fort Smith negotiations, the Choctaw and Chickasaw delegates appealed to have him retained for the duration of their council. These Indian delegates, it appears, would have disagreed with Abel's assertion. They wrote, "[The] fact that the United States Government have seen fit to include a member of an Indian tribe, with its Commissioners, has inspired us with confidence as to its designs and desires . . . and we are anxious to have the benefit of his presence and counsel."[35] The commissioners granted the request, and Parker remained, ultimately trying to aid those delegates as they sought to amend and modify the treaty offered by the federal government. Based on this evidence, it would seem that Parker did not fall into line with the other commissioners—an assumption granted additional validity because the other commissioners rejected these amendments and modifications.

Rather than a "blind" or silent player in western commissions, Parker played an increasingly important, even vital role, lending his voice to Indian complaints. Consequently, it might be useful to examine Parker's role at a subsequent peace council to find greater insight into his alternative perspective.

In 1867, Parker participated in the investigation of the military encounter known as the Fetterman Fight or Fetterman Massacre that resulted in the deaths of eighty U.S. Army soldiers at Fort Phil Kearney at the hands of Great Plains Native soldiers. In meetings with the Lakota, Cheyenne, and other Indians along the Missouri River in Nebraska and the Montana Territory, Parker worked with Indian delegates. While his fellow peace commissioners focused on punishments for the "hostile" Indians, Parker focused on the treatment of "friendly" Indians. "The Great Grandfather will take care of and protect the friendly Indians from their Indian enemies, and from bad whites," Parker told a group of Brule and Oglala leaders at California Crossing on April 20, 1867. He also asked to hear their "complaints of grievances" and promised to open dialogue between them and the federal government.[36] Later, he met with other Brule leaders from the Black Hills region. Parker stressed that he and President Grant wanted "to see everybody friendly" and assured them that they would listen to Natives' concerns.[37]

The commission's final report is a significant and often overlooked source documenting the development of postwar Indian policy. In fact, as mentioned at the beginning of this chapter, Parker and General Alfred Sully provided several recommendations for policy reform that predated and likely influenced the conclusions and recommendations of the better-known Peace Commission of 1868. This is a critical point and helps to illuminate more brightly the role Parker played in policy development in this era.

Parker and Sully argued that rather than fighting western Indian nations, the federal government should provide food for their subsistence, and (employing the ethnocentric language of the time) they asserted that "the Indian is susceptible, by proper management, of a high state of culture and civilization" and that they could ideally become "law abiding citizens."[38] In fact, demonstrating Parker's confidence in Natives' abilities, the report even suggested that "Indian citizens [might be] more pure and more patriotic than many of our white citizens."[39]

Several other key elements of Parker's reform alternatives emerged in this report. First, Parker and Sully blamed white settlers for instigating Indian violence and thus argued that Indian land titles needed to be clarified and protected by the federal government. Second, they asserted that the government should encourage agricultural development on Indian reservations even though they understood that federal officials had to honor treaty stipulations and would need to continue providing rations until Indian people could compete in the agricultural marketplace. Third (and related to the previous point), they argued that the time frame for reform had to reflect Indian expectations—not those of the government. Therefore, widespread results could not be expected for "for some years to come."[40] Fourth, they asserted that trade needed better regulation because an increase in poverty among the Indian people would intensify any underlying tensions between them and neighboring whites. Finally, they recommended that the OIA regularize its practices, particularly by providing more consistent employment and higher salaries for Indian agents, and by allowing Indian communities to select their own representatives, rather than Indian Affairs officials selecting for them.[41]

Only a few days before beginning his work on the Fort Phil Kearney commission, Parker submitted a letter to Secretary of War Edwin Stanton at the request of General Grant outlining some main points for a reform agenda in Indian affairs. The letter reveals significant connections to the final report of the Kearney investigation, and even more importantly demonstrates that it was likely Parker's voice and pen—much more than Sully's—that shaped that report and, subsequently, the recommendations of the 1868 Peace Commission.

Parker's 1867 plan, which he described as a program for "the establishment of a permanent and perpetual peace . . . between the United States and the various Indian tribes," reflected his previous experiences among the Tonawanda Seneca and the Fort Smith commission.[42] Parker's ideas focused on oversight of policy administration by both Native and non-Native individuals and the establishment and protection of specific land rights for Native communities. He also advocated bureaucratic reform through the transfer of the OIA back to the War Department. He argued that this move would curb corruption, allow the military to enforce treaty stipulations (something civil agents failed to do), and insulate the OIA from the influence of land and business interests. Parker also articulated his view that the government should provide money, goods, services, and new opportunities for Native people, particularly in the form of education, in an effort to counterbalance dispossession and the history of colonization.

Together the letter Parker wrote in 1867 and his authorship of the Fort Phil Kearney report revealed the evolution of his reform agenda and went a long way toward establishing him as a leading voice in Indian policy making at this time. As a political entrepreneur, Parker was working to influence powerful potential allies and to carve out the space necessary to develop his policies.

One of Parker's primary proposals in the 1867 letter involved the creation of an oversight committee comprised of private citizens who did not hold current governmental positions. He wanted this committee to monitor the acquisition and distribution of goods and rations to ensure that treaty stipulations were followed. They would "see that every cent due the Indians is paid to them promptly . . . and that proper and suitable goods and implements of agriculture are delivered to them." Perhaps drawing upon his experiences with the Choctaw and Chickasaw delegates at Fort Smith, Parker believed in the importance of instilling confidence in Indian people as a strategy to ease tensions between them and local non-Natives.[43] Upholding the government's end of treaty agreements would go a long way toward that end, Parker argued.

He also suggested the appointment of a second committee, a separate "permanent Indian commission" composed of both humanitarian-minded whites and Indian leaders from different nations. He wanted this group to meet with every Indian community, advocate for general peace, and to explain in the clearest terms that "the waves of population and civilization are upon every side of them; that it is too strong for them to resist; and that, unless they fall in with the current destiny as it rolls and surges around them, they must succumb and be annihilated by its overwhelming force." While the language he used might appear overly pessimistic, he also wanted the committee to "assure the tribes that the white man does not want the Indian exterminated from the face of the earth, but will live with him as good neighbors, in peace and quiet." In regard to putting Indians on the committee, Parker tried to reassure the politicians and military officials whose prejudices might influence his reform agenda that employing Native people on such a commission would be of great benefit because "they are familiar with the best modes of communicating with the tribes." Their presence, much like his own at Fort Smith in 1865, he argued, "would add greatly to the confidence of the tribes in the earnestness, sincerity, and humanity of the government."[44]

Another proposal in Parker's letter reflected his interest in protecting Indian communities as distinct geographic entities within the United States and in streamlining and consolidating Indian affairs as a way to stamp out corruption and mismanagement. Simultaneously, though, this proposal also revealed one of the primary techniques Parker the political entrepreneur would attempt to use to create a monopoly in Indian policy administration. He suggested that the federal government create "a plan of territorial government for the Indians . . . [that] should remain upon the statute books as the permanent and settled policy of the government." He noted that placing "all the Indians on any one territory is perhaps impracticable," but they could "be consolidated in separate districts of [the] country, and the same system of government made to apply to each." Perhaps echoing Supreme Court Justice Marshall's notion of "domestic dependent nations," Parker argued that the boundaries of these Indian territories had to be well defined and that the federal government needed to work to maintain these regions exclusively for Indian settlement. In his appeal he lamented that previous federal treaties had been violated and that Indian nations whose lands were to remain "unmolested by the hand of the grasping and avaricious white man" had in fact been molested.[45]

By proposing the establishment of these well-defined Indian territories with "the same system of government made to apply to each," Parker worked to limit the level of interaction between non-Native and Native people in the short term. As a political entrepreneur, though, Parker was also seeking to create political space to deploy his policy alternatives by limiting the disruptive influence some agents of the federal government had in Indian affairs. In fact, near the end of the letter, he asserted, "A whole army of Indian agents, traders, contractors, jobbers, and hangers-on would be dispensed with . . . it would effectively close to them the corrupt sources of their wealth."[46] At the same time, however, his language and ideas reflected some of the prevailing attitudes of mainstream assimilationists. According to this proposal, once Indian people were situated on permanently protected lands, the "government [could] more readily control them and more economically press and carry out plans for their improvement and civilization."[47]

There was an important coherence to these proposals that reflected not only the emerging programmatic, as opposed to piecemeal, nature of Parker's plans, but also the guiding principles and most distinctive elements of this reform agenda—his willingness to provide Indian communities with time to assimilate on their own terms. Parker wanted the mixed-race commission he advocated to "visit all the Indian tribes within the limits of the United States . . . [to] hold talks with them . . . [and explain] the advantages of their consolidation upon some common territory, over which Congress shall have extended the aegis of good, wise, and wholesome laws for their protection and perpetuation."[48] He envisioned this to be a slow and methodical process that might take "three, five, or ten years." He warned that many "of the tribes would have to be visited several times by the commission . . . and the government and people of the United States would be compelled to exercise the Christian virtue of patience, until the aboriginal mind was fully prepared and ripened to adopt the plans of the government."[49] By advocating a collaborative process and a slow pace, Parker demonstrated the value he placed on Indigenous rationality and just policy administration.

The other major suggestion that Parker made in his 1867 letter was to transfer the Office of Indian Affairs from the Department of the Interior back to the War Department, where it had been initially created in 1824 (it was moved to the Interior Department in 1849). He advanced several arguments in support of this position. First, he asserted that the military was better suited to protect Indian communities from avaricious whites by enforcing existing treaties. He characterized civil agents as "absolutely powerless" in this regard. Strictly enforcing treaty language was one of Parker's guiding principles, and when he observed the interactions between Native groups and invading non-Native settlers, the results disturbed him. As the "hardy pioneer[s] and adventurous miner[s]" traveled west, he noted, they "found no rights possessed by the Indians that they were bound to respect . . . the faith of treaties solemnly entered into were totally disregarded, and Indian territory wantonly violated." If "any tribe remonstrated against this violation of their natural and treaty rights . . . [they] were inhumanely shot down and . . . treated as mere dogs." He concluded that the "military alone can give the Indians the needed protection."[50]

In a related vein, Parker saw the civilian agents working in Indian affairs at this time as especially prone to fraud. He believed that they sought "to avoid all trouble and responsibility, and to make as much money as possible out of their offices." In contrast, the military officer's "honor and interest is at stake, and impels him to discharge his duty honestly and faithfully."[51]

In an effort to regularize trade and consolidate responsibilities for Indian affairs, he suggested that the practice of employing outside traders to supply Indian agencies be ended and instead that the military assume these responsibilities, work that the Army Commissary Department had carried out successfully during the Civil War. Finally, Parker asserted that Native leaders would more likely listen to military officials than they would the civil agents who had mistreated or lied to them or mismanaged affairs in the past.

It seems clear that Parker was not advocating increased military action *against* Indian people (though other reformers and federal agents, such as William Tecumseh Sherman, certainly envisioned this). Instead, Parker viewed the War Department in the postwar years as the most well-developed department in the federal government and therefore a perfect home for a newly reformed and efficient Office of Indian Affairs.

In advocating the transfer, he drew from his experiences both during and after the Civil War. He looked upon these events from the perspective of a bureaucrat, not a soldier, and clearly distinguished individual actions from institutional practice. For example, in the Fort Phil Kearney investigation, he asserted that Colonel Henry Carrington, the commander at the fort, "had no sort of discipline in his garrison" and took "no unusual precautions" against the potential for violence between the Indians and the soldiers.[52] He saw the deficiencies of individual soldiers and officers as the root cause of these institutional failures—not the bureaucratic structures of the military itself. He concluded that the "whole conduct of Indian Affairs shows a great lack of judgment and efficiency on *some one's* part."[53] Parker's own military experience as an "indoor man" may have led him to distinguish between voluntary soldiers or militias and the pared-down, postwar, professional military, which he viewed as much more efficient and trustworthy. Understood in this way, Parker's support for the OIA transfer to the War Department reflected his interest in creating an effective and impartial bureaucracy.

At the end of the Civil War, the War Department housed the most complex and well-developed bureaucratic system of any of the executive agencies. In addition, it was arguably the most smoothly running department. It also consumed the lion's share of the federal budget. Not only did the War Department manage the roughly 2,213,000-man Union army, but beginning in 1863, it administered the draft, as well as managing commutation payments and substitutions.[54] This was a significant expansion of its operations necessary to carry out the day-to-day operations of the military before 1860.[55]

The War Department also played an important role in implementing Reconstruction programs in the South—a role that Parker would find instructive. Once fighting ended, the "military enforced emancipation, and it fed and housed thousands of black refugees."[56] After twelve months of debate, Congress decided that the War Department would be the most effective in controlling the Freedmen's Bureau, whose authority and responsibility were modeled after the military anyway. In fact, General Grant believed the army should have operated it directly. Beginning in 1867, following the Radical Republicans' usurpation of control over Reconstruction programs, Congress placed the ten "unreconstructed" states under military jurisdiction, an action Parker and Grant both supported.[57] All of these developments would have provided additional support for Parker's faith in bureaucracy. Although he was certainly not the only individual advocating the transfer of the OIA, Parker's support differed from other military advocates in that he focused on issues of bureaucratization and treaty enforcement.

Parker received almost immediate support for the ideas outlined in his 1867 plan for Indian affairs reform. Henry Wilson, a leading Republican and Massachusetts senator (1855–73) who would be elected as Grant's vice president in 1872, wrote to him only four days after Parker penned the letter. "I have read your interesting and able report on Indian Affairs," Wilson stated, "and would feel much obliged if you would draw up and send me a bill for presentation to Congress, embodying the ideas and propositions embraced in your report."[58] It seems that because of his work on the Fort Phil Kearney investigation, Parker was unable to fulfill this request. This expression of support, though, was significant.

Even before the Fort Phil Kearney committee completed its work in 1867, and in part based on its early reports that most of the Indians in the West desired an end to the current wars and violence, Congress authorized a separate peace commission to meet with and negotiate peace among many of the same Great Plains nations with whom Parker, Sully, and the others had recently met. This commission occupies a larger space in the historical literature than other postwar commissions for two reasons: first, the 1868 commission was granted treaty-making authority, which many of the others were not; and, second, the men who served on the 1868 commission were powerful and influential in both the civilian and military elements of Indian policy making. Their story has come to dominate the literature, and it is likely the reason that historian Annie Abel made such strange conclusions about Parker's role (or lack thereof) in the Fort Smith Council in her otherwise very astute work. Focusing on the ways the 1868 group had likely been influenced by the earlier commissions points to a greater understanding of Parker's significance in peace policy development.

Members of the 1868 commission included Commissioner of Indian Affairs Nathaniel G. Taylor (Cooley's successor); Samuel Tappan, a noted supporter of Indian rights; Senator John B. Henderson, chairman of the Senate Committee on Indian Affairs; and John B. Sanborn, who had also served on the

"Commissioners at Fort Laramie, 1868." Several members of the 1868
Peace Commission are present surrounding an unnamed Arapaho woman.
Left to right, General Alfred H. Terry, General William S. Harney,
General William T. Sherman, General John B. Sanborn, Colonel Samuel F. Tappan,
and General C. C. Augur. Courtesy of National Anthropological Archives,
Smithsonian Institution, negative 3687, Glass Negatives of Indians, 1850s–1930s.

earlier commission with Parker and Sully. Military officers, General William T.
Sherman, Major General Alfred Terry, and retired general William S. Harney
accompanied these civilian members. Through the end of 1867 and beginning
of 1868, they met and signed treaties with the Comanche, Kiowa, Cheyenne,
Arapaho, Crow, Navajo, Bannock and Shoshone, and Lakota Nations. During
this period, members prepared two reports of their work, one submitted in
January 1868 after several months of negotiations and a second, final report
submitted in October of that year.

In important ways these reports demonstrated the traction that some of
Parker's reform alternatives had quickly gained. They also show that many of
the prominent voices in Indian policy making saw value in Parker's alternative
opinions and goals for reform. Of equal significance, though, these reports
demonstrate how deeply some of the other prevailing attitudes about Indian
affairs remained entrenched in the minds of important policy makers. Historian Andrew Denson has defined this attitude as "a variation on removal with
special attention paid to the civilizing mission."[59]

In their first report, Taylor and the others, echoing Parker and Sully, blamed whites for instigating and intensifying the violence and warfare around Indian communities. "Many bad men are found among the whites; they commit outrages despite all social restraints," they wrote. It was not "astonishing," they concluded, that Indians went to war; they were "often compelled to do so."[60] After lamenting the long history of violence and dispossession, the commissioners suggested, following Parker's (and Sully's) earlier lead, that a shift in focus would be necessary. They urged Congress to clarify and protect the boundaries of Indian nations' homelands. They also proposed to regularize Indian affairs by employing agents who had "unquestioned integrity and purity," and paying them enough to keep them "above temptation."[61]

The peace commissioners' conclusions mirrored Parker's ideas in other ways, too. They argued in both reports that treaty obligations needed to be honored, but instead of providing money annuities, which "more than anything else have corrupted the Indian service," they believed agricultural goods and supplies could be given as a means to develop subsistence and larger-scale farming.[62] In their final report, the commission recommended that the federal government "feed, clothe and protect" all of the Great Plains nations who chose to settle on agricultural reservations.[63]

The peace commissioners asked that trade with Native nations be reformed through a reconsideration of the trade and intercourse laws. The new laws would better protect Native people from fraud and avarice.[64] The commissioners did not imply that westward expansion of the United States would cease but that it could become less harmful to Indian communities if the government adhered to principles of justice and humanity.

It is likely that Parker found much to appreciate in this report. It is also likely that its connections to his own reform alternatives gave him confidence that fundamental change was possible. Their suggestions, however, differed in significant ways, and that should have been an indication that change might not come so easily.

The first report of the peace commissioners, though espousing language of peace and justice, revealed an underlying threat of continued violence or military action and a ready willingness to break treaties. "We do not contest the ever ready argument," the commissioners stated, "that civilization must not be arrested in its progress by a handful of savages. . . . The Indian must not stand in the way."[65] This threatening tone was overt in the commission's final policy recommendations. As they were drafting the latter document, the peace commissioners voted to break the treaty stipulations they had negotiated only months before (likely a response to violence along the Southern Plains), which allowed

"U.S. Army Commissioners in Council with Chiefs Inside Tent, 1868." Members of the 1868 Peace Commission and others are pictured negotiating with several Great Plains Native negotiators. General William T. Sherman is seated near the center of the photograph. Courtesy of National Anthropological Archives, Smithsonian Institution, SPC Plains Dakota BAE 24–39, Photographs of American Indians and Other Subjects, 1840s–1960s.

Indian hunters to roam freely on or off the reservation. They recommended that Plains Indians be allowed to leave their reservations only with "written authority from their Agent or Superintendent." Further, they suggested that "military force should be used" to expedite reservation confinement.[66]

In their final report, the peace commissioners also unanimously adopted a resolution stating, "The time has come when the Government should cease to recognize the Indian tribes as 'domestic dependent nations' except in so far as it may be required to recognize them as such by existing treaties."[67] Although Parker would eventually support this position and advocate for a cessation of treaty making, in 1868 he was not yet willing to go that far.

Another point of division between Parker and the peace commissioners existed in the time frame envisioned for reform. Parker argued that a slow, measured pace was the most appropriate because it would give Indian people time to adapt more comfortably to the government's new orientation toward assimilation. The peace commissioners, on the other hand, appeared apologetic that their recommendations might take awhile. Their plan might experience "slow progress," but if they could "civilize in twenty-five years," it would be a "vast improvement on the operations of the past."[68]

Finally, but most significantly, the peace commissioners, in both reports, grappled with the idea of transferring the Indian Office to the War Department. In their first report, they argued that Indian affairs should not be transferred. They wrote that the new federal policy goals would be "emphatically civil, and not military." They also argued that the Interior Department was not a good home either; instead, they wanted a new "independent bureau or department" for Indian affairs.[69] An independent bureau, they asserted, would help to remove the influence of political patronage from the office, and they even went so far as to suggest that on a given date, Congress should dismiss all employees of the Indian Office, review their performances, and rehire only those who had "proved themselves competent and faithful." They stated explicitly that "professions of party zeal" could not be a factor in reappointment.[70] While all seven of the original commissioners signed this report, it is clear only a simple majority approved of the recommendation against transferring the Indian Office. In an 1869 letter to Senator E. G. Ross, General Sherman revealed that the civilian members of the commission voted in favor of the recommendation, while he and Generals Terry and Harney did not. "We did not favor the conclusion arrived at, but being out-voted," he wrote, "we had to sign the report."[71]

In their final report, the peace commissioners changed their recommendation. As violence reerupted in the Southern Plains in October 1868, the generals, this time with an additional vote on their side (General C. C. Augur had recently joined the commission in an official capacity), were able to sway the opinions of all but one of the civilian peace commissioners. In the debates surrounding this move, Commissioner of Indian Affairs Nathaniel Taylor made an impassioned and strongly worded argument against the recommendation.

Taylor stated that since the Civil War had ended, Congress should support only a small army on a "peace footing"; citizens would not abide the use of tax dollars to fund a large army in a venture that seemed to have no set endpoint or system for measuring success. Moving Indian affairs to the War Department, he continued, would be "offensive" to Indian people and an indication of "perpetual war." It could only result, he believed, in "demoralization and disease." In the past, military management had failed, and it would "always prove a failure." Finally, Taylor asserted that he could find no new evidence to support changing the decision made only a few months earlier not to recommend the transfer.[72] The commission voted to recommend the transfer; Taylor recorded the only "no" vote.

It is interesting to consider this final recommendation in connection to Parker's argument supporting the transfer. On the one hand, while the peace commissioners appeared to be Parker's allies in advocating the move, their motivation was ongoing military action. A statement from the earlier report reflects this standpoint nicely: "If the savage resists, civilization, with the ten commandments in one hand and the sword in the other, demands his immediate extermination."[73] This was a stance that Parker explicitly rejected.

On the other hand, in arguing against the transfer, Commissioner Taylor used a logic that Parker not only supported but also invoked constantly in his agitation for reform. Taylor wrote, "Respect their wishes, fulfill our treaty stipulations promptly and faithfully, keep them well fed, and there will be no need of armies among them."[74] In this sense, Parker's position on this issue can be understood as a middle path, one that might appeal to a broad swath of reform-minded individuals in late-1860s Indian policy making.

INDEED, PARKER HAD many reasons to believe that he was positioned advantageously to lead a successful reform movement. He gained valuable experience in the Fort Smith commission of 1865 and in the investigation of the Fort Phil Kearney incident in 1867. His letter outlining a plan for reform in the Office of Indian Affairs had been well received in 1867, and his contributions to the final reports of the various commissions upon which he served seemed to be echoed by other prominent policy makers. When he entered the Indian Office in an official capacity as commissioner in 1869, then, he had many reasons to be optimistic.

Parker's alternative program displayed several distinctive features. He placed a high value on enforcing treaties and was willing to deploy the military to do so. He wanted to provide Indigenous nations with as much time as possible to incorporate themselves into the broader United States by their own means. Finally, he was fully convinced of Native people's capacities.

Other elements of Parker's reform program appealed to a broad swath of reformers during the Reconstruction era and focused on several related efforts, including making the administration of Indian policy more efficient by consolidating power within the Office of Indian Affairs; streamlining the bureaucracy of that office; providing oversight in the procurement and distribution of Indian treaty rations, supplies, and annuities; and compensating Indian communities for land loss and continuing U.S. colonialism. As the next chapter demonstrates, Commissioner Parker would work to institute these reforms almost immediately, and he and his allies experienced many quick victories.

FOUR

Ely Parker's Moment, 1869–1871

You will endeavor to keep constantly before their mind the pacific intentions
of the Government, and to obtain their confidence by acts of kindness, and
honesty.... Your success in the accomplishment of these objects will depend
greatly upon the efficiency, discretion, and care to be exercised by you in
the economical expenditure of the means placed at your disposal.
—ELY S. PARKER, letter to Indian superintendent Alfred Sully, 1869

Optimism, alliance building, and an attempt to improve efficiency all characterized the efforts of reformers following the peace commissions of the 1860s, especially as they came to view newly elected President Ulysses S. Grant as an ally. In his first inaugural address, Grant stated clearly that he was on their side. "I will favor any course toward [Indian people]," he said, "which tends to their civilization and ultimate citizenship."[1] In fact, one of his administration's first actions involved freeing an Indian appropriations bill deadlocked by a procedural dispute between the Senate and the House of Representatives. House members, whose responsibility it was to provide funding to pay for the Indian Service (as the Office of Indian Affairs [OIA] was also known in the nineteenth century), had become frustrated by their lack of input in the treaty-making process. Furthermore, they resented the Senate, who held sole responsibility for ratifying the treaties. At stake in 1869, though, was $4 million in Indian appropriations. To break the deadlock, Grant used the Board of Indian Commissioners (BIC), the newly established Indian affairs oversight committee, to advocate the passage of the appropriation. They were successful, and Congress provided $5 million to the Indian Service for the annual distribution of treaty goods and annuities and an additional $2 million to pursue reform initiatives.[2] In his first annual report as commissioner of Indian affairs, Ely Parker wrote that because of the additional funds, "mischief has been prevented, and suffering either relieved or warded off from numbers who otherwise . . . would have been led into difficulties and extreme want."[3]

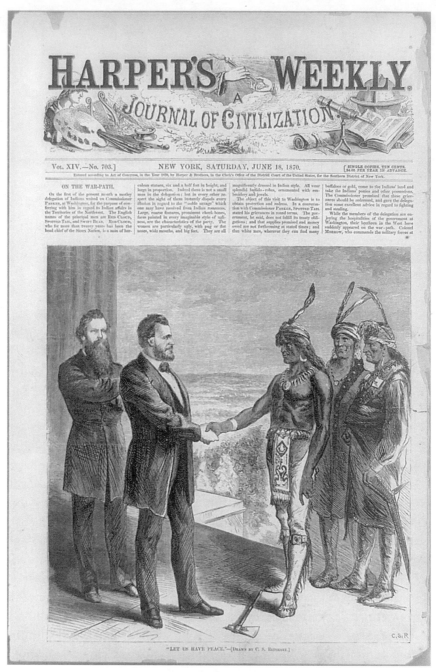

D. S. Reinhart, "Let Us Have Peace," *Harper's Weekly*, June 18, 1870. This cartoon illustrates the optimism many reformers and others felt about the potential for a shift in the trajectory of federal Indian affairs during the early Grant administration. Courtesy of the Library of Congress, Prints & Photographs Division, LC-USZ62–96533.

This chapter illustrates how policy makers began to implement reforms developed in the late 1860s. The quick progress of these reforms within the context of the early Reconstruction era suggests that they constituted a genuine, viable alternative program. In the existing scholarship, postwar Indian affairs have been described as complex and paradoxical, fraught with internal contradictions. For example, some reformers championed "peace" as a guiding principle, but warfare, more than anything else, characterized events in the Plains and far West. Others sought to stamp out corruption in the OIA, but it was during Grant's presidency that the OIA faced investigation and charges of mismanagement at a greater rate than at any previous moment. This was also an era in which the federal government began to shift its assault on Indian nations from an attack on external sovereignty through removal and reservation policies to a chipping away at internal sovereignty through "civilization" and assimilation programs. Importantly, Parker's reform agenda did not move completely away from Indian confinement; in fact, it coincided in important and troubling ways with the prevailing ideas of mainstream reformers. In sum, though, this program did pose alternate and perhaps less disruptive methods to provide Native communities with multiple paths to peaceful coexistence with non-Native ones as their relationships with an expanding settler-colonial United States developed.

A brief anecdote involving two prominent reformers working with the OIA provides some insight into the optimism of this moment. In the summer of 1869, Parker, who had only just been appointed, wrote a letter to Felix Reville Brunot, a member and the soon-to-be chairman of the inaugural BIC, offering some important advice and a brief summary of his thoughts on Indian policy. While he referenced inefficiencies and failures on the part of the OIA, he also noted that "the practice of promising material and moral aid to the Indians when there is no certainty that such promises can be made good" had perhaps caused "greater embarrassment to the administration of Indian affairs" than anything else. He optimistically anticipated an alliance between his office and the new oversight board. "I earnestly hope," he wrote, "you will be enabled to make such suggestions as will assist the Dept. in elevating and making more efficient the present Indian Service and impress the Indian mind with the belief that justice will be done them."[4]

Peace policy studies generally focus on a constellation of initiatives undertaken by the Grant administration in the late 1860s and early 1870s. According to historian Francis Prucha, the peace policy "was a state of mind, a determination that since the old ways of dealing with Indians had not worked, new ways which emphasized kindness and justice must be tried." Because it was a "state of mind" in Prucha's telling, he declares that it could not be "precisely dated" nor "rigidly defined."[5] One of the most studied elements of the peace policy era is the removal of Indian agents at the reservation level and their replacement with army officers or men approved of by Quaker meetings. A second frequently examined element is the establishment of the BIC. As a corollary of this second topic, some scholars have focused on other non-Native reformers involved in policy making, often working in conjunction with the BIC, such as men and women of other religious sects and former abolitionists. Finally, many studies of the peace policy era focus on the military component of post-war Indian policy, especially the protracted and brutal warfare that took place on the Great Plains and far West.[6] These studies provide a general interpretation of this period in Indian policy development and demonstrate Prucha's assertion that the federal government's initiatives lacked a coherent framework. Much of this work, however, omits or underemphasizes the significant role Ely Parker played in the development of the early peace policy. It also fails to acknowledge the viable policy alternatives that emerged and the significance of his advocacy of a strong Indian voice within mainstream structures of governance. While historian Richard Levine notes that the existing literature has not "suggested a single ideological framework within which to fit all the disparate elements of the Grant Indian policy," I argue that Parker's tenure in the Indian Office provides an alternate way to conceptualize these issues.[7]

Promoting Efficiency and Usefulness

Throughout the 1850s and early 1860s, reform-minded politicians and philanthropists suggested that federal Indian affairs were corrupt and inefficient. The commissions of the post–Civil War era confirmed these assertions again and again in their final reports to Congress. In one of the clearest statements of this kind, the Doolittle Commission—whose charge it was to investigate the conditions of various Indian nations and their treatment at the hands of civilian and military authorities in the aftermath of the Sand Creek massacre—reported that "many agents, teachers, and employés of the government are inefficient, faithless, and even guilty of peculations and fraudulent practices upon the government and upon the Indians." The commission's 1867 final report also concluded that the problem was not the federal system of Indian affairs itself but rather the "abuses of that system."[8] When Parker accepted his appointment to head the OIA in 1869, he began almost immediately to streamline policy administration in an effort to combat inefficiency and mismanagement. This was also Parker's attempt to create an OIA monopoly on Indian policy (limiting or completely excluding agents from other departments in the federal government), which could have made his office considerably more powerful.

One of the ways in which Parker sought to improve bureaucratic efficiency was by limiting or ending the practice of appointing special commissioners and special agents to carry out specific tasks on reservations or among Indian nations where a regular agent was currently employed. On May 25, 1869, only a few weeks after beginning his tenure in the OIA, Parker wrote to Secretary of the Interior Jacob Cox to suggest that a special committee working among the Sac and Fox and Potawatomi be dissolved. He cited as his reason the fact that the commission, after six months of work, had "not yet accomplished anything material in the performance of their duties." As an indication of the new focus on efficiency, he added, "The work required can be better and more economically performed by the regularly appointed officers of this bureau."[9] Several weeks later, on July 8, Parker dispensed with another special appointee, this time an agent named George Mitchell, who had worked in the Southern Superintendency for more than three years. He suggested to Secretary Cox that Mitchell was "unnecessary," despite the support he received from southern Indian leaders, and that "the regular Agent can properly attend to the business of his Agency." Also, reflecting the increased effort to employ Quakers and other religious officials in these positions, Parker recommended that if a special agent did become necessary in the future, the secretary should appoint "a member of the society of Friends."[10]

In June 1869, the new commissioner addressed what can only be described as an extreme example of the inefficiencies of the OIA in the mid-1800s when he concluded that there was at least one agent on the payroll for a nonexistent reservation. Henry Oman Jr. had been listed as an agent at Smith's River Reservation in California, but, as he outlined in a letter to Secretary Cox, Smith's River had been discontinued by an act of Congress passed with the Indian Appropriation Bill of July 1868. The Smith's River Indians were relocated to the Hoopa Valley Reservation. Pointing out that Oman had remained on the payroll as an agent at a nonexistent reservation for eleven months, Parker wrote to Cox that it was perhaps time that his "services . . . be dispensed with."[11]

Following his work on the Fort Philip Kearney investigation, retired general Alfred Sully became the superintendent of Indian affairs in the Montana Territory and maintained an active official and personal correspondence with Parker as he assumed his role as commissioner. In his letters, Parker continued to articulate his goal of efficiency and bureaucratic economy. In one early letter, he wrote that Sully's success as superintendent would likely be a result of his "efficiency, discretion, and care" and that he "confidently hoped" that Sully's appointment would prove to be a wise decision.[12] Later, Parker articulated OIA policy in response to one of Sully's questions, and in so doing, gave insight into his strategy of consolidation. When Sully asked if it might be possible to appoint acting agents for particular agencies in Montana, Parker replied that such an action was "wholly without authority of law" and "cannot be allowed." He explained that all appointments had to originate with or be approved by the OIA.[13] Ensuring compliance with this policy would aid Parker's effort to consolidate as much power and control of Indian affairs as possible within the OIA.

Another consistent problem mid-nineteenth-century reformers pointed to were traders (either employed by the OIA or acting independently) who swindled or otherwise mistreated their Indian patrons. Indeed, in his 1867 letter outlining some of his policy initiatives, Parker suggested that the Army Commissary Department carry out trade because it could be more closely monitored. While that reform never came to be, he did attempt to regularize trading practices by permitting only licensed traders to deal with Indian clients and requiring that all licenses be approved by the commissioner's office. He also believed that agents of other federal bureaucracies had been improperly paid out of funds set aside by Congress for Indian affairs.[14] He articulated the OIA's new position most forcefully to Cox: "This office has immediate charge of Indians and the supervision of all their transactions whether between themselves or with white persons."[15]

As described in chapter 3, many reformers championed a proposal to move the Indian Service back to the War Department in the aftermath of the Civil War. Parker was one of its most outspoken supporters, and his advocacy focused upon treaty enforcement that could include using the military to protect Indian communities from surrounding whites, as well as overall bureaucratic efficiency. The "transfer debate," as it came to be known, had strong proponents on both sides. Members of the House of Representatives—the chairman of the Military Affairs Committee and future president James A. Garfield among them—favored the transfer and believed that moving the OIA would streamline policy administration. Always looking for opportunities to influence Indian policy, especially because it lacked a formal role in treaty making, the House passed transfer bills both in 1867 and 1868. Senators, on the other hand, tended to align themselves with civilian reformers, like Commissioner of Indian Affairs Nathaniel Taylor (in 1868), who argued passionately against the transfer. Grant even attempted to circumvent the Senate by encouraging the appointment of army officers as superintendents and agents.[16]

Perhaps recognizing the potential political minefield surrounding this issue and understanding the impediments to the transfer, Parker tried to use his personal connections to influence military decisions and focused more of his attention on bureaucratic mechanisms within his own purview. In the short term, he sought to create a more efficient system of communication between and a clear delineation of the duties of his OIA and the military. In an early letter to Secretary Cox, he suggested the importance "of having a perfect understanding respecting the treatment of the Indians by the civilian and military authorities." He went on to assert most adamantly that the army "should not be called in except as a last resort."[17] This belief distinguished him from the adventuresome and hard-line army officers, such as Generals Sherman and Sheridan, who were more willing to employ military violence.

In his first annual report, Parker noted a break from the previously complex and confusing relationship between the civilian and military branches. He wrote, "[There is] now a perfect understanding between the officers of this department [OIA] and those of the military, with respect to their relative duties and responsibilities in reference to Indian affairs."[18] Parker also circulated to the members of the Interior Department a statement indicating the proper protocol for the administration of Indian affairs and asked that military leaders issue similar orders. The result of this, Parker reported, was a "harmony of action between the two departments" with "no conflict of opinion having arisen as to the duty, power and responsibility of either."[19]

Religious organizations, such as the Society of Friends, criticized the transfer proposal. In a memorial to Congress in 1869, the Friends stated that they appreciated the "evident desire of Congress to remedy the gross evils and abuses of our Indian system" and that they were sure that the "proposal to place the Indian affairs in the control of the War Department has been dictated by motives of humanity, both to the interest of the Indians and the honor of the nation." But they argued that the transfer should be stopped because of the deleterious effect of alcohol consumption that often characterized interactions surrounding western forts and that in many cases led to violence. The "loathsome disease [alcoholism] which has destroyed thousands," they argued, could be "traced to licentious intercourse between the soldiers and the Indians."[20] Still, these criticisms did not ultimately prohibit the transfer.

In January 1870, General Phillip Sheridan authorized an attack on Piegan Indians in northern Montana (Department of Dakota) to punish them for harboring a Native man wanted in the murder of a white settler. In what would become known as the Marias massacre (or Baker massacre), Major Eugene Baker and the soldiers of the Second Cavalry attacked thirty-seven Piegan lodges— Chief Heavy Runner's settlement—a group that had been granted "safe conduct" by the Indian Office. This was the wrong camp; Baker's men mistakenly attacked Piegans who had maintained peaceful relations with the United States. They killed 173 Indians (at least 53 of whom were women and children) and took another 140 prisoner.[21] The attack raised important questions about the military's ability to simultaneously punish so-called hostile Indian groups while protecting "friendlies." When John A. Logan, Illinois congressman and then chairman of the Committee on Military Affairs of the House of Representatives, read the details of the massacre in early 1870, "his blood ran cold in his veins" and he asked the committee to "let the Indian Bureau remain" where it was. The committee agreed.[22] In an effort to further curtail President Grant's interference in congressional patronage in the Indian Service, the House and Senate also made regular army officers ineligible for civil positions.

Later congresses took up the transfer question. In both 1876 and 1878 the House proposed to move the OIA to the War Department, but neither proposal found widespread support. As perceptions of Indian violence diminished in the 1880s and 1890s, so, too, did congressional interest in the transfer.[23] Despite the setback in 1870, Parker continued to seek bureaucratic efficiency and a clear relationship between the military and his office. Even as Congress limited Grant's power and ended the transfer movement, the president encouraged Secretary of the Interior Jacob Cox "to harmonize the action of the two branches." He argued that this, more than anything else, would "promote the efficiency and usefulness of the Agents in charge of the Indians."[24]

Feeding versus Fighting

The 1867 final report on the investigation into the Fort Philip Kearney fight stressed the importance of the federal government's role in creating programs that counterbalanced Indigenous land loss and continuing colonialism. For example, Parker and Sully asserted that while Native nations worked to develop subsistence and ultimately commercial agriculture, "it would be necessary to feed them for a few years" and that this "would be cheaper than fighting them."[25] Indeed, in his 1867 letter to Secretary of War Edwin Stanton, Parker lamented the high costs of Indian wars and suggested that peace could be established, lives could be saved, and the "Indian race" could be perpetuated in a much more economical fashion.[26] With these goals in mind, he began to build early in his tenure a compensatory foundation in the OIA's work. Reflecting the recommendations of the earlier councils and his own distinctive reform position and displaying a keen awareness of the overall orientation of the federal government in the Reconstruction era, Parker demanded that the OIA honor treaty promises, but he also fought to provide new opportunities, including education, that he believed would allow Native individuals to assimilate into the expanding United States at their own pace.

Shortly after assuming control of the Indian Service, Parker was confronted with several challenges that forced him to articulate the "feeding instead of fighting" mandate. In late summer, R. B. Mitchell, the governor of New Mexico Territory, issued a proclamation that declared Navajo and Gila River Apache people to be outlaws. It further authorized citizens to detain, by force if necessary, any Indians not on reservation lands or in the company of a U.S. soldier, "even should it result in the killing" of those Indians. Parker immediately protested to his superiors in the Departments of the Interior and War "to prevent the carrying into effect the indiscriminate slaughter authorized" by the proclamation.[27] His appeal referred directly to an editorial titled "Indian Difficulties: The True Remedy" published in the *Santa Fe Weekly Post* on October 16, 1869, in which A. P. Sullivan called for an "indiscriminate slaughter of the Red Men of New Mexico." In a letter to Secretary Cox, Parker not only asserted that the editorial directly disregarded "the present Indian policy of the Administration" but also noted that A. P. Sullivan was "a federal office-holder," which gave the editorial an air of official approval. With the aid of New Mexico congressman Jose Francisco Chaves, Parker petitioned Grant for Sullivan's removal from office.[28] As commissioner, Parker also sought to end one of the standard military practices employed in Indian country: the use of Indian scouts. He argued that while Indian scouts were "no doubt . . . useful to the military," their involvement in military action was "not in harmony" with the emerging peace policy.[29]

The more significant test of the "feeding vs. fighting" mandate occurred in the summer of 1870. In the Dakota Territory, Indian communities had begun to experience severe food shortages. There was a very real fear among policy makers and Indian agents that without rations, starving Indian people would seek alternate ways of procuring food, likely by "raiding" local white settlements. In fact, the governor of Dakota Territory wrote to Parker, stating, "We must feed or fight the Indians in this superintendency."[30] Parker had imagined this scenario and early in his tenure had sought alternative approaches to honoring the treaty stipulations and compensating nations for continuing American expansion. In particular, he employed the Army Commissary Department to supply food beginning in the summer of 1869 and even arranged to have "one year's supply . . . left and stored" to avoid "extra handling and transportation."[31] In July of that year, Parker reported that the arrangements had been made with the army and if any delays happened to occur, "the Commissary of the Department of Missouri was instructed . . . to issue to the

Indians [rations] ... from the military stores on hand until the Indian supplies could reach the territory."[32]

In early 1870, though, it appeared that problems with these plans were on the horizon. The Army Commissary Department gave notice that it would be unable to continue supplying the Missouri River Indians after July 1. In addition, the 1870 Indian appropriations bill had stalled in Congress, as had been the case with the 1869 bill (described at the beginning of this chapter). Without funding, the OIA could not purchase the necessary rations. In April 1870, Parker wrote to Cox that "should the feeding of the [Arapahoe, Cheyenne, Apache, Kiowa, and Comanche] be stopped after the first of July, they will again scatter to the Plains, being compelled to do so to procure food." It could be assumed, he argued, that "they would commit depredations which would result in another war."[33]

In an effort to avoid hostilities, Parker contacted a large contractor, James W. Bosler, based out of Carlisle, Pennsylvania, to provide beef and flour to the Missouri River Indians. Later—facing a House of Representatives investigation into his conduct as commissioner—Parker revealed that he had no prior connection to Bosler but knew that the contractor previously had supplied army posts along the Missouri and dealt with the Peace Commission of 1868. Both parties took risks when they entered into a contract in 1870. Bosler risked accepting a deferment in compensation until Congress passed its appropriation bill, a likely but certainly not foregone conclusion. Parker risked a potential break with new protocols—designed to weed out corruption and fraud—that he and other reformers were beginning to establish in the purchase and distribution of Indian goods. In particular, he did not take the time to accept competitive bids, nor did he inspect Bosler's products. Expediency was the order of the day. During the House investigation, Parker reported that all of the risks had been worthwhile since the Indian Office had been able to provide the necessary rations to the Missouri River communities. He added that "the manner in which [Bosler] executed his contract fully justifies the confidence the office placed in him" and that "an abundance of good provisions was soon supplied, the Indians did not abandon the agencies, and an apprehended expensive Indian war was averted."[34] The BIC, though, would not be satisfied with this.

The Indian peace policy initiative was not the first or only government project that emphasized education as a means of improvement. As historian Eric Foner has described, one of the most striking illustrations "of the freedmen's quest for self-improvement" in the Reconstruction period was "their seemingly unquenchable thirst for education."[35] In fact, it was in the development of educational opportunities for ex-slaves that the public-private hybrid approach to reform in the postwar state was most apparent. Northern benevolent societies, state governments, the Freedmen's Bureau, and local churches in the South all provided funding and support for freedmen's schools. Many northern teachers traveled to southern districts to work among the former slaves, but often the most significant initiative came on the local level among the freed people themselves. Parker and other Reconstruction-era Indian reformers shared these ideals and worked to provide educational opportunities as a part of their compensatory programs.

Parker, in fact, viewed education to be one of the most important pathways for Indian advancement and reflected often on the role it had played in his life. In an 1885 letter to his friend Harriet Maxwell Converse, an aging Parker wrote, "[The] only salvation for the Indians and the only solution of the great Indian problem is to give them secular and industrial schools in abundance. . . . This alone will perpetuate their life."[36] Parker attributed his professional success to the educational opportunities offered him due to his own hard work and his friendship with Lewis Henry Morgan. As a youth, Parker studied at both Yates Academy and Cayuga Academy in upstate New York.[37] Morgan often encouraged him through their correspondence and instilled in him the idea that education was the key for Native people. In an 1848 letter, Morgan commented on Parker's efforts to study law. "I am glad to hear that you are attending diligently to your studies," he wrote. "All eyes will be upon you and if you establish a good character as a student and as a man, and I have no doubt you will, you will find something . . . worth having."[38]

Parker developed schools and educational programs in conjunction with mission work. In his first annual report as commissioner, Parker argued that the improvement in Indian affairs during the previous year was directly attributable to "supplying them [Indian communities] with means . . . for their education and moral training."[39] Using language that today seems offensive but at the time reflected common perceptions, Parker asserted that through education, "the clouds of ignorance and superstition in which many of this people were so long enveloped have disappeared . . . and opened up a brighter future."[40] Later in his report, Parker commented that among the Seminoles of the Southern Superintendency, "schools are well attended and a deep interest is apparent in regard to the subject of education."[41] Concerning his own New York communities he wrote, "An increase is manifested in reference to education . . . twenty-six schools are in operation."[42] Throughout his tenure in the OIA, he emphasized "education to be made first above all. . . . Other good things will follow."[43]

Treaties and Land

The final reports and recommendations of both the Fort Philip Kearney investigation and the Peace Commission of 1867–68 stressed the importance of honoring existing treaties with Indian nations. In fact, Parker was even willing to deploy the military against non-Natives surrounding Indian communities to this end, as he outlined in his 1867 letter. Both Parker and Sully asserted that the federal government should stress agricultural development but recognized that it would need to continue providing rations until Indian people could compete in the agricultural marketplace. The peace commissioners' report mirrored this idea and suggested that while honoring treaty stipulations, the government should provide agricultural tools and supplies in lieu of money. As OIA commissioner, Parker followed these recommendations and sought to institute a policy of strict adherence to treaty language.

In an early-1870 letter to Secretary of the Interior Jacob Cox, Parker outlined this policy most clearly. He wrote that it was "of the utmost importance . . . that a strict and faithful observance of all the Indian treaties should be maintained by the government and thus avoid the evils and horrors incident to, as well as the expense attendant upon a general Indian war."[44] In another he wrote, "This office [Indian Affairs] *must* be governed by the treaty."[45] In his first annual report, Parker argued, "In regard to treaties now in force, justice and humanity require that they be promptly and faithfully executed, so that the Indians may not have cause of complaint, or reason to violate their obligations by acts of violence and robbery."[46] Although these statements seemed to refer to the benefit this policy might hold for the non-Native population, in practice, it could have had quite radical results in the West. If treaty language had been adhered to as strictly as Parker had intended it to be, it is likely that the wars and violence that characterized the West in the 1870s would not have occurred in the ways they did. Speculation aside, the high value that Parker placed on honoring existing treaties distinguished his alternative approach from that of mainstream reformers in the postwar period.

As Parker and others attempted to introduce economic and educational opportunities for Native people, Congress intensified its assault on tribal sovereignty. Formal treaty making ended in 1871 by way of a rider attached to the Indian appropriations bill that year. In the immediate post–Civil War context, the emphasis on state-building, western expansion, and the stability of U.S. sovereignty in the wake of a traumatic war facilitated a process of temporal confinement. Historian Kevin Bruyneel has asserted that "an extended look into Parker's argument shows that the linked articulation of progress, rule, rationality, and the state led to formal creation of a paradoxical status for many indigenous tribes." He characterizes Parker's argument as indicative of a "post-colonial paradox" of the postwar era, particularly in the "idea that although indigenous tribes were becoming increasingly bound by and within the rationality and rule of the new American state, they were deemed neither sufficiently rational nor self-ruled to be able to respond to this changing situation."[47]

Indeed, judging by many of Parker's own statements, it would appear that Bruyneel's interpretation is correct. In his first annual report, Parker suggested that the question of whether the treaty system should continue had become a "matter of serious import." He argued that it should not continue, and further—denying Chief Justice John Marshall's findings earlier in the century—he asserted that "Indian tribes of the United States are not sovereign nations, capable of making treaties."[48] In a letter to William Welsh, the first chairman of the BIC, Parker foreshadowed congressional actions: "Congress intends a radical change in the Indian policy by discontinuing the treaty system and hereafter legislating for Indians as for wards of the government which they really are."[49] He also argued in support of an allegedly fraudulent treaty with the Wyandot Nation from 1855 when some members protested in 1871 that they had never consented to the agreement. On its face, this seems like an odd position for him to take, considering his role in the Seneca effort to prove the fraudulent nature of the 1838 Buffalo Creek Treaty and the Compromise Treaty of 1842. Citing *Blacksmith v. Fellows*, a Supreme Court case that originated from the Seneca experience, Parker argued that even though Wyandot leaders charged that U.S. negotiators had committed fraud, "the courts cannot go behind an Indian treaty when ratified, to inquire whether or not a tribe was properly represented by its head men."[50] Parker's opinions certainly seemed to support the larger trends of Indian confinement, as Bruyneel has suggested.

There is an alternate interpretation, however. As a leading voice in the Seneca resistance campaign against forced removal in the 1840s and 1850s, Parker saw firsthand how devastating political discord could be—even within a powerful and populous Indian community. He watched as numerous western New York tribes jockeyed for position against one another and then, in 1848, as a political revolution swept through the Allegheny and Cattaraugus communities. At that time he asserted that internal political conflicts had "made so much trouble" and "caused so much bitter and hard feeling among our leading men."[51] "If ever the Tonawandas were required to be united in their plans and purposes," he advised his own community, "it is now."[52] His position on treaty making in 1871, then, might be understood as an expression of realpolitik.

In Parker's experience, Native communities lacked the political, economic, and military might to force external agents of colonialism (land speculators and other private interests) to negotiate fairly or to compel the federal government to honor its treaty agreements. The resulting pressures caused destructive political disputes that further weakened Indian nations.

We can return to Parker's own words as commissioner to see that this experience indeed motivated his support for an end to treaty making. In the same annual report in which he asserted that Indian tribes were not sovereign nations, he argued that "great injury has been done by the government in deluding this people into the belief of their being independent sovereignties, *while they were at the same time recognized only as its dependents and wards.*" He also suggested that no Indian nation had "an organized government of such inherent strength as would secure a faithful obedience of its [*the United States'*] people in the observance of compacts of this character."[53] In other words, he was suggesting not that Indian nations maintained a premodern, anachronistic existence but rather that the federal government took advantage of Native nations by encouraging them to sign treaties they could not negotiate fairly or enforce.

Even after he left the OIA, Parker continued to criticize the federal government's contradictory stance on tribal sovereignty. In a draft of a lecture he was preparing in 1878, Parker wrote, "Here I may mention the absurdity of the United States Gov't making treaties with the Indian tribes of the country. . . . They have all been declared the wards of the government, and they all live within its jurisdiction, and yet these dependent people are treated as though they were independent sovereign nations." He continued:

> I perhaps ought to be the last person to find fault with such a condition
> of things. I suppose that I ought to be very proud, I ought to swell out as
> a turkey cock that with a few hundred ignorant Indians at my back I can
> consider myself the head of a strong independent sovereignty, and treat
> with the great United States as if I were Russia or Germany or China or
> Japan. But I have no such feeling. On the contrary I am humiliated. For I
> know too well the great wrecks of violated Indian treaties that are strewn
> in the historical pathway of the U.S. I know too well that a violation of
> a treaty on the part of the Indians means their forcible expulsion from
> their homes and their extermination. These things are like the handle to
> a jug. The advantages and the power of execution are all on one side.[54]

In the end, he appealed to policy makers for a "wise, liberal, and just" approach to Indian affairs, because, though pessimistic, he realized this was the best hope for Indian people.

It is also important to note that scholars Vine Deloria and Raymond DeMallie have suggested that the 1871 rider was as much a product of Reconstruction-era politics as it was an assault on tribal sovereignty.[55] The congressional debates surrounding the cessation of treaty making and the passage of the appropriations bill rider involved numerous topics, some only tangentially related to Indian affairs. For example, Congressman James Beck, a Kentucky Democrat and former law partner of John C. Breckenridge, commented on the jurisdictional benefits the end to treaty making provided to the House of Representatives. "I desire to say that the House, in my judgment, has gained almost everything that it had a right to expect," he said. No longer would the House have to figure out ways to fund the treaty annuities ratified by the Senate alone. The bill formalized "a distinct agreement between the two Houses," thereby ending the Senate's exclusive control of Indian policy.[56]

Senator Eugene Casserly, a California Democrat, argued that the procedure by which the rider had been developed—through a committee of conference—was a threat to transparent legislating in Congress. He stated that the trend was to remove important bills from open debate and "decide them by conferences held in some committee-room, with closed doors, without the knowledge of either House, and without any practical capacity in the members of either House to reject what had been done."[57] Building on Casserly's argument, Garrett Davis, a Democratic senator from Kentucky, objected to the rider on the grounds that the treaty making relationship between Indian tribes and the federal government was "as fixed and immutable in the foundations of the Constitution as any other power" and that no committee of conference, not even the Senate or House, could change that.[58]

Democratic senator Willard Saulsbury Sr. responded to these arguments with attacks on his political enemies in Congress. Saulsbury is perhaps best known for his 1863 intoxicated outburst on the Senate floor when he called President Lincoln an "imbecile." Although he would lose his Senate seat to an older brother in late 1871, Saulsbury fanned the partisan flames, arguing that Radical Republicans had no respect for the Constitution and therefore any argument appealing to constitutional law was useless. Davis (his colleague), he sarcastically asserted, needed to banish from his mind the "absurd notion" that "the Constitution of the United States is authority in the Congress of the United States." Davis, recognizing Saulsbury's sarcasm, replied optimistically, "When the party now in power [Republican Party] is dispossessed, the principles of the Constitution may be dug up again and restored to their former supremacy."[59] Senator Casserly concluded the debate. "I know what the misfortune of the tribes is," he said. "They hold great bodies of rich lands, which have aroused the cupidity of powerful corporations and of powerful individuals. . . . I greatly fear the adoption of this provision . . . is the beginning of the end in respect to Indian lands. It is the first step in a great scheme of spoliation, in which the Indians will be plundered, corporations and individuals enriched, and the American name dishonored in history."[60] His words seem eerily prophetic to modern ears.

Casserly's prognostication points toward another way in which Parker's alternative reform agenda conformed to larger ideas of Indian confinement: his effort to clarify and protect Indian land titles while simultaneously supporting U.S. territorial expansion. Influenced by his early career as a leader in the Tonawanda resistance campaign and by the recommendations of the peace commissions and councils of the late 1860s, Parker's OIA endeavored to maintain and define Indian nations as distinct entities within the United States, even supporting the establishment of a Native-run coalition government in Indian Territory. In his correspondence with other policy makers and reformers, and in several public statements, however, Parker indicated the opposite—that "consolidation" and ultimately allotment in severalty were inevitable policies.

In his first annual report, Parker outlined many of the steps his administration had begun to take in clarifying and upholding Indian land titles. He attributed any improvement in general Indian affairs to the availability of "suitable reservations" and challenged Congress not only to continue "fulfilling all treaty obligations" but also to provide the OIA with adequate funding and the "powers to adopt the requisite measures for the settlement of all tribes, when practicable, upon tracts of land to be set apart for their use and occupancy."[61] He also argued strenuously in favor of "a general council in the Indian territory" that would be composed of delegates from the various nations there and endowed with the power to legislate as a "territorial form of government." The local government would be controlled by Indians. The next step, he hoped, would be the admission of the Indian Territory "into the Union as a State." In the face of intensifying U.S. expansion after the Civil War, he believed that this would provide Native nations with a sense of security and the political mechanisms necessary to maintain the "permanent possession" of their lands.[62]

The territorialization of the Indian Territory (in other words, placing the territory on the path toward statehood) had in fact been a goal of non-Native policy makers for several years. It was a move that American expansionists hoped would open new lands for non-Native homesteaders and place Native communities there under the institution of American territorial law. It was a development that few Indian leaders supported.

In December 1870, the intertribal Okmulgee Council met to discuss the creation of a Native-initiated constitution, a document that, in its original form, might have maintained the Indian Territory as a homeland for Native American nations and placed its governance beyond the scope of U.S. authorities. Commissioner Parker attended the council and in his address to the delegates called it "the most important council ever held among the Indian tribes of the country." He also said that it was an opportunity for them to encourage Congress to recognize their right to self-government and a chance for them to block any future attempt "of having a territorial government forced upon them."[63] Ultimately, President Grant weakened the Okmulgee Constitution by recommending that it be amended to conform to standard territorial law, a paternalistic action that effectively killed the constitution itself. Nonetheless, OIA support for the Okmulgee Council indicates strongly Parker's and other reformers' efforts to clarify and maintain Indian land titles.[64]

At the same time, though, the OIA under Parker's leadership seemed unable to divorce itself completely from the path of Indian confinement espoused by mainstream assimilationists. Even as he laid out his thoughts on preserving Indian homelands in his 1867 letter to General Grant, Parker indicated a tacit support for U.S. expansion. Because of the "immense augmentation of the American population . . . throughout the entire west, covering both slopes of the Rocky mountains," he said, Indian communities would need to be "consolidated in separate districts of country." Later in the same document he suggested that one of the benefits of his policy alternative was that it would allow for settlement on lands that were currently held by "hostile bands of Indians."[65]

In private correspondence during his term as commissioner and in several public statements, Parker also demonstrated support for allotment in severalty. In a June 1869 letter to William Welsh, he wrote that he would "prefer to operate upon the now civilized Indians for allotments of their land in severalty before attempting the experiment upon the wild bands of the prairies."[66] To Secretary of the Interior Columbus Delano he wrote that Native and non-Native societies differed in their view of landownership in that Indigenous communities only held land in common, but he assured Delano that "the policy of allotting lands in severalty has been advocated by all the true friends of the Indians for years past."[67] Finally, to the principal Choctaw delegate in Washington, D.C., Peter Pitchlynn, Parker asserted that holding land in severalty would prepare Native individuals for the responsibilities of "American Citizenship" and keep them from being lost in the "advancing wave of white civilization."[68] His 1870 annual report advocated for the federal government to begin to institute a general policy of allotment as soon as feasibly possible.[69] Although Parker and other postwar reformers sought alternative approaches to recasting Indian/ white relations and questioned the pace and goals of U.S. colonialism, larger trends and trajectories in Indian confinement proved overwhelming pervasive.

Oversight and Collaboration

Almost all of the Indian policy reformers of 1860s argued that the OIA was a corrupt and inefficient agency sorely in need of some kind of oversight. Indeed, in Parker's 1867 letter to General Grant outlining his policy program, nearly half of his recommendations involved the establishment of oversight committees (described in detail in chapter 3). He hoped to create one committee to monitor the purchase and distribution of annuity goods for the Indian Service and a second committee of Native and non-Native leaders to serve as a liaison between the government and Indian nations. The creation of an oversight board in the early peace policy era, though, had other points of origin as well.

Following the 1862 United States–Dakota War in Minnesota, Episcopal bishop Henry Whipple outlined an idea for a "council of appointment" as a means to end corruption in and mismanagement of Indian affairs. Through the 1860s, Whipple, William Welsh, a Philadelphia philanthropist, and the Society of Friends urged the federal government to create a national board of inspectors to monitor the Indian Office. They cited as precedents both the United States Christian Commission that operated during the Civil War and the Freedmen's Bureau that followed.[70] The government had financed both of these organizations, which were jointly administered by civilian and military officials.[71] Their proposals, however, differed in one significant way from those that Parker set forth in his 1867 program of reform. While Parker sought to employ both Native and non-Native individuals, Whipple and Welsh envisioned the control of Indian policy solely in the hands of wealthy, Christian, non-Native individuals who would proselytize and focus mainly on "civilization" programs.[72]

In 1868, Peter Cooper, a New York philanthropist and reformer, called together like-minded individuals through his Cooper Institute to form the United States Indian Commission, an institution whose stated mission was to protect and elevate the Indians by working directly with the U.S. government (even though it had received no official sanction). The United States Indian Commission tapped men like William Dodge and Vincent Colyer to work directly with the OIA.[73] At the same time, William Welsh called together humanitarians and philanthropists to discuss the new president's interest in "civilization and ultimate citizenship" for Indian people.[74] They met with President Grant and Secretary of the Interior Jacob Cox throughout 1868. One of the prominent members of this group was George Stuart, a friend of Grant's and a wealthy Philadelphia merchant. Stuart had been an active antislavery and temperance crusader, as well as a leader in the Young Men's Christian Association and in the Sunday school movement. The editor of Stuart's autobiography characterized him as "zealously Christian and diligently a man of business."[75] As a result of this lobbying efforts, on April 10, 1869, Congress authorized the president to appoint a committee of men, "eminent for their intelligence and philanthropy, to serve without pecuniary compensation . . . [to] exercise joint control with the Secretary of the Interior over the disbursement of the appropriations made" to Indian communities.[76]

The Board of Indian Commissioners, as it became known, resembled more the body Whipple, Welsh, and Stuart envisioned than the one Parker proposed. Grant asked his friend Stuart, a veteran of the Christian Commission during the Civil War, to nominate several men to serve on the board. His nominees hailed from different regions of the United States, though only as far west as Missouri, and were affiliated with the Episcopalian, Presbyterian, Congregationalist, Methodist, and Baptist Churches. The group included Felix Reville Brunot, a Pittsburgh businessman who worked on the Sanitary Commission during the Civil War and had fought for temperance and other conservative reforms as a college student; William Dodge, a member of the United States Indian Commission, a former dry goods merchant, and a partner in the copper firm of Phelps, Dodge & Company who earned a fortune in business and in the Lake Superior copper industry; and Robert Campbell, who, as a young man in St. Louis, amassed a fortune as a fur trapper and competitor of the American Fur Company and previously served Millard Fillmore as a commissioner in the Fort Laramie councils in 1851.[77]

Stuart also nominated John Farwell, another successful dry goods merchant in New York and Chicago, where he eventually sold his companies to Marshall Field and Potter Palmer; Vincent Colyer, a New York artist and activist who served as a colonel in an African American regiment during the Civil War and a member of the United States Indian Commission; Henry Lane, a former "Indian fighter" from Kentucky who moved to Indiana, became a state legislator, U.S. senator, and governor, as well as a founding member of the Republican Party; John D. Lang, a former Quaker preacher and successful blanket manufacturer; William Welsh, the Philadelphia merchant, philanthropist, and Episcopal layman; and Nathan Bishop from Boston, the former executive chairman of the Christian Commission, the manager of the American Bible Society, and a member of the Evangelical Alliance.[78] Grant approved the list, but added George Stuart's name. The board selected Welsh as their first president.

The BIC began its work in earnest in mid-1869 after successfully lobbying Congress—at the behest of President Grant—to pass the Indian appropriations bill for that year. And Parker, perhaps recalling the successful alliances he built with local non-Native leaders in New York State during the Seneca resistance campaign, sought to lay the groundwork for a productive partnership with the BIC. However, it had to be clear to him at this time that the oversight board he imagined in 1867 and the one that became a reality in 1869 had little in common. That summer, the OIA began accepting bids and proposals from suppliers for Indian annuity goods, and it would be for the first time the responsibility of the BIC to monitor these purchases and the distribution of the goods. "I shall be very happy to see you here when the proposals for Indian goods are opened," Parker wrote to George Stuart, stating that he believed it was "doubtful" anyone else could do as thorough a job.[79] Even when he complained about the slow pace of the inspections, Parker chose his words carefully and diplomatically, employing a passive tone: "It is agreed to be of the utmost importance that all unnecessary delays . . . in getting the goods started to the Indians should be avoided."[80]

William Welsh found the relationship between the BIC, OIA, and Interior Department ill-defined and problematic. Welsh felt that the board should have held a central position in the Interior Department. Indeed, in a pamphlet written later, he stressed the notion that the BIC's authority, as established by Congress, should have been equal to that of the commissioner of Indian affairs. "Instead of giving the Board the joint control as indicated in the Act of Congress," he said, "its powers were limited to that of a mere council of advice."[81] Welsh believed that President Grant supported Parker out of friendship, and after only a month on the BIC, he resigned.[82] Welsh noted in his letter of resignation that he had "the kindest personal feelings to the Secy & the Commissioner [Parker]" but "could not act the part of a man if [he] allowed [himself] to be emasculated."[83] Welsh publicly pledged to "serve the cause as a private citizen," and the BIC appointed Felix Brunot as their new chair.[84] Privately, though, Welsh and his allies began plotting ways to wrest control from Parker and other alternative reformers.

Welsh's resignation could have been perceived as a hostile action, but Parker and Jacob Cox continued to work hard to maintain a positive reform alliance.[85] Parker, unaware of the plans being made to facilitate his downfall, wrote to Welsh, "I sincerely regret that you thought it your duty to resign your place. . . . Let me assure you that any information as may be in my power to give you to advance your efforts will be most cheerfully given."[86] To Felix Brunot, Cox wrote that he "very deeply regret[ted]" Welsh's resignation and expressed his "anxious desire to make the co-operation of the Commission (BIC) with this Department (Interior) entirely pleasant and satisfactory."[87]

THE EARLY YEARS of the peace policy era were characterized by optimism. As Ely Parker stepped into his role as commissioner, he sought to translate the important recommendations advanced by the peace commissions of the 1860s into viable alternative policies. His efforts centered on regularizing Indian administration and creating a power monopoly in the OIA, honoring treaty stipulations and providing food, money, and educational opportunities, to clarifying and protecting Indian land titles, and building alliances with other reformers. Simultaneously, though, some of his actions, including his advocacy of the discontinuation of treaty making and his support of continued U.S. expansion, coincided with larger trends and trajectories of American colonialism typified by an ever-increasing confinement of Indian nations.

FIVE

A Contentious Peace Policy, 1871–1875

I have little or no faith in the American christian civilization methods of
healing the Indians of this country. It has not been honest, pure or sincere.
Black deception, damnable frauds and persistent oppression has been its
characteristics, and its religion today is that the only good Indian is a dead one.
—ELY S. PARKER, letter to Cousin Gayaneshaoh (Harriet Converse), 1885

Far from the optimism that characterized the Office of Indian Affairs (OIA)
in the late 1860s, cynicism and paranoia pervaded in the following decade.
In 1871 the House of Representatives launched an investigation into charges
that Commissioner of Indian Affairs Ely Parker had committed fraud against
the federal government when he contracted with J. W. Bosler to provide food
and supplies to Indian nations along the Missouri River. Upon completing its
hearing, the House Committee on Appropriations found "much to criticise
[*sic*] and condemn," though they ultimately uncovered no evidence implicating
Parker in wrongdoing.[1] It would be easy to dismiss this as simply another investigation into the much-maligned Grant administration, but the actions and
intentions of those who filed the initial charges and who testified in the hear-
ings provide important insights into the repression of viable reform alternatives symbolized by Parker's efforts on the federal level. In fact, the speed and
strength with which mainstream assimilationists opposed Parker's alternatives
indicate the very real threats his programs posed.

William Welsh and the Board of Indian Commissioners (BIC) led the
opposition, and it was their repressive efforts that led to the 1871 House investigation. Their vision of Indian affairs rested upon the concept that the government had the power to coerce Native peoples to assimilate. These men,
while initially seeing Parker and other reformers as potential allies, advanced
a policy agenda that focused on confining Indians within increasingly smaller
reservations and cultural assimilation by any means necessary. Welsh and the
BIC ultimately took advantage of this transitional period by wresting power
from men such as Parker, a fact often overlooked in the scholarly literature.[2]

94

Their driving philosophy, animated by Welsh's evangelism, argued that the wealthy, educated, Christian philanthropists of the United States understood the best interests of Indian peoples, better than Indian peoples themselves. The findings of the House Committee, then, influenced an entire generation of policy makers who worked on Indian affairs and ushered in a particular form of Indian policy that proved disastrous for Native communities.

In this chapter I argue that mainstream assimilationists opposed to Parker's alternatives seized a moment in the early 1870s to repress them and sought instead to use federal programs to accelerate dispossession, to coerce assimilation, and promote Indian confinement. At stake for them was nothing short of their vision for the proper role of the federal government. When Parker, a Native man, assumed control of the OIA seeking alternative policies, Welsh and the BIC felt threatened, and their actions before and after, as well as their language during the House investigation of 1871 revealed their perceptions of Indians as racially and socially inferior and in need of uplift.

William Welsh

William Welsh developed an interest in Indian policy reform late in life. As a young man he had been active in the Episcopal Church and amassed a fortune by importing West Indian sugar, working closely with his brothers John and Samuel. He promoted various philanthropic causes in his early adulthood and founded several churches and a hospital in Philadelphia.[3] He also authored several books about home missions and the role of church laity. But by 1862, Welsh had devoted himself to the development of Indian policy, thanks in large part to the influence of Bishop Henry Whipple. Although Welsh was considered one of the "most earnest and devoted" of all the Indian reformers, he also frequently rubbed his contemporaries the wrong way. His conflict with Parker in 1870–71 was not an anomaly; he also clashed with President Grant, Interior Secretaries Jacob Cox and Columbus Delano, BIC members including Felix Brunot and eventually his close and trusted friend Bishop Whipple.[4]

From 1862 until his sudden death in 1879 during a meeting of the Philadelphia Board of Trusts, Welsh attempted to mold Native Americans to fit into his elite, Christian vision of "civilized" people by eliminating tribal autonomy and destroying Indian communities. More than anything else, Welsh's religious background drove his reform efforts. He believed in the "evangelical theory of lay responsibility for the world," arguing that by failing to encourage the laity to pursue social justice and individual spiritual welfare, the church had operated in error for hundreds of years. Furthermore, as he asserted in his 1872 book,

William Welsh, first chairman of the Board of Indian Commissioners
and a proponent of coercive assimilation. From Charles Morris, ed.,
The Makers of Philadelphia (Philadelphia: L. R. Hamersly, 1894).

Women Helpers in the Church, the wealthy should feel especially compelled to
activism because "education, social position, and money are all trusts involving
a fearful personal responsibility."[5]

In a short 1869 book titled *Taopi and Friends; or, The Indians' Wrongs and
Rights*, Welsh outlined his ideas for Indian reform. He argued that Indian
policy in the nineteenth century had not successfully promoted "civilization"
among the Indians. He believed that treaties should no longer be made with Indian communities, and—in stark contrast to Parker—that those "which allow
Indians to retain large tracts of land . . . must, of necessity, be broken."[6]

A cornerstone of Welsh's reform agenda was faith in the process of Christianization. The first step toward this goal, he believed, was Indian confinement.
"Efforts thus far made to extend the saving influence of the Christian religion
to the Indians in their nomadic condition," he wrote, "have generally been so
unsatisfactory as to dishearten most of those who have undertaken this work."[7]
While almost all reformers, Parker included, supported the reservation system

to some extent, their purposes often differed. Parker sought to provide space and time for Native individuals to assimilate on their own terms and within their own time frame. For Welsh, the reservations provided laboratories where experiments in "civilization" could be practiced and Native people could be located in place and time. Confinement was the key, and Welsh argued that Indians who would not go willingly to the reservations should "be driven by force or exterminated in the process."[8] Later he supported the creation of the North Pacific Railroad in 1872 because, as he asserted, it would "bring the lawless Indians of the North into subjection, and thus aid effectively the religious bodies charged with bringing Christian civilization."[9]

Welsh also saw corruption in Indian appropriations as a major problem and asserted that nepotism and political patronage within the Indian Office "render every attempt to civilize the wild Indians utterly abortive."[10] It was this component of his agenda that led Welsh to charge Parker with fraud and corruption, and demonstrated what most scholars have considered one of Welsh's major faults: an almost obsessive suspicion. Welsh vigorously challenged any opponent whose ideas appeared to pose a threat to his plans. As one historian put it, Welsh's "greatest weakness was a nagging suspicion of conspiracies, a trigger judgment that anyone who disagreed with him on Indian affairs was a member of the Indian Ring."[11]

Welsh's preoccupation with corruption, however, did not make him unique among many other activists of the period. In fact, his use of corruption allegations as a political tool situates Welsh more completely within the Reconstruction-era context and perhaps demonstrates that he was less an outlier in his techniques than previously assumed. As historian Mark Summers has asserted, during the Grant presidency, "corruption [actual corrupt activity] had less important consequences than the *corruption issue* [a political tool]." Welsh, as an astute political observer, grasped the utility of this political technique and used it frequently and with significant success. "The great reforms," Summers argues, "did not occur in spite of the corruption around them, but in large part *because* of it, and more, because of incidents that were misread as corruption."[12]

Due to his role in Indian policy advocacy in the 1860s and his connection to outspoken reformers like Bishop Whipple, William Welsh emerged as a top candidate on George Stuart's list of nominees to the BIC in 1868 (and served briefly as its first president). On the final list of nominees (described in detail in chapter 4) were men whose backgrounds, educations, philanthropic interests, and religious affiliations were entirely homogenous. Although Felix Brunot's biographer referred to the group as "every way a representative body of men," none of them were Native people, none of them lived farther west than St. Louis, and aside from Robert Campbell, Henry Lane, and Welsh, none of them had much previous interaction with Indian communities. Interestingly, almost all of these men maintained business interests in the dry goods, shipping, mineral extraction, and transportation industries. These industries stood to benefit from Indian confinement in the West, which suggests that their personal interests influenced their Indian policy work and their support of coercive reservations.

Despite Parker's alliance-building efforts, Welsh maintained that Congress intended the BIC to hold a central position in the OIA, equal to that of the commissioner of Indian affairs himself. Welsh feared that Parker sought merely to use the board as a "council of advice," and after only a month, he resigned. In public he stated that he would continue to support the OIA and "serve the cause as a private citizen." Behind closed doors, though, he vowed that "Col. P[arker] will have to leave."[13]

In late 1869, in response to a series of questions posed by Commissioner Parker, the BIC members outlined a policy agenda that fit well with Welsh's larger philosophies. Their proposed agenda also contrasted in important ways with Parker's alternatives, especially their aggressive time frame and their focus on Christianization. They unanimously agreed that the reservation system should be continued and that Indian people were "wards of the United States government, which should exercise over them the care of legal guardians, with a view to prepare them to become citizens as soon as practicable."[14] In a letter dated November 23, they stated that the "policy of collecting the Indian tribes upon small reservations . . . seems to be the best that can be devised." There, Indians "should be taught as soon as possible the advantage of individual ownership of property . . . and the tribal relations should be discouraged." Finally, they asserted that Christian missions should be established on all the reservations, because the "religion of our blessed Saviour is believed to be the most effective agent for the civilization of any people."[15]

The key features of this policy agenda were dispossessing Indians of their lands and undermining internal tribal sovereignty (which they referred to as "tribal relations"). This was a crucial moment following the Civil War. The federal government had begun experimenting with compensatory legislation and social policy making through Reconstruction programs such as the Freedmen's Bureau that shifted and expanded its powers. The political climate in Washington, D.C., seemed poised to support radical changes in racial politics, even in Indian affairs, yet the BIC advanced policies that differed in no significant way from those for which earlier western politicians fought.

The contentiousness that framed this period in Indian affairs in many ways mirrored the larger struggle for power in the postwar federal government. This struggle—founded on optimism for the reconstructed nation—not only resulted in an "unfinished revolution" for African Americans; it also presented a missed opportunity for Native communities.

The BIC could have provided transparency and public oversight of the policy-making process. It did not. Instead, it sought to limit public access to Indian policy, while placing it in the hands of a small circle of respected white elites who shared similar religious, business, and social interests. When the OIA drafted its communications with contractors in 1871, the BIC sought to signify its (perceived) superior position by adding the words "under the supervision of the Board of Indian Commissioners."[16] Welsh and the BIC campaigned against and successfully removed federal officials who did not agree with their positions: first Ely Parker and then his successor, E. P. Smith, and Secretary of the Interior Columbus Delano. Most significantly, in 1874, the BIC proposed to separate the OIA from the Interior Department and establish it as an independent, executive-level agency. They argued that this would protect it against political patronage, a broader Reconstruction-era issue that had become a rallying cry for disaffected Democrats and reform-minded Republicans in the Republican-dominated years of the Grant administration. But their proposal also bore the marks of an effort to control access to the mechanisms of political power. Ultimately, it failed, and in response, six of the original members resigned en masse.[17]

Prior to this development, in the years between 1869 and 1874, Welsh and the BIC established a policy framework that at its foundation held a belief in Indian confinement and assimilation by any means necessary, animated by an expressly elitist, evangelical Christian approach to policy making. Advancing their agenda between 1869 and 1874, these reformers effectively derailed any progress Parker and his compatriots had made in developing an alternative agenda. Indeed, their programs helped cement, for the next several generations at least, the notion that non-Native people understood the best interests of Native communities and the idea that the federal government could, in a short period of time, destroy Indian autonomy and distinct Indigenous communities for the betterment of Indian people and the United States.

Indian Policy Alternatives on Trial

Parker spent the month of December 1870 attending the Okmulgee Council in Indian Territory. There he voiced his support for the creation of a Native-run coalition government, a distinctive element of his policy agenda—"a government exclusively of Indians, ultimately to become one of the States of the

Union."[18] With the commissioner out of the capital and unable to respond immediately, Welsh published an open letter to Secretary of the Interior Columbus Delano suggesting that Parker was guilty of "frauds in the purchase and transportation of goods for the Indian service."[19] On December 12, the House of Representatives adopted a resolution that called for an investigation into Welsh's charges.[20] The *New York Herald* speculated that if the charges were to "prove true upon investigation, it is believed that General Parker will be removed, to say the least, from the position he now occupies."[21]

When Welsh filed his charges against the commissioner, he was motivated partially by a personal animosity toward the approach Parker took in Indian affairs. He believed that, as long as Parker remained in control of the OIA, the vision of Indian policy he shared with mainstream assimilationists would never come to fruition. As early as March 1869, Welsh began slowly advocating for Parker's removal from office, writing first to Secretary Cox "that Gen. Butler and others are strongly opposed to the present Commissioner of Indian Affairs."[22] Welsh also recognized Congress's concern that Grant exercised too much control over Indian affairs, as it had passed a motion on July 15, 1870, prohibiting army officers from serving in the Indian Office and limiting the president's power.[23] Welsh looked to exploit the executive/legislative split on Indian issues and used the political division to his advantage.

Welsh's charges also demonstrated his use of the corruption issue. At a meeting with Indian agent Edward Smith in December 1870, Welsh suggested that Parker was "very closely in with the [Indian] ring." Smith, however, believed that Welsh lacked evidence and that his actual complaints originated in the fact that Parker did not consult with him or support his agenda. He concluded that, in any case, Welsh would stop at nothing to have Parker removed from office, just as he worked to remove Indian communities from their homelands.[24] For his part, Parker saw Welsh as "a presumptuous person who would use any pretext to gain private ends."[25] Parker asserted that the charges were "but a determination to carry out certain theories put forth by Mr. Welsh in 1869."[26] Most scholars have interpreted Welsh's charges and subsequent investigation as a personal attack, revealing the acrimony between the two men.[27] However, an examination of the ways Welsh used the corruption issue as a political tool and of the racialized language used in the course of the investigation broadens our understanding of the conflicts in Indian affairs in this period. It also places these conflicts within the larger context of Grant's administration and demonstrates how the investigation itself highlighted larger issues with profound and long-term significance for the federal government and Indian people alike.

The House of Representatives hearing served as a turning point in the move-ment to repress the viable reform alternatives in the early peace policy era. It also sealed the fate of many Indian communities because it helped foster an approach that drove federal policy over the following decades. In early Janu-ary 1871, William Welsh assembled and filed an official report outlining thir-teen charges against Parker. Among them was the assertion that in June 1870 Parker purchased cattle, flour, and other food from Carlisle contractor James W. Bosler without publicly advertising for bids and thereby circumventing federal protocol. In addition to being "in direct violation of a law . . . which requires such supplies to be advertised . . . in the public newspapers," Parker failed to consult with the BIC concerning "extensive and important expendi-tures of money."[28] It is likely that, among all of the charges, this was one that Welsh found particularly irksome, given his intense efforts to control Indian affairs through the BIC.

Welsh also charged that Parker's purchases violated the Indian appropria-tions bill passed on July 15, 1870, that he paid exorbitant rates for the transpor-tation of goods to the Missouri River communities, and that he forced Indian agents to accept inferior quality or less than adequate quantities of goods. In addition, Welsh argued that Parker defied a congressional and presidential mandate when he failed to consult with the BIC concerning the purchase of treaty goods. Finally, echoing a familiar refrain voiced often during the Grant presidency, he charged that Parker had appointed officers in the Indian service upon the sole merit that they had been "strong political friends." Welsh con-cluded that Parker committed a "grievous wrong to the Indian service . . . by which the Government has been defrauded."[29]

The House of Representatives Committee on Appropriations interviewed several contractors, federal officials (including Parker and the by then former secretary of the interior Jacob Cox), as well as members of the BIC, military leaders, and Indian agents; in total they heard testimony from thirty-four men. They also granted William Welsh wide latitude, perhaps indicating the layman's influence as well as the growing support for repressing Parker's and the other reformers' alternatives. Welsh questioned these individuals and built his case, all the while corresponding behind the scenes with prominent BIC members.

In a letter to BIC secretary Vincent Colyer written from Philadelphia on December 17 (just five days after the House of Representatives resolved to in-vestigate his charges), Welsh noted, "Last night I made up my full statement for Mr. Sargent," referring to the chairman of the appropriations committee and lead investigator, Aaron A. Sargent of California. Welsh enlisted Colyer, who was based in Washington, to complete some important political maneuvering in advance of the hearing. He suggested that Colyer discern whether Sargent wanted to "make clean work." If he did, then the secretary should "beg him quietly but effectively to secure all the private papers belonging to" contractors Wheeler, Bosler, and Smith, along with several others. He went on to suggest that Wheeler was a key player in the so-called Indian Ring, a term used by many reformers to refer to a shadowy and ill-defined group of politicians, agents, and contractors who benefited financially by defrauding the Indian service. Wheeler "played a deep and adroit game," Welsh wrote, and had several senators firmly in his debt.

In the same letter, Welsh also revealed his paranoid nature. Referring to the impending House hearing, he suggested, "If we cannot expose the whole affair they will be at it again. That they pulled wool over Secretary Cox's eyes, I have no doubt."[30] A few weeks later, on January 2, 1871, Welsh again wrote to Colyer, and this time he referred to Parker directly. Welsh called him an "unrighteous steward" and, employing a paternalistic tone that no doubt emerged out of his evangelical philosophy of lay responsibility, added, "[I] did not have any unkind feelings to the poor fellow and if I knew *how* to bring him to repentance . . . I would like to do it."[31]

It was Norton P. Chipman, though, a lawyer and Mason from Iowa and Parker's attorney, who ultimately persuaded the House Committee that his client was innocent of wrongdoing. Chipman demonstrated that the BIC failed as an oversight board because it did not call Parker's attention to any of the problems or inconsistencies outlined in Welsh's charges. Instead, at Welsh's request, it had kept meticulous records and secretly worked to build a case against him.[32] Chipman singled out BIC secretary Vincent Colyer, arguing that more than any other member he had misled Parker. Rather than offering aid, as was his responsibility, Colyer conspired with Welsh "in the accomplishment of a purpose to remove the Commissioner of Indian Affairs."[33] In fact, additional evidence came to light during an 1876 investigation that exposed a plot between Welsh and the BIC to oust Parker. During that investigation, W. J. Kountz, a contractor and supplier of Indian goods, stated that his "unpardonable offense against the Indian Bureau" was that he "was the cause of the removal of Indian Commissioner Parker." Kountz may have been one of the contractors with whom Welsh conspired to entrap Parker.[34]

During his examination of J. W. Bosler and other businessmen, Chipman showed that the prices Parker paid for beef and other foods were acceptable because the agencies that he supplied along the Missouri River had run out and the Indians there were in danger of starvation. Parker believed that if he did not act, the Indians would leave the reservations to search for food, leading to the potential for a military conflict. Chipman told the committee that Parker's actions were completely consistent with emerging policy of "feeding rather than fighting the Indians."[35]

Interestingly, Parker at first defended his actions but under continued questioning backpedaled and appeared less and less secure in his position. "I have spared no pains, no sacrifice of personal convenience and pleasure," Parker stated, "to discharge my whole duty faithfully." But he went on, "I do not claim that I have made no mistakes . . . [but] I have never profited pecuniar[i]ly, or indeed otherwise, by any transaction in my official capacity."[36] Upon completion of testimony, the committee published its findings and exonerated him, though the tone of their statement was far from positive. It noted that "the testimony shows irregularities" but it had "not found evidence of fraud or corruption." Furthermore, there was "no evidence of any pecuniary or personal advantage sought or derived by the Commissioner, or anyone connected with his Bureau."[37] Although it would seem that Parker was now free to pursue his reform agenda without further interference, a closer examination of hearing testimony and events of this time demonstrates that quite the opposite was true.

When J. W. Bosler testified before the House Committee, he revealed an issue that pervaded the thought of mainstream assimilationists and emerged frequently in their language. Welsh and the BIC believed that only the wealthy, educated elite should direct policy and, through their attacks on Parker, sought to destabilize the position of Indians, and anyone else who they deemed unfit, in federal policy making. Indeed, Welsh told Bosler that if the other BIC members had followed his lead when he resigned in 1869, "they would have had Parker out of office at that time; that the matter would have been ended there." Welsh revealed his own racial/cultural prejudices when he stated that Parker was "the representative of a race only one generation removed from barbarism" and that he was no match for "parties who were his superiors in the matters of business." According to Bosler, Welsh believed the only reason Parker maintained his position was due "to the President's goodness of heart."[38] Indeed, in an open letter to Grant published later in the *New York Times*, Welsh wrote, "Your protection of Gen. Parker . . . seems wholly unaccountable, except on the hypothesis that love in you is blind."[39]

Bosler also testified that Welsh asked if he "had ever seen General Parker drunk." Here, Welsh's racial/cultural prejudices and his use of the corruption issue combined when he suggested that contractors and supply companies, looking to defraud the government, "feasted and wined" Parker. Playing on the expectation of Indian alcoholism, Welsh concluded that because Parker was an Indian, he "did not have the moral courage to withstand temptation."[40]

Interestingly, in an 1873 letter to Lewis Henry Morgan, Welsh—obviously aware of the his friendship with Parker—wrote patronizingly that "Parker meant well." But, reflecting the assumption of Native alcohol abuse, he noted, "conviviality and a fashionable wife made him the prey of astute and polished augers. I always pitied him."[41]

Other members of the BIC used similarly paternalistic language that revealed racial and cultural prejudices. In a letter to Vincent Colyer, for example, John D. Lang wrote that Indian people were "an unfortunate portion of our fellow beings, who need the help of our more enlightened and favored position."[42] In another example, board member Nathan Bishop wrote to Colyer asking that he send him some of their "new supply of 'civilized paper'" as all he had at the moment was "this 'savage stuff.'"[43]

William Welsh's paternalistic and racist attitudes revealed themselves in other ways, too. Penning a tardy reply to a telegram from J. D. Cox, Welsh assured the Interior secretary that he would have responded sooner but the original telegram had been sent to his brother Samuel's house on Spruce Street, where "a very stupid housekeeper" had misplaced it. The federal census for 1870 reveals that Samuel Welsh, also a wealthy shipping merchant, employed four domestic servants, a French butler/chef, and three Irish women, so it is likely that the "very stupid housekeeper" to whom he referred was one of these young Irish women. Despite Welsh's lay evangelism, or perhaps because of it, he seemed to display no real qualms about these racial/ethnic prejudices.[44]

Parker and his lawyer used the 1871 hearing to draw attention to the larger implications of Welsh's and the BIC's repressive efforts. In his concluding remarks to the House Committee, Chipman argued,

> If Mr. Welsh desires to keep the Indian office free from outside rings and corrupt combinations, heaven help him, but if he expects to reform our public service by wholesale charges of corruption that have no foundation except in his own fertile brain, if he hopes to elevate the Indian by openly declaring, as he has, that the President put into office . . . one who is but a remove from barbarism, thus stigmatising [sic] the whole race . . . if in short, he intends to work out certain theories of his own, under cover of Christian philanthropy . . . he will find he has undertaken that which will recoil fearfully upon him.[45]

It is clear, however, that Chipman and Parker were incorrect in this assumption. The agenda that Welsh and the BIC advanced did not recoil upon them; rather it represented an ideological "fit" with the ideas of many other political officials.

An 1870 Senate debate over the Indian appropriations bill (HR 1169) revealed that several western politicians shared Welsh's and the BIC's racial/cultural expectations and political philosophies. Echoing broader notions about external tribal sovereignty and Indian confinement, Senator Thomas Tipton, a Republican from Nebraska, argued that the early peace policy reforms had been a failure: "You say that Quaker policy is a success, and the only way to keep the peace is to feed and feed and feed, and let one portion of this country work and work and work and toil, in order that your agents may go and feed and feed and feed to save the lives of the rest of the population." Tipton implored his colleagues to demand a change in policy stating, "The system is rotten; the system is false; the system can no longer be maintained or endured." The only wise Indian policy, he said, would be to place Native people on "reservations guarded around by bayonets; reservations over the limits of which the Indians shall not pass . . . reservations with walls as high as necessary, and with pitfalls as deep as necessary."[46]

Other senators chimed in, though using less dramatic language. Senator John Thayer of Nebraska argued that treaty appropriations needed to be reevaluated because many treaties had been negotiated with tribal nations whose numbers had dwindled significantly and, consequently, the "benefit to each Indian [was] much larger than was intended at the time the treaties were made." Senator Joseph Fowler, a Tennessee Republican, employing similar logic and, ignoring the far-reaching implications of continued colonialism and confinement, reasoned that Indians in the state of Nebraska were, due to treaty annuities and federal appropriations, "individually far richer in capital than any other portion of our population."[47] Senator John Sherman of Ohio, younger brother to General William Tecumseh Sherman and the principal author of the Sherman Antitrust Act (in 1890), compared Indian appropriations to Civil War pensions. As historian Theda Skocpol has argued, at this time policy makers were beginning to view the soldiers' pension program with some skepticism, and by the end of the 1800s, it had little unified support.[48] Sherman asserted that the federal government provided to Indian people "a higher compensation, a higher annuity than we are giving to the same number of families consisting of widows and orphans of our soldiers." He admitted that "a degree of liberality . . . ought to be bestowed on Indians," but he concluded that "there is a limit to it."[49]

The senators then moved on to a specific discussion of Parker's role as commissioner. Senator Fowler stated that, in his mind, the goal of the federal government regarding Indian nations was to "Christianize, and thus render a permanent contribution to the world's civilization." Referring to Parker, though, he added, that at "the head of this fountain of spiritual light is placed, not one of the highest, but the lowest types of humanity." Even as an Indian man, Fowler argued, Parker was never a "respectable specimen of his race." He found it "ridiculous in itself" that from the commissioner's office "is to flow this flood of Christian light that is to civilize these wild Indians," when Parker "is a wild man himself!" Echoing the notion that only non-Native philanthropists understood the best interests of Indians, he said that Parker was not "capable of inaugurating a great policy that is to illuminate these benighted creatures," because he was not even "at all equal to the very humblest of the Quaker sect."[50]

Welsh and the BIC, through the House investigation and hearing, successfully unsettled Parker's position in the federal government and used a language of racial prejudice and cultural expectations to repress the reform alternatives represented by his work in the Indian office. Although he was exonerated, Parker realized that his opponents and their political allies expected Indian people to be subjects of federal policy—not voices in its creation. Moreover, he recognized that those directing federal Indian affairs would no longer listen to his voice as an Indian man.

Welsh and the others continued alleging abuse, fraud, and misconduct, even in the aftermath of the hearing. In an April 1871 letter to Vincent Colyer, Welsh referred to the "fraudulent design" of Indian office advertisements and asserted, "The impression is, that Wheeler and Bosler have concocted them." He also alleged that "the Indian Office is under the control of Wheeler and Bosler."[51] A few weeks later, though several months before Parker's resignation, BIC member Robert Campbell urged BIC chairman Felix Brunot to continue the attack. He suggested that they needed to give to President Grant "a true statement of Parker's conduct. Which I consider most outrageous." He added that the president's Indian policies would no doubt fail if Parker retained his position.[52] A few days later, George Stuart wrote to Parker directly to inform him that the BIC found his recent actions, specifically the fact that he reopened bidding on a transportation contract after the BIC had already approved a successful bidder, to be problematic. In fact, Stuart threateningly concluded, Parker's actions were "so remarkable" that he would withhold comment until he had "completely examined the law and conferred with [his] colleagues."[53]

It appeared, too, that Parker's resolve was wearing down. Following the hearing and the continued assault from Welsh and the BIC, the commissioner began yielding in the jurisdictional conflicts that had plagued their relationship since the board's inception. On April 22, 1871, Parker wrote to BIC secretary Vincent Colyer that board members were "authorized to make any changes in the advertisements they deem proper and necessary."[54] The letter carried the heavy tone of defeat. Then in June, Congress passed a bill requiring that the BIC supervise all expenditures made by the Indian Office. Parker asked Secretary of the Interior Delano for clarification and learned that he would, in fact, be required to submit all expenditures for approval. The message was clear; the humiliation stung.[55]

In his resignation letter later that summer, Parker conceded that Welsh and the BIC had successfully wrested control of policy making from him and those he thought shared his reform agenda. The Indian Bureau, he asserted, had been divested of "all its original importance, duties, and proper responsibilities." He added that his position had become simply that of "a clerk to a Board of Indian Commissioners, operating wholly outside of and almost independent of the Indian Bureau." The latter point was not a mere emotional reaction. Parker believed this was reflective of the larger political wrangling between Congress and the president.[56] Others did not share Parker's views. "The snake [the Indian Ring] has been scotched," heralded the *Nation*.[57] Parker's departure from the Bureau of Indian Affairs, the paper continued, signaled "the complete overthrow of a most gigantic system of wrong, robbery, hypocrisy, greed, and cruelty, and the triumph of right, of official integrity, of administrative economy, and of the principles of a Christian civilization."[58] According to the *Nation*, the corrupt influences of the Indian Ring, whose temptations Parker could not avoid, would now have to contend with a new commissioner, and mainstream assimilationists offered Felix Brunot, the current chairman of the BIC, as a suitable replacement. Brunot's views were completely consistent with Welsh's and the BIC's policy agenda, but he ultimately turned down the position, believing he would have more political latitude without the bureaucratic responsibilities of the office.[59]

Parker and his allies may have lost a major battle in the wake of the House investigation, but they also won a minor one in early 1872. In April of the previous year, a group of Mexicans, Papago Indians, and whites rode onto the Camp Grant reserve to the northeast of Tucson, Arizona, and massacred 118 Apaches, only 8 of whom were adult men. BIC secretary Vincent Colyer, Welsh's co-conspirator, visited the region as a representative of the federal government. Arizona residents heckled and harassed him in person and in print, and when he returned to Washington, he penned a scathing account of the massacre, placing blame squarely on the whites. Even though Colyer's appraisal may have been accurate, Secretary Delano seized this moment to suggest that "for the welfare and prosperity of [our] part of the public service," the BIC would benefit from its secretary's resignation. As a result, in February 1872, Colyer resigned.[60]

Between 1873 and 1875, Welsh and the BIC continued their efforts to repress viable policy alternatives and used the corruption issue as a fruitful political tool by filing often-groundless charges of fraud and insinuating that their opponents colluded with shadowy contractors and suppliers. In 1873 Welsh began an attack campaign against Delano—perhaps as retribution for Colyer's forced resignation—arguing that the secretary had approved $300,000 worth of fraudulent vouchers for supplies. In 1874, William Dodge, a prominent member of the BIC, testified vaguely before Congress that the Indian Ring was still operating, but he could not provide specific names or examples of fraud. Welsh also attacked the new commissioner of Indian affairs, E. P. Smith, who he believed misrepresented events at the Red Cloud agency in an effort to discredit the Episcopal Indian agent there.

All of the original BIC members resigned en masse in 1874. Despite assurances from President Grant, they had come to believe that the entire Indian affairs bureaucracy, from Secretary Delano on, was a tangled web of corruption and that no amount of oversight could prevent ongoing fraud. Nonetheless, the events they and Welsh set in motion came to fruition in 1875 when both Commissioner E. P. Smith and Secretary Delano resigned out of humiliation and anger, as Parker had four years before. The BIC continued to operate after the mass exit, but it never again mustered the power and influence it held between 1869 and 1874.[61]

While Parker no longer directly influenced policy making on the federal level after 1871, one of the central tenets of his reform agenda had critical significance in the development of Indian affairs in the late nineteenth century. By encouraging the development of an efficient bureaucracy in Indian affairs to protect it against the influence of land speculators and business interests, Parker actually contributed to the expansion of administrative capacity in Indian affairs. Ironically, the expansion would provide mainstream assimilationists with the mechanisms necessary to institute the Allotment Act in 1887, a law that forced Native people to create individual family farms, dispossessed them of much of their remaining communal lands, and broke apart tribal relations—all of which required considerable bureaucratic management.

When he fought to transfer the OIA to the War Department after the Civil War, Parker envisioned placing it within the most developed and efficient bureaucracy in the executive cabinet at that time. After the passage of the Allotment Act, the Indian Office itself expanded to incorporate more clerks, agents, and officials than ever before. By advocating for oversight committees, Parker focused on the importance of monitoring and verifying appropriations and supplies. As the allotment program progressed, the Indian Office itself overtook this responsibility, maintaining meticulous records on every aspect of Indian life on the reservations. It created tribal rolls that translated and standardized Indian names. It also kept records of demographic information, including genealogical data and dates of baptisms, confirmations, and deaths. In an effort to stamp out corruption, Parker sought to "make the government the purchaser of all articles usually brought in by the Indians."[62] The allotment program also monitored all production and consumption on the reservations, from agricultural output to purchases of supplies such as shoes, socks, hammers, and nails. Regulating the purchase and sale of goods became one of the most important functions of the OIA in the allotment period, and while he did not anticipate this development, Parker clearly envisioned this as one of the OIA's responsibilities as part of his reform agenda.

Historian Philip Deloria has characterized components of the allotment program as an effort to "transform Indian people from conquered enemies into colonial subjects, people who were—and who saw themselves as—part of the American state." The knowledge contained in these meticulous records, he argues, "could be translated into power over Indian people. . . . To be known by name, date and location of baptism, rations drawn, and enrollment number, was to be made visible to the colonial bureaucracy."[63] Although Parker certainly could not foresee it, his reform agenda contributed to one of the most disastrous policies in the history of Indian affairs.

HISTORIAN ROBERT KELLER has written that just "as United States history too often is written omitting Indians, Indian history can be written as if it were central to America's past. It was not."[64] This statement reveals how scholars and other American citizens often dismiss the significance of Indian history and the development of Indian policy in the nineteenth century. This chapter, however, demonstrates that policy makers, reformers, and journalists invested a significant amount of time and energy in Indian affairs.

Politicians who directly shaped Indian policy—the senators who debated Parker's strengths and weaknesses in the halls of Congress; the U.S. representatives who investigated the OIA; the elite, Christian philanthropists who fought to repress opposing alternatives; the members of two executive departments, War and Interior; the president himself and his close Seneca friend—all considered Indian affairs a top priority. So too were other politicians, some far removed from Washington, who were not directly involved in policy making. These men and women followed and commented upon developments in Indian affairs. In 1870, for example, E. B. Washburne, the U.S. minister to France, forwarded a letter to Parker at the OIA from his colleague C. C. Andrews, the U.S. minister to Sweden. In the letter, Andrews complimented Parker and the Grant administration on their efforts to reform Indian policy and wanted to "urge upon the Administration the great importance of at once setting in motion" additional reforms.[65] The *Nation* poignantly described elements of the peace policy as "a revolution in a most important branch of public affairs."[66] When Indian affairs are viewed within this context, the larger significance of the policy debates and conflicts between Parker, Welsh, and the BIC becomes clear.

The contentiousness between these men extended beyond differences in personality or issues of personal gain. When Ely Parker argued that the primary role and responsibility of the federal government in regard to Indians was to counterbalance financially and socially an economic and political system of domination that had dispossessed Indian peoples of land, resources, opportunities, and sovereignty, he was suggesting nothing short of a reorientation of the national state. In his desire to expand the bureaucracy and administrative capacity of the Indian Office to insulate it against the influence of land speculators, business interests, and other nonstate actors, he actually suggested that politicians in Washington, D.C., take a more active approach to the social welfare of the population. When mainstream assimilationists argued that they understood the best interests of Indian people and that only a small group of elite, white citizens should make policy, they, too, sought to impose their vision of the role of the state in the everyday lives of its citizens/wards. They saw that the federal state would likely move to confine Indians further, and they wanted to use it as a tool with which they and their peers could create what they envisioned to be the ideal society.

At the end of the Civil War, the reformist spirit of the Reconstruction program and the legacy of wartime events and developments in the borderlands of Indian-white contact inspired some individuals to break from a policy of government action that had promoted dispossession and forced assimilation. But while the early peace policy era represented a moment when a shift in the trajectory of Indian affairs seemed possible, two different policy directions emerged from the in-fighting among those who influenced Indian affairs the most—Ely Parker, William Welsh, and the BIC. These reformers fought bitter and complex battles, but at a most basic level, they each contested the other's notions of who best represented Indian people. Scholars have dismissed Parker's career too easily perhaps because he yielded and alternative policies were repressed. But an understanding of his failures and flaws, as well as his modest successes, offers new and better ways to make sense of this complex period.

The conflicting visions of the role and responsibilities of the OIA effectively provided the foundation for the late-nineteenth-century programs of coercive assimilation.

The ultimate tragedy of these events, of course, is one with which scholars of Native American history are actually quite familiar. The well-intentioned efforts of Ely Parker to reform Indian affairs had the unintended consequence of facilitating an exponentially more disruptive policy. The scope of the allotment program, which sought to govern every aspect of Indian lives in an effort to speed along assimilation, would not have been possible without the well-developed bureaucratic framework that Parker's reforms helped to create. Scholars of Native American history, however, might also recognize a significant difference between this and other examples of well-intentioned efforts in Indian affairs that resulted in unintended consequences. In this case, the well-intentioned reformer was a Native person himself. Although Parker fell as a casualty in this battle between opposing government agendas, his pleas for increased Indian involvement in the crafting and administration of U.S. Indian policy did not go unheard.

SIX

Thomas Bland's Moment, 1875–1886

The manifest duty of the Government is to protect the Indians in their
reservation rights, aid and encourage them in stock raising and farming, [and]
establish schools on or near the reservations for the education of all the children.
—THOMAS A. BLAND, "Intemperate and Ill-Directed Zeal," *Council Fire*, 1885

Alfred B. Meacham believed in the peace policy. The former superintendent
of Indian affairs for the state of Oregon and founder of the Indian reform
newspaper the *Council Fire* argued in 1878 that it was the "best" program
for Native communities "ever attempted by this Government."[1] Meacham
had been appointed to his position early in Parker's tenure as commissioner
and corresponded with him frequently, often discussing opportunities for
the Klamath and Modoc Nations. Most mainstream assimilationists did not
agree with his assessment. In fact, by the mid-1870s, many, especially elite
philanthropists in the eastern United States, began to advocate a movement
away from the slow-paced, community-oriented, "civilizing" process of the
programs initiated by Parker, Grant, and others. In this constitutive moment,
reformers and activists reconsidered racial politics, assimilation, citizenship,
tribal sovereignty, and the financial costs related to the administration of the
Indian service.

The generation of reformers who emerged in the late 1870s and 1880s focused a considerable amount of attention debating legislative proposals to divide tribally held lands, dissolve tribal relations, and force Indigenous people
to assimilate in as little time as possible. The General Allotment Act of 1887
and subsequent similar legislation were the result of these debates. The allotment act, known also as the Dawes Act (the bill's sponsor was Senator Henry
L. Dawes), authorized the president to break up reservation lands into single
plots for individual and family ownership, which would be held in trust by the
federal government for twenty-five years. The Dawes Act promised to encourage individual property ownership and an adherence to free market economic
values among Indian people.[2]

Thomas A. Bland, founder of the National Indian Defense Association and co-editor of the *Council Fire*. From the frontispiece of his self-help/medical book, *How to Get Well and How to Keep Well* (Boston: Plymouth Publishing, 1894).

In these debates, Thomas Bland—a close friend of Alfred Meacham who was primary editor of the *Council Fire* and a founder of the important but often overlooked reform organization called the National Indian Defense Association (NIDA)—supported a series of policy reforms that rejected forced assimilation and focused instead upon using the federal government to provide resources and opportunities for Indigenous nations while simultaneously protecting the integrity of communally held land. His ideas represented a viable alternative to the existing trends in Indian policymaking, which valued increasing confinement and diminishing tribal sovereignty. Herbert Welsh— William Welsh's nephew and ally, along with the members of his organization the Indian Rights Association (IRA) (a significant contingent of the self-styled "Friends of the Indian," a group of mainstream assimilationist, reformers, and activists)—advocated policies that fit well with existing trends in Indian policymaking. Welsh and the IRA advocated coercive assimilation, a continued attack on tribal sovereignty, spatial confinement on increasingly smaller plots of individually held land, and social confinement within certain prescribed roles.

More important than the similarities the two organizations shared with pre-vious reformers, though, were the differences that emerged in their work—both across time and between one another. The NIDA and the IRA, beginning in the 1880s, situated their arguments about Indian policy within a framework that tied developments in Indian affairs to larger concerns about the role and nature of the state, as well as the relationship between the government and its citizens and wards. As historian Heather Cox Richardson has made clear, questions about the federal government's role and its relationship to its citizens were by no means new in the late nineteenth century, but they took on new importance because Congress imposed national taxes during the Civil War. How those taxes were to be used and who had a voice in this decision moti-vated reformers and policymakers. In addition, the Civil War constitutional amendments were the first to expand, rather than limit, the power of the fed-eral government.

Questions about inclusion and exclusion, as well as the rights and respon-sibilities of citizenship, were layered atop the debates surrounding land allot-ment and forced assimilation. Land allotment and forced assimilation were potentially to serve as the means, with citizenship and all that that status entailed (including the end of tribal sovereignty and tribal relations) as the end.[3]

Thomas Bland approached policy reform as an outsider espousing view-points deemed radical by his opponents. His midwestern upbringing and de-votion to working-class and agrarian causes put him at odds both with eastern, elite philanthropists and western policymakers. Though he did not support the antigovernment rhetoric that was becoming the rallying cry of former Confederates and far western radicals at the time, his fears and criticism of unrestrained wealth and power won him few friends among the recipients of patronage and nepotism. He and the other members of the NIDA believed that land allotment legislation would disrupt the separation of the powers in the federal government either by strengthening or by undermining the power of congressmen and senators. They also believed that land allotment would threaten the balance between state and federal authority to the detriment of all citizens. As they made these arguments, Bland and the NIDA hoped to create a permanent alternative to the assimilation process by providing incentives to Indian communities and allowing Native people to embrace mainstream culture and societal values only if they chose to do so. They simultaneously suggested that the state itself should serve a protective role for the nation's most needy and disenfranchised citizens and wards, much in line with larger populist agitation during this time period.

Thomas Nast, "Give the Natives a Chance, Mr. Carl," *Harper's Weekly*, March 13, 1880.
This is probably the most well-known cartoon relating to Indian affairs in the buildup
toward the passage of the allotment law. While it is often misinterpreted as a
representation of Nast's support for Indian communities, it was more likely an
expression of his distaste for Carl Schurz, who was secretary of the interior during
the Hayes administration. The cartoon shows three Indian men examining a glass
globe beneath a crude picture of a freedperson and German and Irish immigrants
who had been "civilized by the ballot." Courtesy of the Library of Congress,
Prints & Photographs Division, LC-USZ62–78252.

Herbert Welsh and IRA, whose political and social connections extended throughout the ranks of eastern and western politicians and philanthropists, attempted to tie Office of Indian Affairs (OIA) reform to civil service reform in the broader federal government and to demonstrate the importance of federal economic regulation. They hoped to use the federal government to create a society that fit their vision of a proper polity with economically motivated, religiously devout, and politically homogenous citizens. In a way, these reformers embraced an emergent middle-class ideology, premised upon economic and social harmony, that attacked "special interests" (such as labor activism, populism, and racial activism), while upholding a mythic notion of American individualism.[4] The federal government, they believed, should serve an activist role, but only insofar as it could stifle these special interests and (paradoxically) aid individualism. Thus in the late nineteenth century, Indian policy reform, and the Office of Indian Affairs specifically, became critical sites where reformers developed and debated ideas about the evolution of the state.

The majority of historical studies that address late-nineteenth-century Indian policy reform portray participants as primarily of one mind: "to be pro-Indian . . . was to be pro-allotment and pro-assimilation."[5] Scholars note that reformers—including the "Friends of the Indians," the IRA, the Women's National Indian Association, the Boston Indian Citizenship Committee, and the attendees at the annual Lake Mohonk Conference in upstate New York— shared similar social, religious, and economic backgrounds that shaped the coherence and harmony of their campaign to bring about these programs.[6] Indeed, if scholars address conflict among policymakers in this era at all, they generally note that while most activists favored some form of coercive assimilation, there were extremists who considered genocide to gain access to Indian lands and resources. Based on these interpretations, it is hard to imagine any possible outcome other than a linear progression toward and ultimate passage of a land allotment law at the end of the century.[7]

As this chapter demonstrates, however, a focus on the significant contestation between rival reformers and the emergence of policy alternatives in this era leads to a more nuanced interpretation. Thomas Bland's NIDA was both an important and a numerically significant organization whose members not only opposed land allotment and coercive assimilation but also provided viable alternative policy reforms. In a study that seeks to break from this consensus history trend, historian Benjamin Johnson concludes that many scholars have "either misunderstood or ignored Bland and the NIDA because they also assume that a monolithically capitalist white America wielded irresistible power in its quest to destroy Indian landholding."[8]

GIVE THE RED MAN A CHANCE.

Make him a citizen, with all the *privileges* which that implies.

Thomas Nast, "Give the Red Man a Chance," *Harper's Weekly*, September 24, 1881. More interesting and perhaps more difficult to interpret, this cartoon was published several months after "Give the Natives a Chance, Mr. Carl," and it appeared small, toward the back of the issue. It is likely that Nast was poking fun at the assimilationist reformers who saw citizenship as the primary goal in their reform efforts. It is less clear, though, if the noose represented Nast's belief that it would have been better to eliminate Native people altogether (he certainly portrayed them unfavorably in most of his cartoons), or if it was a play on the notion that suffrage would "kill the Indian and save the man," as Richard Henry Pratt, the founder and superintendent of Carlisle Indian School, would put it eleven years later, in 1892. Courtesy of the Library of Congress, Prints & Photographs Division.

A fuller incorporation of Bland's and the NIDA's work into the history of the allotment controversy presents many interpretive possibilities. First, as Johnson noted, it demonstrates that "there was more fluidity, contingency, and common ground between whites and Indians in the late nineteenth century than we have previous recognized."[9] Second, it encourages us to push backward chronologically by situating the allotment debates within a longer reform tradition from the peace policy era. In this way, we are more likely to draw important connections across time and space. Third, it requires that we envision these reformers as part of a much larger, even national conversation about state development in the late nineteenth century, much as they would have understood their work themselves.[10] Envisioning these men and women as part of a larger national dialogue reveals that the nineteenth-century Indian experience was more crucial to the U.S. narrative than previous work has portrayed. Finally, it illustrates a second constitutive moment in post–Civil War Indian policy reform when viable alternatives were actively targeted and repressed by opposing activists.[11]

Critics of Coercive Assimilation

Thomas A. Bland was not initially drawn to Indian policy reform. His parents had been members of a North Carolina Quaker colony and then settled in Indiana in 1817. Bland was born in 1830 and had only seven years of formal education as a youth. In 1852 he married a Virginian named Mary Cora Davis. As a young man, Bland farmed, but once he married, he studied medicine at the Eclectic Medical Institute in Cincinnati, Ohio, where physiology and phrenology were his specialties. "Eclectic medicine" in the nineteenth-century United States focused upon the use of botanical compounds and herbal treatments and traced its heritage back to Native American medicinal traditions. Its adherents considered themselves "medical protestants" against the prevailing orthodoxies of therapeutic practice who offered "a viable alternative to those . . . who had wearied of allopathy's pretentions and failures."[12] It was a near-perfect career path for Bland, reflecting important elements of his character. He opened a practice six miles from the village of his birth. During the Civil War, he served a commission as an army surgeon, then with his wife Cora, who had been studying medicine as well, embarked on a joint career divided between medical, literary, and philanthropic interests, moving around the country every few years.

Little is known about Cora Bland, but from the broad outlines available, it seems that Thomas found a most appropriate spouse. At a time when few women were able to enter into the ranks of professional life, Cora taught and practiced medicine. In the U.S. capital, she helped to found the American Red Cross and served as president of the Women's National Health Association.[13] The couple established several journals, including the *Home Visitor* in Indianapolis, the *Northwestern*, which became the *Indiana Farmer*, and *Ladies' Own Magazine*, for which Cora served as editor in chief.

The Blands lived in Chicago in the early 1870s and moved to New York in 1874. They sold *Ladies Own Magazine* that year as Cora completed her medical degree. In 1878 they moved to Washington, D.C. Cora practiced medicine, lectured on health, and endorsed personal fitness products like the "Pocket Gymnasium," which she believed was the "most complete and perfect system of physical exercise ever invented."[14] Thomas focused on his literary and reform work, publishing ten books between 1870 and 1906.

Bland's work demonstrated an intense distaste for concentrated economic power. As Benjamin Johnson noted, his writing and policy advocacy was animated by the "deeply anticapitalist strains of American politics."[15] Bland's books protested railroad monopolies and the establishment of a national bank and advocated for populist causes, the Greenback Party, and medical as well as religious reform. While Bland may not yet have articulated it as such in the late 1870s, his emerging interest in Indian policy reform and especially his efforts to protect communally held Indian lands connected quite clearly to his arguments in support of democratic self-determination and a federal government that performed a protective role in some form or another.

Bland's books reflected these interests, as did his membership in a number of political parties and organizations that espoused these values. In the 1870s he published *Farming as a Profession* (1870), *How to Grow Rich* (1879), and *The Life of Benjamin Butler* (1879).[16] The first was a novel about a young man named Charley who chooses to farm despite a successful Harvard education and against the prodding of his elitist friend and fellow Harvard graduate, Fred. When the two men meet later in life, Fred (then a Boston attorney) is unmarried, unhappy, and barely getting by; Charley is living happily and profitably with his wife. In the end Fred chooses to farm as well. The message is clear: honest labor, community ties, and family together yield personal happiness. In *How to Grow Rich*, he attacked monopoly, arguing that it was easy to accumulate wealth if one was willing to go about it ruthlessly. In Benjamin Butler's biography, Bland applauded the subject's support for labor regulation and women's rights and his attacks on corporate and government corruption. It also focused intently on the "greenback" issue and celebrated Butler's advocacy of fiat currency. (Butler would run for president as the candidate of the Greenback and Anti-Monopoly Parties in 1884.)

Bland believed that the federal government should issue paper money, and he vehemently opposed bankers. "Banks are foes to justice and equality always," he argued.[17] In a capitalist society, honest farmers and the working classes would always operate at a disadvantage. It was the role of the state, Bland suggested, to compensate for the shortcomings of a capitalist economy and level the economic playing field. As a Greenbacker, Bland supported labor against capital, the eight-hour workday, the establishment of an income tax, and women's suffrage.[18] He also took issue with railroad monopolies; this, in fact, dovetailed nicely with his efforts at Indian reform, and was the subject of his fourth book, *The Reign of Monopoly* (1881).[19]

In 1892 he returned to his interest in challenging bankers and published *Esau: or the Bankers Victim*, in which he railed against hard currency and the dangers of unrestrained capitalism. In this, as well as several of his previous works, Bland juxtaposed local, small-town, community-mindedness with ruthless corporate development and the inequities of economic growth. Also in 1892, he published *People's Party Shot and Shell*, which addressed the reform agenda of the upstart Populist Party.[20] His interest in populism reflected not only his notions of state responsibility and fears of uncontrolled capitalism but also his support for agrarian radicalism.[21]

In 1875 Bland attended a lecture given by Alfred B. Meacham, former superintendent of Indian affairs in Oregon and former peace commissioner, at the Cooper Institute Hall in New York. Walking across Boston Common later that year, the two men encountered one another and struck up a conversation. This lecture and subsequent chance meeting sparked Bland's interest in Indian affairs—an interest that would help shape the debates over land allotment and forced assimilation, to which Bland devoted more than ten years of his life.[22]

Though he was no longer officially employed by the Indian Service in 1872, Meacham served at President Grant's and Secretary of the Interior Delano's request as a negotiator on the peace commission sent to Captain Jack and the Modoc Indians near the Tule Lake on the California/Oregon border. In yet another failure of federal removal and reservation policies, the Modoc had been removed to the Klamath Reservation in Oregon, a region already occupied by their longtime rivals. After suffering poor treatment from Klamath Indians, the Modoc left the reservation, a violation of federal treaty law. Meacham recommended that they be given a separate reservation. On April 11, 1873, however, frustrated and desperate Modoc men attacked Meacham and several other peace commissioners. Meacham was shot four times (including in his left eye), partially scalped, and left for dead.[23]

He recovered rapidly but incompletely. During his convalescence, Meacham continued to advocate for the Modoc, even his attackers, offering at one point to serve as their legal counsel. And in late 1873, feeling compelled "to do something for these poor despised down-trodden misunderstood people," he took to the lecture circuit, delivering a talk titled "The Tragedy of the Lava Beds."[24] Meacham became a proponent of tribal sovereignty and believed that more than anything else the Indians should be allowed to express their own opinions and ideas about the allocation of treaty annuities and issues of federal governance.[25] He also argued that the "tragedy" would not have occurred if the Modoc had been protected from the Klamath, if white settlers had not become involved in the violence between the Indians and the military, and if the government focused more attention on educating and providing opportunities for Native people.[26]

The origins of the *Council Fire* can be traced back to the aftermath of the attack. Meacham's tour failed as a financial venture and his health deteriorated, but Thomas Bland pledged his and his wife's medical, literary, and oratorical talents, as well as monetary support, to Meacham's cause.[27] The solutions to Indian land issues that Meacham proposed appealed to Bland's antimonopoly ideology, and he came to believe that it was railroad companies who had the greatest interest in divesting Indian communities of their lands.[28] Over the next several years, with the Blands' assistance, Meacham continued lecturing and began to publish the *Council Fire*, a corollary medium designed to educate the public on Indian issues.

As editor of the *Council Fire*, Meacham expressed a fierce devotion to the tenets of the peace policy. In the late 1870s and early 1880s, Meacham and Bland used the journal to fight against the transfer of the OIA to the War Department and to support the reservation system as a method of protecting Indian communities and communally held land. The journal also expressed the men's support of Standing Bear and the Ponca and other tribal nations in their opposition to federal removal policies and of an assimilation process carried out only at a pace dictated by Indian peoples.[29] When Meacham died in 1882, the Blands assumed co-editorship of the journal. As editors, they maintained Meacham's advocacy of gradual assimilation "through rational educative measures."[30] In the 1880s, as agitation for Indian policy reform intensified, Bland invited the reform organizations to use the *Council Fire* to spread their message.

By 1883, Bland had come to believe that Indian affairs was "growing on public attention much faster than did the question of negro rights during the early years of anti-slavery agitation."[31] He celebrated the fact that reform organizations were emerging in "Philadelphia, New York, Boston, and other cities for the purpose of giving systematic force and effect to the sentiment of justice in the public treatment of the Indian question." One of the most promising groups, according to Bland, was the IRA, to whom he extended a formal greeting and offered the pages of the *Council Fire* "to communicate with each other and the general public."[32] He even joined the IRA for a brief time. It soon became clear to the editor, however, that the IRA's support for Indian confinement and assimilation differed greatly from the reform ideas shared by the Blands and their allies. This was especially true following a series of controversies that developed on the Pine Ridge Reservation between the Oglala and their neighbors.

In the early 1880s, army surgeon Valentine T. McGillycuddy served as the federal agent at the reservation, and his actions, particularly his efforts to undermine the customary leadership of the Oglala Lakota, served to polarize philanthropists and reformers. As a supporter of Indian confinement, McGillycuddy employed all possible techniques, including reducing treaty-stipulated rations and pitting Native leaders against one another, to pressure the Oglala to abandon customary social, cultural, and political practices. Doing so, he believed, would not only force them to assimilate but also facilitate the process of dispossession and provide land and financial opportunities for non-Native settlers.[33] As historian Jeffrey Ostler has argued, "No one personified the spirit of coercive assimilation at the heart of U.S. policy better than McGillycuddy."[34]

Herbert Welsh, IRA founder and a driving force behind the movement for coercive assimilation, believed McGillycuddy was exactly the type of Indian agent who could control customary chiefs and destroy tribal/community relations, a necessary process if Native communities were to embrace nineteenth-century Euro-American values. Welsh would later refer to McGillycuddy as "a man of remarkable ability" and praised in particular his capacity to discourage "the non-progressive element at the Agency."[35] Upon returning to Philadelphia after a visit to the reservation in 1883, Welsh complimented the agent's ration reduction strategy, asserting that treaty appropriations led to "idleness and pauperism."[36]

Bland, in sharp contrast, despised McGillycuddy and publicly challenged his approach. He pledged his support to Chief Red Cloud and other Oglala leaders who sought McGillycuddy's removal in the early 1880s, calling the agent "an epicurean in his habits of diet, a fop in dress and manners, and a petty tyrant in character."[37] In 1882, he wrote that McGillycuddy was "a petty, vindictive, revengeful tyrant, who was robbing the Indians . . . [and] enriching himself at their expense."[38] The conflict between Bland and McGillycuddy exposed some of the important differences among opposing reformers in this period and revealed the critical role Native people themselves played in the viable alternative reforms proposed by the NIDA.

Although the relationship between Red Cloud and McGillycuddy seemed to be improving in 1883, the agent's continued efforts to isolate the chief and his support for the Dawes Sioux Bill, a plan to reduce the size of the Great Sioux Reservation and allot tribal lands (a precursor to the broader and better-known Dawes Allotment Act of 1887), reignited the conflict. In early 1884, McGillycuddy organized an agency council at Pine Ridge made up of representatives from different villages, whom he characterized as the "working and progressive element" of the Oglalas who supported "proper management of the agency irrespective of the Indian Chiefs."[39] McGillycuddy's short-term goal involved ending the Sun Dance, and he selected only the most supportive delegates. He also intended to weaken Red Cloud's influence, as well as others whom he saw as "nonprogressive." McGillycuddy argued that he was creating a uniquely "American" form of government, but Jeffrey Ostler has referred to it as "simply a tribal council limited to leaders from the bands of the agent's choice."[40]

In the spring of 1884, Bland received permission from Secretary of the Interior Henry M. Teller to visit the reservation. Teller was sympathetic to Bland's position and even skeptical of allotment schemes himself, but he warned him not to "interfere in the affairs of the agencies."[41] Bland may not have intended to interfere directly, but he no doubt planned to encourage the Lakota to resist the Dawes Sioux Bill. Bland and Red Cloud were friends; during trips to the capital in the late 1870s, the Oglala leader had visited the Blands' home. Now he appealed to his ally for help in removing McGillycuddy.

During his trip through Rosebud Reservation, on the way to Pine Ridge, Bland stopped and spoke to many different Indian people, encouraging them to voice their concerns and complaints, and taking their ideas seriously. He referred to one Lakota leader, Quick Bear, as "a very sensible chief" and reported that another, Red Leaf, declared that his band could "get along pretty well" if only they could "get seeds to plant and farm tools."[42] From there, Bland traveled west to meet with Red Cloud at Pine Ridge.

On a hot late-June day, Red Cloud and an entourage of fifty to eighty other Lakotas greeted the doctor. They stopped at midday while on the reservation. During lunch, Indian police officers, instructed by McGillycuddy, arrived to arrest the visitor. At the agency office, the two men engaged in a heated debate that almost ended in a fistfight. When McGillycuddy threatened to have him removed, Bland reportedly exclaimed, "I'm a citizen of the United States with a letter from the Secretary of the Interior giving me permission to come here."

McGillycuddy replied that they were not in the United States; they "were on an Indian reservation" where he was in "supreme command."[43] The agent disregarded the letter and instead issued ammunition to the Indian police officers. He ordered them to escort Bland off the reserve and authorized them to use force if necessary. Bland reportedly left the office screaming, "My wife said I was a fool for visiting your agency."[44] McGillycuddy's commissary clerk, Frank Stewart, allegedly replied, "Well, all I've got to say is that your wife has a damn sight more sense than some people."[45] It is little wonder that Bland ultimately concluded that the reservation had become "the little monarchy over which McGillycuddy reigns."[46]

Bland stayed at a nearby ranch and continued to meet with Red Cloud, assuring him and other Oglala leaders that he would see McGillycuddy removed from the agency as soon as he returned to Washington. He perhaps believed that McGillycuddy's refusal to accept Secretary Teller's letter was a punishable offense. In fact, Teller was likely willing to accept Bland's story, but McGillycuddy had powerful friends, including Massachusetts senator Henry L. Dawes, one of the leading political supporters of the IRA and successor to legendary abolitionist Charles Sumner. In reports to his superiors, McGillycuddy portrayed himself as valiantly fighting to maintain order among a hostile and aggressive Indian community. Lacking an expedient solution, Teller sent a federal investigator to Pine Ridge in November.[47]

Throughout 1884 and into 1885, the editors of the *Council Fire* and IRA leaders fought openly in the newspapers and through a voluminous pamphlet literature. In one notable article, published in the *Springfield Republican*, Senator Dawes stated that Bland was "a very strange man . . . making trouble and mischief with everybody who is trying to help [the Indians]."[48] The IRA printed 3,000 copies of the article and distributed it widely. Bland responded in the *Council Fire* that perhaps the name "Indian Rights Association" was a misnomer: "The Indian Rights (?) Association of Philadelphia professes . . . to exist for the sole purpose of defending the rights . . . of the Indians; . . . [instead they] defend a thieving Indian agent against the truthful complaints and charges of the Indians he is robbing."[49] For the time being, at least, McGillycuddy remained in place.

The National Indian Defense Association

As the McGillycuddy/Oglala Sioux controversy continued, Bland and like-minded individuals intensified their challenge to the Indian Rights Association and in late 1885 founded the National Indian Defense Association, "for the purpose of protecting and assisting the Indians of the United States in acquiring the benefits of civilization, and in securing their territorial and proprietary rights."[50] Perhaps playing off his opponents' self-appointed title "Friends of the Indian," Bland referred to the NIDA as "friends of a sound and humane Indian policy."[51]

At the founding meeting of the NIDA, Bland and his compatriots outlined the organization's three fundamental tenets. In some ways these principles represented an extension of Ely Parker's earlier reform agenda. They asserted first that civil, criminal, and property laws of the United States should be used to protect Indian people within their communities against encroachments and actions of non-Native people. In addition, they stressed that tribal sovereignty and land rights should be federally and permanently protected. Second, they declared that the "tribal condition," which they defined as communal landholding and customary practices of tribal governance, should be maintained until, at a point in the future, they could be incorporated "into some political institution in harmony with the general system of our Government." And finally, they stated that Indian communities should be given secure patents for their land to protect them from dispossession.[52]

The organization elected as their president General James W. Denver, a former governor of Kansas Territory, former commissioner of Indian affairs, and former member of Congress. Reverend Dr. Byron Sunderland, the longtime pastor of the First Presbyterian Church in Washington, D.C., and former chaplain to the U.S. Senate (1861–64, 1873–79), served as the first vice president. Judges A. J. Willard and E. J. Ellis, Reverend Alexander Kent, Professor Bernard Janney, and Thomas Bland rounded out the first executive committee. Bland was optimistic. The "new association starts under favorable auspices," he wrote, "and will, we believe, be a potent factor in solving the Indian problem."[53]

In this constitutive moment of Indian policy reform, the National Indian Defense Association used historical examples to situate their reform arguments. Rather than simply outlining problems in the administration of Indian policy, they championed several specific policy correctives, experiencing at least a modicum of success in stalling forced allotment and in encouraging policymakers to consider viable alternatives. Importantly, their relationship with Native people differed in significant ways from that of other reform organizations. While others saw Indians as recipients of the largesse of non-Indian philanthropists, the NIDA appealed to Native people for their input, encouraged them to participate actively in reform, and provided opportunities for Native people to present their ideas. Perhaps this reflected Bland's own interest in grassroots reform and community-oriented life. Most significantly, the NIDA vehemently opposed the ideology, methods, and goals of the Indian Rights Association and other self-styled "Friends of the Indian."

As they began their campaign against the IRA in 1885 and 1886 (during the critical build up toward legislative action on allotment proposals in Congress), Bland and the NIDA drew evidence from recent events and experiences in Indian affairs to support their reform objectives and persuade *Council Fire* readers to support their alternatives. In an article titled "Why Not Profit By Experience?," Bland argued that the United States had already found a satisfactory answer to the "Indian Question" when it gave patents in fee to the Cherokees, Creeks, Choctaws, Chickasaws, and Seminoles of Indian Territory. The term "patent in fee" refers to the title deed by which the federal government transfers landownership to different people. Receiving a patent in fee nullified the trust relationship or "trust patent" previously established between the government and Indian nations. Patents in fee could be granted to entire communities, as Bland suggested. In essence, he was arguing for the creation of "tribal title" to reservation lands. This property law concept is different from that of "fee simple." Under fee simple ownership, an individual, not a community, holds a title to specific property.

Ending the trust relationship in landownership, Bland and the NIDA believed, would empower Indian communities and help insulate them against additional land loss. "Those five tribes," Bland continued, "still own and occupy the lands then secured to them . . . and they have solved the problem of civilization for themselves and in their own way."[54] The emphasis on tribal sovereignty and Indian self-determination here is evident. He later wrote, "If the policy of uniting tribes with internal powers of self-government is extended to the mass of the Indians, it will produce the long desired outcome of the Indian question."[55]

Bland further asserted that the experiment of signing forced land allotment treaties with individual Indian communities such as the Delawares had been a failure, and he compared their experience with that of the Indian Territory nations. The Delawares suffered because "the greed and shrewdness of their white neighbors proved too strong for the Indians." In the end, they "were cheated out of their lands and were obliged to ask the Government for new reservations or get some more fortunate tribe to adopt them and give them homes."[56] Another prominent NIDA member, former commissioner of Indian affairs George Manypenny, outlined in the *Council Fire* the process by which the Delawares were dispossessed. He focused on the treaties of 1854, 1860, 1861, and 1866, demonstrating how in the 1854 treaty, "the initial step was taken to disinherit them; a gap was made in the barriers which had shielded and protected them from the invasion of the whites for nearly twenty-five years." Each successive treaty "widened the breach" and chipped away at Delaware sovereignty and their land base; by 1866 the secretary of the interior was able to authorize a sale of all lands owned by the tribe to the Missouri River Railroad. The Delawares were then transferred to Indian Territory and forced to pay the Cherokee for lands allotted to them. Manypenny reminded readers that the Delawares had supported the revolutionaries against England in the 1770s, they were U.S. allies in the War of 1812, and they fought for the Union in the Civil War. But "while the Delawares were thus patriotically engaged in the Union army the process of disinheriting them of their noble lands . . . was being wrought out by the civil agents of the Government."[57]

Bland was convinced that NIDA agitation was working and frequently noted a sea change in thought on Indian affairs. While he lamented that "tired benevolence and the land appetite" combined at the end of the 1870s and early 1880s to create an overarching opinion that "the Indian was an obstacle . . . he must be got out of the way," he believed that the NIDA had created "an awakening of the public conscience to the recognition of what is due to the Indian."[58]

Education was a key pillar in NIDA policy reform. NIDA members filled the pages of the Council Fire with pleas for expanded educational opportunities. Bland once wrote that education was "the primary factor in a true system of Indian civilization." He believed that a well-rounded, liberal arts education should serve as the first step of any policy reform and that no significant changes should be made to the legal status or property of Native people until after a new system of Indian education had been implemented.[59] This was one of the most significant ways in which Bland differed from mainstream reformers in the 1880s; they saw little benefit in such classical education for Indian people beyond what they thought was necessary for assimilation. Instead, they primarily advocated vocational training that would instill Euro-American gender roles. NIDA leaders recognized the educational potential among the Indians but also believed that it would be a slow process and that "until then the Indians must have special protection against the avarice and dishonesty of the white man."[60] In fact, in the aftermath of the allotment controversy, Bland found one positive effect of the Dawes Act and its corollary assimilation program. A "hopeful feature of the present situation," he wrote, "is found in the fact that . . . the present administration is preparing to do what the Council Fire has from the first urged should be done—educate every Indian child." But he added, "This is the only ground of hope."[61]

Throughout 1885 and 1886, Bland and other NIDA leaders, most notably A. J. Willard, a former chief justice in the South Carolina Supreme Court, criticized specific programs and legislation championed by the IRA and the "Friends of the Indian." In their critiques, they also drew attention to their alternative policy reforms and identified protecting Indian communities, fulfilling treaty obligations, and fortifying tribal sovereignty as the most significant elements of their own agenda (next to providing educational opportunities).

Responding to the 1885 platform outlined by the "Friends of the Indian" during their annual meeting at Albert K. Smiley's Lake Mohonk resort in New Paltz, New York, Bland passionately stated, "What the Indian stands in need of to-day is the faithful fulfillment of the obligations of the Government toward him." These obligations included protection of reservation lands, a federal investment in farming and employment opportunities, the creation of reservation schools, and "the exercise of genuine friendship."[62] In 1886, Senator Dawes reintroduced legislation that would reduce in size the reservation lands "occupied by the various tribes of the Sioux Nation . . . [and] transfer to the United States a large portion of the lands ceded to those tribes by the treaty of 1868 . . . [to become] a part of the public domain of the United States."[63] Bland and his allies immediately challenged this plan in the pages of the Council Fire. If "the Indians are entrusted with a suitable degree of the power of self-government, and have the title to their lands," A. J. Willard declared, "they can protect themselves against [such] injurious intrusions."[64]

Willard also argued that "tribal relations should not be hastily or suddenly ruptured" and that land titles had to be secure.[65] Bland reminded readers of the Council Fire that the federal government had already recognized and agreed to protect Indian land titles in the treaties it had negotiated. "To ignore this title . . . and break up the system of holding land . . . all supposed to be protected by the solemn covenants entered into between the Indian tribes and the United States Government," Bland stated firmly, "would be an act of bad faith."[66]

As an alternate approach to the Sioux Bill, Bland and Willard suggested (as Bland had alluded to earlier) that the federal government issue land patents in fee to the Indians. Doing so, they argued, would codify tribal title and empower the Lakota as a tribal nation to manage its "self-support and general advancement." It would also "simplify the relations of the Indians to the Government." They appealed to Congress to consider their suggestions before moving on the Dawes proposal.[67] Some congressmen, it seems, listened.

On February 23, 1886, Bland and NIDA leaders James Dorsey, a Smithsonian anthropologist, and Colonel Samuel Tappan appeared before the House of Representatives Subcommittee on Indian Affairs to protest the passage of the Sioux Bill. Bland reported on the hearing in the Council Fire. Among other reasons for opposing the bill, they argued that it would require the government to pay the Lakota "a price far below" what their land was worth and to use the money from the land sale to pay for supplies and services that the government was already obligated to provide (according to previous treaties in 1868 and 1876). Most importantly, however, the Lakota leaders were not willing to sell any portion of the Great Sioux Reservation. As evidence of the last point and demonstrating the important role Native voices played in NIDA reform proposals, Bland read a statement provided by Chief Red Cloud that indicated he was "not in favor" of the bill and did not believe that the federal government would "forcibly take our last home from us."[68]

Never one to miss an opportunity to attack an opponent, Bland also added that it was "evident . . . that those who desire to break up the Sioux Reservation and rob these Indians of their lands regard McGillycuddy as an important agent in carrying out their selfish scheme."[69] He also noted that during the hearing Herbert Welsh spoke and defended McGillycuddy but did so in a way that might not have been palatable to other members of IRA. McGillycuddy is "very despotic" and "rules with an iron hand," Welsh said, according to Bland's report, "but . . . that is necessary." Bland agreed that an agent needed to be firm indeed, but that his "firmness should be tempered with kindness."[70]

Shortly after this meeting with the House subcommittee, McGillycuddy's reign at Pine Ridge ended. This not only was an important political victory that bolstered Bland and the NIDA, but it also demonstrated how Indian affairs issues were connected to broader political developments like civil service reform and patronage. The federal agent sent to investigate the controversy on Pine Ridge back in 1884 concluded that McGillycuddy acted appropriately in expelling Bland. Almost simultaneously, Grover Cleveland was elected president, the first Democrat to be placed in that office in twenty-four years. Secretary Teller—fearing widespread patronage turnover—reappointed the Republican McGillycuddy for a four-year term just before Cleveland took office. Having campaigned on civil service reform, though, Cleveland was loath to remove agents without just cause, even if he was persuaded by the NIDA's and Red Cloud's arguments.[71]

The Cleveland administration did not act immediately, instead choosing to wait for the results of yet another congressional investigation at Pine Ridge, this one led by Democratic congressman William S. Holman from Indiana. Republican members of the committee blocked a recommendation to dismiss McGillycuddy, but in the end, the patronage machine won out. OIA officials provoked McGillycuddy into a punishable offense by ordering him to fire his clerk in May 1886. He refused, and Secretary of the Interior L. Q. C. Lamar permanently suspended him.[72] The new agent appointed to Pine Ridge was a Democrat from Indiana.[73]

Although broader political issues played a critical role in these events, Bland, as a political entrepreneur, took credit. He suggested that this dismissal was especially significant because Henry Dawes was both a McGillycuddy supporter and the chairman of the Indian Committee in the Senate and, as such, controlled personnel decisions in the Indian Service. That Secretary Lamar supported an NIDA initiative indicated to Bland increasing political influence for his organization.

NIDA leaders recognized that their alternatives might be viewed as an effort to promote racial difference and inhibit the incorporation of Indians into mainstream society. Many mainstream assimilationists did indeed criticize them on these grounds. Reverend Alexander Kent, an NIDA executive committee member, sought to disarm their critics: "Opposition of the National Indian Defense Association to the land in severalty bill [allotment program] . . . has been characterized by the advocates of that measure as a fight against progress, an effort to perpetuate barbarism," he wrote in the *Council Fire*, adding that some critics even suggested that the NIDA sought "to keep the Indian perpetually in his present relations, and to prevent progress toward manhood and citizenship."[74] He assured his readers, however, that while the NIDA did support a notion of assimilation, it opposed the allotment program because it ignored "the Indian's wishes, feelings and convictions . . . [and was] a deliberate and intentional disregard of Indian rights."[75] As an example of the NIDA's willingness to consider compromises, Kent noted that despite its opposition to the Sioux Bill, it was agreeable to the United States buying land from the Sioux, if the Indians themselves could name the price. This was a natural extension of their advocacy of sovereign rights in the 1880s.

More than anything else, the NIDA's focus on the opinions, ideas, and voices of Native people made the organization an exceptional and forceful opponent of the supporters of coercive assimilation and dispossession. At NIDA meetings, Native people were given the opportunity to speak, and Bland frequently published letters, speeches, and other material from Native writers in the *Council Fire*, as in 1886, when he published a letter written by Chief Red Cloud. In it, the Oglala Sioux leader expressed his support for the NIDA agenda and said he spoke for Native people across the nation. He wrote that Indians opposed selling their remaining reservation lands through the allotment program.[76] Later, "a Cherokee" concurred, writing that "all [Indians] are opposed to allotment."[77] The editors filled the pages of the *Council Fire* with letters and statements such as these.[78]

In powerful ways, Bland's alternative notions of federal policy, influenced by broader populist efforts, and the value placed on Indian voices in the NIDA combined to shape the organization's campaign against allotment and forced assimilation. In Bland's vision of American democracy, Indian people could participate fully, on a level political, economic, and social playing field. One of the strongest arguments NIDA leaders made against allotment legislation, therefore, was that it did not provide Native communities with any element of self-determination; they had no voice in their own future.

Not only did Bland provide opportunities for Native people to speak out in the *Council Fire*; he also sought to involve them in policymaking more directly. In January 1887, for example, Bland was invited to represent the NIDA at a meeting with the Board of Indian Commissioners and other "Friends of the Indian," including the IRA. Once there, he asked that his seat be given to General Pleasant Porter, a representative of the Creek Nation and an NIDA member. During the meeting, Porter outlined the NIDA agenda, which called for treaty fulfillment, education in "literature and industrial arts," an acknowledgment of Indians' right "to hold their lands," and finally, a requirement that any proposed legislation designed to shrink the Indian land base include a clause requiring tribal approval.[79]

Bland often disregarded Indian Service officials and counseled Native people to resist federal policies, and his actions drew the ire of IRA. In late 1886, Peoria chief W. C. Lykins alerted Herbert Welsh that after Commissioner of Indian Affairs J. D. C. Atkins met with the Peoria to encourage them to accept land in severalty, "Doctor T. A. Bland appeared and held a meeting in our school house . . . urg[ing] us to hold our lands and never consent to severalty, claiming that he and others would see that no laws were passed that would affect us in any way." But while Lykins and other Indian leaders who stood to profit from allotment complained, most Indian people appreciated and supported the NIDA. Bland took a similar approach with the Kiowa and Comanche, persuading them to fight allotment. It appears the IRA took Bland's actions quite seriously; in mid-February 1887, C. C. Painter, the organization's Washington lobbyist, wrote, "I certainly think that something must be done to counteract Bland's pernicious influence."[80]

Most existing literature fails to recognize the NIDA's significance, not only in its political accomplishments but especially in the ways it appealed to Native people. If the NIDA's self-reporting is to be believed, they had an equal or larger membership than any other Indian reform group, including the IRA, and certainly a larger Indigenous membership. In late 1886, Thomas Bland toured the southeastern states to encourage membership and support. Nearly one-fifth of those who joined were Native people.[81] Between May 1886 and February 1887, 425 people joined the NIDA; Bland reported in the *Council Fire* that "not less than 200" of them were members of various Indian nations.[82] The NIDA "embraces over 200 of the most intelligent Indians of Indian Territory," he noted, "including the governors and other public officials of all the five civilized nations, and also over 40 white Christian missionaries, who have spent years among those people and whose opinion of Indian policy is entitled to respect." In addition, he reminded his readers that the NIDA had "a large membership in Boston and other cities of the East as well as Washington."[83] Actual NIDA membership was approximately 1,000 in 1885.[84] That year the IRA claimed only 250, and their numbers did not exceed 1,000 until 1888 or 1889.[85] Nevertheless, the editor acknowledged that even with significant numbers, the NIDA faced an uphill battle against the older, well-funded, and well-connected IRA. The NIDA struggled financially, and he appealed to his friends and readers, emphasizing that they were "engaged in a conflict of ideas and of interests with powerful combinations . . . rich in material resources and strong in political influence. . . . Our resources in those regards are not large."[86]

THE YEAR 1886 turned out to be a banner one for the NIDA, and no doubt frightened IRA leadership. The first victory came in the form of Agent McGillycuddy's permanent suspension. Bland relished the moment, noting that the NIDA offices found it "gratifying" and received "congratulations constantly."[87] Next, a political compromise with the Board of Indian Commissioners helped build momentum.

The board had continued its advisory work with the Office of Indian Affairs through the 1870s and 1880s, and on January 21, 1886, Bland, along with Dr. C. C. Painter of the IRA, and Rev. M. E. Strieby, a representative of the American Missionary Association, were appointed to serve on the BIC resolutions committee. The group was unable to agree on a resolution concerning the newest version of the severalty bill proposed by Senator Dawes. Bland submitted a minority report insisting that "patents . . . be issued by the Government to the Indian tribes, to be held in common until by education—literary, industrial, and political—they should be prepared to safely have the land divided and patented to them in severalty."[88] As he had previously, Bland argued that patents in fee benefited Indian nations and allowed them to maintain their land base better than fee simple. In addition, the time frame he described and his suggestion of educational opportunities to compensate for dispossession closely followed the NIDA platform. Painter and Strieby argued that education should follow allotment, not precede it.

After heated discussions, the *Council Fire* editor agreed to support the majority view provided that the resolution was reworded to state that treaty rights would be maintained until, at some point in the future—when the Indians themselves deemed it appropriate—tribal relations could be dissolved and lands divided.[89] In effect, the revision was intended to provide Indian communities a more comfortable time frame, a longer period of support from the federal government, and a greater voice in whether or not this program would ever come to fruition. Later, when the Dawes Allotment Bill moved through Congress and senators excluded a critical clause requiring Indian approval of the allotment program prior to its being instituted on individual reservations, Bland and NIDA pressured the House to amend it. They succeeded, and the bill moved forward with an amendment "to prevent its enforcement upon tribes of Indians until two-thirds of the men shall have signified their consent."[90]

Finally, the NIDA successfully blocked the IRA-supported Sioux Bill in March, an issue to which Bland had devoted significant attention since 1884. In mid-1886, the allotment bill, following Senate approval, stalled in the House of Representatives. Despite IRA efforts, it would not come up for a vote by the time the session ended in August.[91] The NIDA's opposition to immediate severalty in late 1886 received an important endorsement when President Cleveland suggested that he shared Bland's philosophy. In an interview with "that well-known friend of the Indians, Huldah H. Bonwill," a Philadelphia reformer who worked among the Quapaw people for more than sixteen years, the president stated that "we must not go too fast in this. . . . I want practical suggestions."[92] Bland was present during the Bonwill/Cleveland interview and found the president's disposition much to his liking. The NIDA celebrated its victories in 1886, preparing to enter the new year with strengthened resolve. IRA members, smarting from their recent setbacks, likewise began to prepare for what they believed would be the most significant battle over the future of Indian policy of their generation.

SEVEN

The Allotment Controversy, 1882–1889

[The Allotment Act is] the embodiment of despotism and injustice.
—THOMAS A. BLAND, "Injustice Sustained by Falsehood," *Council Fire*, 1887

Herbert Welsh and the Indian Rights Association (IRA) championed a policy of dispossession and assimilation in the 1880s, and much of the historical literature has focused on their story. These individuals argued that the Office of Indian Affairs (OIA) was a corrupt and mismanaged agency and led the movement for immediate land allotment and citizenship rights and responsibilities for Native people, as well as the abrogation of treaty appropriations and the opportunity to open reservation land for white settlement and economic development. Their policy reforms focused in some very specific ways on managerial techniques and administrative technologies. Their ideas emerged from the reform traditions already established in the Philadelphia area, a strong religious (Protestant, mostly Quaker and Episcopalian) conviction, direct political connections to powerful legislators, and a vision of the federal state as a mechanism that should shape the polity according to ideals and principles that fit their vision of a modern nation.[1] Their campaign orbited around a constellation of expectations that included spatial, social, and political confinement of Indian communities as a necessary step toward complete, compulsory assimilation. If Bland's National Indian Defense Association (NIDA) can be characterized as reflective of broader Populist concerns with concentrated economic power and decidedly undemocratic political power combinations, Welsh's IRA might be characterized as a reflection of larger protoprogressive efforts to instill efficiency and accountability within the mechanisms of governance.[2]

The IRA's policy work was innovative and energetic. It employed a full-time lobbyist in Washington D.C., which was an important development not only in Indian policy reform but also in social policy reform more generally. IRA members built relationships with senators and congressmen who represented land/resource-hungry constituencies and corporations.[3] Significantly, they did not simply dismiss the NIDA or Thomas Bland—as some scholars have

assumed—but understood, particularly in 1886 and early 1887, that these opponents posed a real threat to their vision of Indian policy. Consequently, the
IRA launched a public attack on the NIDA in order to discredit it and its alternate approaches toward Indian policy.

This chapter argues that the IRA, Herbert Welsh, and their allies led a successful campaign in the newspapers and throughout Washington, D.C., to misrepresent and repress the NIDA, Bland, and their alternative approach. The
IRA's success may be best understood in terms of how the organization managed to expel the NIDA and Bland from the historical literature. This chapter
asserts that, far from being a simple linear progression toward the ultimate
passage of the General Allotment Act in 1887, Indian policy reform in this
period was marked by significant contestation.

The Indian Rights Association and Forced Assimilation

Born in 1851 to a wealthy Philadelphia family, Herbert Welsh grew up surrounded by philanthropy and business success. His father, John Welsh, and
his grandfather were both successful merchants, and his brother, also named
John, prospered in the railroad, steel, and banking industries.[4] While Herbert
Welsh decided not to follow in the footsteps of his predecessors, he probably
received early encouragement for his philanthropic interests from his aunt and
uncle, William and Mary. William Welsh—the Episcopal missionary and first
president of the Board of Indian Commissioners (BIC)—and his wife, Mary,
founded the Indian's Hope Association, a branch of the Episcopal Church's
Women's Auxiliary to the Board of Missions. Herbert's father, too, was well
known in Philadelphia for his public service. He took a leading role in the creation of the Centennial Exhibition in 1876 and endowed a chair in literature
at the University of Pennsylvania.[5] Welsh's elite upbringing and wealthy family
background were typical of many nineteenth-century eastern philanthropists.

In 1882, thirty-one-year-old Welsh and his friend Henry Pancoast traveled
to the Great Sioux Reservation and visited several agencies in Dakota and Nebraska.[6] Moved by the poverty and hardships of reservation life and impressed
by both the potential they saw for assimilation and the interest they believed
Native people had in mainstream society, Welsh and Pancoast returned to the
East and began to consider creating an organization to pressure the government for changes in Indian policy. Welsh published a brief pamphlet in which
he recounted his trip and suggested changes in the government's approach to
Indian legislation. His account appeared, on the surface, to support legislation that compensated Native people for dispossession and protected Indian

Herbert Welsh, hiking in the woods, date unknown. Courtesy of the Historical Society of Pennsylvania, Herbert Welsh Collection, Photos Box 1.

communities from ruthless speculators. It was likely because of these early sentiments that Bland offered the pages of the *Council Fire* to carry Welsh's message. Welsh wrote that the "government owes them such assistance [rations, etc.] in consideration of the many injuries inflicted upon them, and the wholesale appropriation of their land."[7] He followed this statement, however, by asserting that the government should hasten a movement away from honoring treaty stipulations and instead provide "the gift of severalty" and "sound education."[8]

While on its surface this final suggestion might seem to be a point of similarity between Bland's and Welsh's views, Welsh believed in a specific kind of industrial and religious education that promoted immediate assimilation, which differed significantly from the classical liberal arts education program Bland espoused. Pancoast also wrote a pamphlet that recounted their trip, and like Welsh, argued that severalty, industrial education, and the usurpation of tribal sovereignty would serve to remove the barriers that separated Indians from mainstream society.[9]

These pamphlets attracted wide readership and indicated an increased interest in Indian reform in eastern cities, including Boston, New York, Washington, D.C., and Philadelphia. In 1882, Herbert Welsh and his father invited like-minded individuals to found a reform organization based in their city.[10] The meeting brought together forty philanthropists, both young and old. The mayor of Philadelphia, Samuel G. King, presided, and many of the leading citizens of the city attended, including a large number of Episcopal and Quaker leaders. Interestingly, among the older attendees were many merchants and magnates in steel, oil, and railroad industries, including John Wanamaker, H. H. Houston, and William Sellers.[11]

While it most likely did not occur to the meeting attendees, much of the initial interest and financial support came from industrial leaders who profited from mineral and resource extraction and transportation development, suggesting that perhaps business concerns were one of the key reasons why the IRA so vociferously supported allotment legislation and dispossession. They nominated Wayne MacVeagh, a former minister to Turkey and attorney general, as president. Herbert Welsh became the corresponding secretary, and Henry Pancoast and Quaker leaders Dr. James Rhoads and Philip Garrett made up the executive committee.[12]

The IRA made two decisions early in its development that proved significant both for its reform agenda and for the broader history of social reform in general. The first involved an institutional innovation adopted from the Society of Friends: employing a lobbyist in the capital. During the Grant administration the Society of Friends had stationed a full-time agent in Washington, D.C., to serve as a contact and liaison to Congress and the Indian Service. At the suggestion of Dr. Rhoads, Herbert Welsh tapped Charles C. Painter, an experienced activist for African American rights and a former faculty member at Fisk University, for this position. Interestingly, Welsh and the IRA considered purchasing the *Council Fire* from the Blands and installing Painter as the editor.

Painter initially approved of this idea, provided that he could get it "away from the Cora Bland atmosphere and surroundings."[13] He was perhaps suggesting that with Cora Bland as an editor, the newspaper had a feminized or sentimental tone. Due to financial exigencies, however, the paper remained under the Blands' control and Painter traveled to the nation's capital to serve as lobbyist, a full-time position that he held until his death in 1895.[14]

Though the IRA did not purchase the *Council Fire*, it decided that controlling newspaper coverage would be one of its main tactics in shaping public opinion. This second innovation was also significant in the broader history of social reform. To build public support and influence popular opinion, the IRA created a Committee on Public Information, which served as one of the most important components of IRA strategy; through it, IRA members actively engaged in public discourse through pamphlet literature, letters to the editors of national and regional newspapers, and lecture tours.[15]

Its rhetoric to the contrary, the IRA platform included a number of policy directives directly connected to the work of earlier mainstream assimilationists, including William Welsh and the BIC. The general principles of its platform were support of allotment legislation, "practical" education, the extension of civil law to the reservations (indicative of the continued assault on tribal sovereignty), and immediate citizenship—all premised upon Indian confinement and a coercive form of assimilation. The marked difference between this program and those championed by earlier generations had more to do with a timetable than actual policy innovations. For the IRA, these changes needed to be instituted immediately.

An 1885 pamphlet titled "What the Indian Rights Association Is Doing" argued, first, that the legislation it supported included stipulations for the "assignment of land in severalty to the Indian under such restriction as will secure him the enjoyment of its title."[16] As a component of this plank, the IRA sought to break apart tribal communities. The "organization of the Indians in tribes is, and has been," it declared, "one of the most serious hindrances to the advancement of the Indian . . . every effort should be made to secure the disintegration of all tribal organization." To that end, the federal government needed to cease recognizing Indian "political bodies or organized tribes." IRA members were thankful that some agencies "diminished" or "ceased" their distribution of treaty-stipulated rations.[17] This practice, they argued (despite the fact that the United States was obligated to uphold treaty agreements), inhibited assimilation. Withdrawing rations would force Native people to assimilate and participate in a market economy—or starve.

The IRA considered the institutionalization of "practical education" for Indian people to be of the utmost importance.[18] It particularly supported the work of off-reservation boarding schools, and it publicly advocated for additional federal funding at the Carlisle, Hampton, and Lincoln Institutes. IRA leaders, interestingly, also supported reservation schools, and even argued in favor of allowing Indian children to use their native languages, but only when it aided missionaries in their efforts to teach the Gospel. "Promises of schoolhouses and teachers for these ignorant people already contained in existing treaties should be speedily fulfilled," Welsh argued.[19] While this was most certainly a point at which the IRA and NIDA platforms intersected, Welsh and his organization believed that education should hasten the process of assimilation along a timetable established by the federal government. Bland, on the other hand, asserted that the government should assist Indian communities so they might compete successfully in mainstream society—if they chose to do so—at their own pace and on their own terms.

The IRA also argued that state and territorial laws should be extended to Indian reservations. In the IRA's first annual report, Henry Pancoast argued that laws should "be enforced upon these Indian reservations, so that the Indians finally should exist not as a separate and distinct people, but should become part of our own nationality."[20] It is important to consider this assertion within the larger context in which it was made. The IRA's first annual report was completed in 1884, prior to the passage of the Major Crimes Act of 1885; however, Pancoast's argument was certainly part of an older, broader, and very powerful assault on internal tribal sovereignty. The act defined seven "major crimes," including murder, rape, arson, assault with intent to kill, manslaughter, larceny, and burglary, and extended federal criminal jurisdiction over all Indian nations (although the Five Civilized Tribes and several others were excluded).[21] While extending U.S. law to Indian reservations might seem like a well-intentioned objective, what this suggestion proposed was nothing short of an end to tribal sovereignty. Not only was this unconstitutional, as the U.S. Supreme Court had deemed it in several cases since the 1830s, but it also directly opposed the NIDA's stance on sovereignty.[22] Another way this element of the IRA's agenda connected to the broader national context was that it demonstrated how members envisioned a certain kind of (qualified) inclusive polity. Native people should become citizens, they argued, forcibly if necessary, but in the process they should abandon the elements of their heritage (language, art, social structures and relationships) that made them unique and give up their legal and political status that predated the constitution.[23]

In a brief pamphlet published in 1884, the IRA reaffirmed its goals and methods, namely that the organization aimed "to secure for these 'Wards of the Nation' education, law, and a protected and individual title to land" and that they sought "to make the Indian first a man and then a citizen, subject to the responsibilities and endowed with the privileges accorded to all other citizens of the United States." Finally, it asked that "the Government adopt toward the Indian a policy wise, firm, and continuous, neither capricious nor vacillating, cruel nor sentimental."[24]

In their public rhetoric, IRA leaders may have argued that their reform agenda had Indian interests at its foundation and that altruistic, philanthropic notions animated their work, but, in their effort to repress NIDA alternatives, they appealed to legislators by reminding them that their policy reforms would not only "solve" the "Indian problem," but also that non-Natives stood to benefit in significant ways. In a pamphlet distributed to congressmen, Welsh wrote that severalty was in "the interests, not only of the Indians, but of the white settlers contiguous to Indian Reservations."[25] In 1885, the IRA sent a letter to President Grover Cleveland in an effort to amend the faltering Sioux Bill. The amendment was designed to protect non-Native settlers who had taken homesteads on the Crow Creek and Old Winnebago Reservations. Urgent notices, IRA leaders informed the president, had arrived from settlers "to the effect that great injury will be done then when they are obliged to leace [sic] the lands where they have settled." adding that it was "a matter of the highest importance not only carefully to guard the rights of the Indians . . . but also to shield such settlers as have entered the reservation in good faith from pecuniary loss."[26] The fact that much of the early interest in and financial support for the IRA came from industrial leaders who stood to gain from severalty legislation also suggests that the organization may not have been as concerned with Indian interests as it claimed to have been. Moreover, that much of the interest came from this group may help to explain their support for dispossession and coercive assimilation.[27]

Beyond simply providing financial support, leaders in business and industry actively sought out the IRA to discuss tactics to pressure legislators to pass dispossession legislation. Welsh and the IRA seemed open to these alliances. During the severalty debates, B. J. Templeton, the president of the Pierre (Dakota) Board of Trade, wrote to Welsh to discuss the upcoming legislative sessions involving allotment bills. Templeton wrote that he and his associates were "making preparations for a renewed effort to secure passage of the Dawes Bill" He told Welsh that they had the utmost confidence in his judgment and that they wished to know if there was anything they could "do at the present time or at anytime prior to the convening of Congress?" He also let Welsh know that they had "lately arranged for an interview with the NW R. [Northwest Railway] officials to have a plain 'Medicine talk' on the R[ail] R[oad] clause in the

Bill."[28] These kinds of relationships distinguished the IRA from the NIDA and other alternative reformers, who associated primarily with retired politicians, former Indian Service employees, judges, and intellectuals. It is likely that this was exactly what Bland meant when he told *Council Fire* readers that their opponents were "rich in material resources."

The IRA supported several pieces of legislation that featured severalty and forced assimilation among their main components: the Sioux Bill, the Coke Bill (another precursor to allotment), and the General Allotment Act (Dawes Severalty Bill).[29] As the IRA worked to build public support for these bills it forged many important alliances. Welsh, Rhoads, Painter, and other IRA leaders, for example, often spoke at the annual Lake Mohonk Conference of the Friends of the Indian, held in upstate New York at the behest of Quaker schoolteacher Albert K. Smiley.[30] The IRA also worked closely with the Women's National Indian Association (WNIA), the Boston Indian Citizenship Committee, and the BIC.[31] The members of the latter often nominated Welsh and other leaders for subcommittee and advisory positions. Interested individuals like the Wahpeton Dakota physician Charles Eastman and his non-Native wife Elaine Goodale Eastman supported the IRA's educational stance, as did Carlisle Institute director Richard Henry Pratt.[32] The IRA also established close relations with powerful senators such as Richard Coke and Henry Dawes.[33]

These mainstream assimilationists operated with a certain amount of unanimity, as they all supported a similar model of Indian policy focused on dispossession and confinement. The NIDA may have represented a real challenge to the success of their policy agenda (described in chapter 5) and the IRA took it very seriously.

Through newspaper articles and pamphlet literature, they presented to the public a framework for Indian policy that appealed to a broad array of non-Native interests. Of equal significance, they also portrayed anyone who argued against them or the "Friends of the Indian" as eccentric or as espousing an agenda that would adversely affect the financial interests of non-Native people and the well-being of Indian communities. This is important in that not only did the tactic hinder Bland's and the NIDA's efforts to influence policy in the late nineteenth century, but the IRA records, meticulously maintained by clerk Matthew Sniffen, continue to shape scholarly interpretations of this period.

While the NIDA could count on the *Council Fire* to publicize and generate support its campaigns for compensatory legislation, the IRA noted that the "newspapers of the country, both secular and religious, have not only commented favorably upon the aim and methods of the Association, but have lent their powerful influence in support of that reform in the management of

Indian affairs which we are seeking to effect." Welsh attributed its success to "the cordial and practical sympathy which has been manifested by the editors of our leading papers."[34] And, indeed, Welsh included a special thank you to newspaper editors in every annual report he wrote.[35]

The IRA newspaper campaign proved significant at several key moments in the debates between the two organizations and their leaders. During the controversy involving Pine Ridge agent Valentine McGillycuddy in the early 1880s, the IRA and its associates not only defended the agent in the public press but also painted Bland as unworthy of the public trust. In an 1884 letter to the editor of the *Springfield Republican*, Henry Dawes referred to Bland as "a very strange man, having some notions about Indians which seem kind, but on the contrary making trouble and mischief." He "has the confidence of no one in Washington . . . [and] is as wild in his attempts to state facts as he is in his ideas of what is the proper policy toward the race he thinks he serves." Finally, Dawes characterized Bland's approach to Indian policy as conservative and a stumbling block to progress: "Chief Red Cloud and Dr. Bland are for the old order of things, when chiefs ruled and made themselves rich out of the Indians."[36]

Later, after Bland publicly criticized IRA support of allotment legislation, Herbert Welsh wrote a letter to the *Boston Herald*, "not so much for the purpose of correcting Dr. Bland's misstatements—this were an endless task—but to make clear an irreconcilable difference of opinion . . . which separates him and his association from Senator Dawes and other prominent defenders of Indian rights." He wrote that Bland wanted to keep "the Indian as he is, his tribal relations untouched, his reservations intact; and in opposing the sale of his unused lands, upon no matter how equitable conditions, for white settlement," arguing that the NIDA "theory is prejudicial to the best interests of the Indians . . . it is wholly impracticable."[37] We cannot know the immediate impact of this newspaper campaign, but it likely was effective because Welsh and the IRA continued this tactic into the late 1880s.

Following the passage the Dawes Allotment Act in 1887, Bland and other NIDA members met with many Indian communities to strategize possible responses and the best course of action. The NIDA planned to test the constitutionality of the law in the Supreme Court and traveled to build support. After one of these meetings, the IRA published an account in several newspapers alleging that Bland asked the Indian communities to support these efforts financially. In a *New York Tribune* article, Welsh claimed that the "Kiowas and Caddos, were glad to know they had friends in Washington, but were doubtful about a friendship for which they were asked to pay."[38] Welsh implied that the

NIDA generally found little support among Indian communities and among policy makers in Washington.

C. C. Painter, the IRA lobbyist, also published a pamphlet at this time, in which he argued that the NIDA was "managed and controlled by two or three white men, who, while they assume the role of special defenders of the Indians, appeal to them for support, and ask that a part of these same tribal funds shall be devoted to this purpose." Because it looked for financial support from Indian communities directly, he concluded, the NIDA had to be considered a biased organization.[39] Other evidence suggests that such actions were not typical of the NIDA and Thomas Bland, however. In 1879, during the Standing Bear controversy, Bland publicly criticized the western journalist Thomas Tibbles for creating undue discontent among the Poncas and for "using the situation to solicit funds [from Indian people] to pay for a court test."[40] Ultimately, though, the validity of the allegations was probably not particularly important to the IRA, the allegations alone shaped public opinion.

During this period, the IRA also circulated a story alleging that three prominent members of the NIDA—E. John Ellis, a former member of the House of Representatives who served as the chairman of the subcommittee on Indian appropriations; General J. W. Denver, a former commissioner of Indian affairs; and Colonel Samuel F. Tappan—signed a declaration endorsing the allotment program. In the *Boston Post*, Welsh reported that "the [National] Indian Defense Association is not harmonious in its membership." According to Welsh, the NIDA had brought together a committee of six members in an effort to create a resolution to help stop the president from signing the Allotment Act into law, but "three of the committee . . . signed a report declaring it an excellent measure."[41]

Bland responded in the *Council Fire* that it was actually only Tappan who supported the measure and that he had tricked Ellis and Denver into signing the report. Tappan reportedly told Denver that the document he signed was simply a report outlining the NIDA's view of the allotment bill. Denver later reaffirmed his support for the NIDA: The "Indian Rights Association is managed in the interest of the whites, and is a deadly foe to the Indians."[42] Ellis related a similar story and declared that he was "in full sympathy with the National Indian Defense Association."[43] Although they had been caught in a lie, Welsh and the IRA never owned up to it; rather, they reprinted the *Post* article in the form of a pamphlet, titled "Allotment of Lands, Defense of the Dawes Indian Severalty Bill." The story had been proven false, but since it was circulated widely, the damage had already been done. Later, Bland revealed that a correspondent for the *St. Paul Pioneer Press* who was friendly to the IRA had also fabricated stories about the NIDA and its leadership.[44]

The NIDA continued to fight back in the pages of the *Council Fire*. In the same five-page response where he refuted the notion that the NIDA was split on the allotment proposal, Bland also outlined other allegations Welsh made in articles in the *Boston Post*, the *New York Sun*, the *New York Post*, the *Pioneer Press*, and the *Friends Review*. Bland argued that the allotment program was "the embodiment of despotism and injustice" and that if "its true intent could be laid bare before the whole country, the public conscience would revolt, and the great majority of the people would demand its repeal." In his most direct reprisal, Bland wrote, "Dawes and his backers . . . exert their utmost abilities in efforts to clothe it [the severalty law] in a garb of fictitious virtue and to misrepresent the views of those true defenders of the rights of the Indians who oppose this infamous scheme of despotism and robbery."[45] Because this response was published only in the *Council Fire*, however, it is unlikely that it reached a broad audience.

Bland and the NIDA were not the only ones to experience character assassination at the hands of Welsh and the IRA. Indeed, one might even understand these actions as a political strategy. When Sarah Winnemucca, the outspoken Paiute critic of forced assimilation, for example, received a position as a teacher in a school run by Boston philanthropist Elizabeth P. Peabody and funded through private donations, C. C. Painter was asked to investigate her background and personal life. In his vitriolic report, Painter declared that Winnemucca was an immoral person who, among other things, lived with a man who was not her husband, gambled, fraudulently sold Indians' wheat, drank frequently, and had committed assault with a brick and a "grip sack." In sum, Painter concluded, she was an "unmitigated fraud."[46]

Later, the IRA investigated Alice Fletcher. Though Fletcher was a proponent of the IRA's coercive assimilationist stance, the investigation yielded findings similar to those in the Winnemucca case. Hiram Chase wrote to Welsh from the Omaha reservation that "among Miss Fletcher's favorites is Frank La Flesche, who accompanied her in her work . . . camping out together alone . . . and it is believed that undue intimacy existed between them." He also noted that she fraudulently administered allotments.[47] When the IRA turned its rhetorical attentions toward entrenched policy makers, though, it experienced some pushback.

In 1886, Welsh publicly attacked Secretary of the Interior Lucius Q. C. Lamar and a clerk at the Standing Rock Agency, arguing that they were both unfit for service in Indian affairs. In the latter case, Commissioner of Indian Affairs J. D. C. Atkins wrote to James McLaughlin, the Standing Rock agent, asking whether Welsh had fabricated the allegations or had McLaughlin failed to report on the conduct of his clerk.[48] The fact that Atkins believed Welsh's allegations could be false demonstrated his familiarity with the IRA's tactics, including filing baseless charges of fraud or mismanagement. Welsh's attack on Lamar was perhaps retribution for his dismissal of Agent McGillycuddy, Welsh's ally. Earlier that year, Welsh published a statement in the *Civil Service Record* suggesting that Secretary Lamar had mismanaged the agency and that Indian policy under his watch had been misdirected. Lamar responded in a scathing personal letter to Welsh, asserting that although he believed Welsh had a "sincere desire" to help Indian people, his method of making unfounded allegations in the popular press was damaging and counterproductive. He argued further that Welsh could be more effective if he brought his complaints to public officials directly.[49] Unfortunately, these kinds of reprisals were infrequent, and the IRA continued to use the newspapers to sully individuals' reputations.

The Allotment Controversy and State Development

Although the IRA, the NIDA, and their principle spokespeople drew some of their ideas and traditions from earlier Indian reform, they also broadened their arguments in the 1880s. As pressures for land and resources mounted in the late nineteenth century, both the IRA and the NIDA framed their arguments in such a way as to demonstrate that the direction of Indian policy was a critical front in the development of the role and power of the state in this era. But whereas the NIDA's envisioned the state as a protective agency for the nation's most needy inhabitants, the IRA believed that it was the state's responsibility to shape the polity according to the values and interests of the wealthy elite.

Examining the ways in which both the IRA and the NIDA situated their arguments within this larger debate about Indian reform reveals that, to both reform organizations, there was much more at stake than just reservation policies. In the 1870s and 1880s, interest in Indian policy reform intensified across the nation. When activists linked Indian policy to broader concerns about federal power and individual liberty, though, even larger numbers of policy makers became fully engaged in the cause.[50] The major players in Indian reform in this era were not, as they have frequently been portrayed, marginal special interest groups; rather, they spoke for a majority of the population and represented widely held viewpoints. To understand this, however, one must widen the analytical lens to include issues not always examined in Indian policy studies.[51] By expanding the framework of Indian policy debates, reform organizations made the OIA a crucial meeting ground upon which policy makers and others attempted to address issues related to role of the state in this time period.

In their fight against severalty legislation, the NIDA first attempted to frame their arguments within the context of legal philosophy. Bland and NIDA leaders suggested that the question of allotment presented a legal contradiction and in a fundamental way would destabilize or at least reshape congressional power, the authority of the states, and the ability of municipalities and private corporations to operate with minimal federal regulation.

In the October 1885 issue of the *Council Fire*, Bland published the transcript of a minority report filed in the House of Representatives by Russell Errett of Pennsylvania, Charles Hooker of Mississippi, and T. M. Gunter of Arkansas that pointed to one of the primary contradictions of the severalty bill: that Indian people would hold a paradoxical position before the law. The first part of the allotment program, argued Errett and his colleagues, treated the Indian "as a man in giving him land and exacting from him the duty of maintaining himself upon and off of it." However, "as soon as we do this, we proceed to treat him as a child, an infant, a ward in chancery, who is unable to take care of himself and therefore needs the protecting care of the government."[52] Like the men who filed the report, NIDA leaders believed that this program would set a poor and contradictory precedent. Ostensibly, it would place Native people on an equal legal footing with other members of the polity, but it would simultaneously disadvantage them by withholding the franchise and stripping Native people's right to elect leaders to represent them. The allotment program took a similarly contradictory approach in terms of economic development on the reservations: the government would pressure Indian farmers to participate in commercial agriculture but hold their profits in trust accounts to which they were not given complete access.

The more noteworthy NIDA argument, however, came in the form of an extended discussion of the role and power of Congress and the impact that enacting allotment legislation might have. In an 1887 *Council Fire* article, Judge A. J. Willard pointed out that the land rights of Native people "are vested in the tribe as a corporate body" and that the tribes held political authority over these lands in the same ways that private corporations and municipalities held their property. This was significant, Willard wrote, because, if Congress could arbitrarily "distribute the tribal property among the members of the tribe" through the allotment program, then it could just as easily divide the lands held by municipal corporate charters or private companies "among the individuals constituting such corporate bodies." With this precedent, Congress could dispossess city governments and private landholders alike. Were the people of the United States willing to extend such extraordinary powers to Congress? Willard asked. The issue was no longer simply a question "of robbing the Indian, but . . . a question whether Congress shall enter upon a career of legislation that embodies the worst principles . . . upon the stability of social institutions."[53]

The NIDA continued to connect Indian policy to broader political issues in the United States in published materials even after the allotment act was passed. In an 1889 *Council Fire* article, Willard warned of the dangers inherent in the allotment legislation, for Indian people and non-Natives alike. Speaking for the NIDA, he asserted that it was Congress's responsibility to compensate for dispossession and the history of colonization by providing opportunities for Indian communities and continuing to distribute treaty appropriations. The allotment program, however, removed Indian affairs from congressional jurisdiction because the Constitution, which established congressional authority, assumed the existence of tribes, and once tribal land was allotted, the individual landholders would no longer maintain tribal status.

The new law, Willard asserted, "destroys the tribal condition and assumes to place the Indian on the same footing within the States as their white citizens." This development would unsettle the balance of federal and state power, an issue that, less that a generation before almost tore the nation asunder. The history of Indian-white contact, Willard continued, demonstrated that when Native communities fell under the jurisdiction of a state or territory, local politicians and settlers often had little interest in protecting them and their lands. He concluded that the allotment program broke the "solemn trust" between Congress and Indian people, but, more importantly, undermined the power of Congress and the federal government more generally.[54]

As the NIDA expanded the framework of its arguments, so too did the IRA; and Herbert Welsh's interests in Indian policy reflected his broader reform interests and ideology. Welsh tied allotment to a larger process of civil service reform, writing, "This Indian question, like the national evil of slavery in the past or the corruption of the Civil Service in the present, was a great national question."[55] Other IRA leaders highlighted their belief in the connection between the state and the economy. Through civil service reform and the professionalization of the Indian Service, they asserted, corruption would cease. In addition, it was the responsibility of the state to foster economic development by opening land, resources, and markets for American entrepreneurs.

In the 1880s, Herbert Welsh, partly motivated by the patronage politics of the Cleveland administration and bolstered by the passage in 1883 of the Pendleton Act, became a devoted proponent of civil service reform and its extension to the Indian Office.[56] He solicited information from and built friendships with several important leaders of the movement, including Dorman B. Eaton, the man who drafted the Pendleton Act, Richard H. Dana, the editor of the *Civil*

Service Record, and George W. Curtis, the editor of *Harper's Weekly* and president of the National Civil Service Reform League (NCSRL).[57] Curtis and Welsh coordinated strategies, consulted other civil service reform leaders, including Theodore Roosevelt and Secretary of the Interior Carl Schurz, and looked for opportunities to publicize their cause.

Early victories for Welsh and the IRA in this campaign came when the NCSRL passed a resolution in 1886 to advocate the application of civil service rules to clerks in the Indian Service and when the "Friends of the Indian" passed a similar resolution at Lake Mohonk that year.[58] In his speech at Lake Mohonk, which the IRA published in the form of a pamphlet, Welsh told the stories of Morris A. Thomas and Dr. J. J. S. Doherty to illustrate the need for civil service reform in the Indian Office. These two men, he said, had been accused of fraud but were subsequently appointed to important positions in the Indian Bureau—Indian inspector and government physician.

Welsh also recounted the story of General R. H. Milroy, former Indian agent from the Yakima Agency. According to Welsh, after Milroy's political enemies forced him to resign, conditions at the reservations under his agency's purview quickly deteriorated. Welsh concluded that to protect against such actions, "the reform civil service spirit, and, in some shape, the civil service rules should be extended to the system which controls the appointment and removal of inspectors, agents, chief clerks, farmers, and other subordinates in the Indian service."[59]

Milroy's personal letters to Welsh in which he asked for help in appealing his removal and questioned the fitness of his replacement are revealing. Milroy argued that the new agent was a Catholic and smoked tobacco, thus making him unsuitable for the position. In addition, perhaps appealing to their shared political philosophies in the Republican Party, he waved the bloody shirt, referring to Secretary of the Interior Lamar, a Democrat, as a "darn Reb."[60] While Milroy's comments may appear to be an emotional reaction to what he perceived as unjust termination, they were intended to win the political favor of the letter's recipient—Welsh, a staunch Republican who demonstrated an anti-Catholic bias, particularly in Indian education.[61]

While reading about the history of civil service reform in the United States and Great Britain, Welsh fixated upon the idea of competitive examinations. In England, one of the most significant features of the new system, Welsh observed, was "that it substituted an open competitive examination, as a means of testing the qualifications of those seeking place in the Civil Service of the Government, for the former methods of influence and pressure."[62] He perhaps believed that through civil service reform it was possible to shape the policy agenda and administration of the Indian Office by controlling who became administrators.[63] Welsh might have considered these examinations as a means to ensure that only properly educated individuals who shared a particular ideology would pass.

Such a notion would not have been foreign to him; his uncle William Welsh and the Board of Indian Commissioners (BIC) tried to control who had access to political power within the OIA in the 1870s, most notably in the allegations made against and subsequent trial of Ely S. Parker. In fact, Herbert Welsh often praised the original BIC, once calling it "an important link between the educated Christian people of the country and the Executive." (It is worth noting, too, that his language here revealed his elitist vision that the "educated Christian" members of the polity were best suited to direct policy.) He also stated that while "the board proved of great value," he believed that it had not been able to go far enough in its efforts to control who had access to policy making. He concluded, perhaps referencing the 1871 Parker controversy, that the BIC "failed to accomplish the full measure of the purpose which General Grant had in view . . . owing to the firm grip with which political corruption held the Indian service, and because of the President's own fatal unwillingness to 'desert his friends under fire.'"[64] Welsh recognized the utility of shaping the makeup of the Indian Office and, through civil service reform, attempted to control and shape Indian policy with the same methods the OIA used to make appointments.

In the late 1880s and 1890s, civil service reform began to occupy more and more of Welsh's time, and he shifted the direction of the IRA to incorporate these ideas. In the Lake Mohonk conferences of the late 1880s, Welsh and the IRA devoted a good deal of attention to their concerns about the connections between patronage, corruption, and mismanagement in the Indian Service. In 1890, the IRA published a pamphlet, titled A Hideous System, outlining these arguments. In 1891, following the Wounded Knee massacre and the assassination of Sitting Bull, Welsh penned an article in Scribner's Magazine in which he acknowledged that the horrible tragedies there had unfolded because of the hunger, poverty, and desperation that had followed dispossession and the reduction of reservation land. His prescription, though, was not an end to allotment, dispossession, and confinement but rather that the Indian Service should be "conducted in absolute harmony with the principles of Civil Service Reform—the principle of merit, not of spoils."[65]

The IRA also argued for increased governmental intervention into the economy. In his presentation to the "Friends of the Indian" assembled at the seventh annual Lake Mohonk Conference, C. C. Painter argued that in order for the allotment program to be successful, the government should help establish contracts between the Indian allotees and landless white men. The white men would help break and cultivate the land for a period of years, while the Indians would work as paid laborers on their own acreage. At the end of the period, the white men would move on and the Indians would keep the ready-made farms.[66] Two years earlier, in a pamphlet titled "The Dawes Land in Severalty Bill and Indian Emancipation," Painter asserted that by breaking apart tribal relations, creating individual farms for commercial agriculture, and disposing of "surplus" lands to white settlers, the government would not only hasten the assimilation process but also stimulate an economic windfall for the federal coffers.[67]

It appears that the question of the viability of farming on the reservations never significantly entered into IRA leaders' thinking, but after the passage of the Allotment Act, many Indian agricultural developments failed, for a variety of reasons. Consequently, Indian people were forced to lease their lands to non-Native farmers, homesteaders, and mineral extraction companies.[68] In championing commercial agricultural development through allotment, IRA leaders envisioned a greatly expanded federal bureaucracy with economic regulatory powers previously unseen. Creating contracts between landholders and laborers or lessees would expand state power into the economic structures of various regions, a move that many believed to be wrongheaded. In fact, in its support of an expanded federal bureaucracy, the IRA's ideology was typical of the larger social and political reform movements of the Progressive Era.

The IRA agenda also fit nicely with Welsh's other reform interests. For example, Welsh participated in the Philadelphia and National Municipal Leagues, working to combat corruption in city governments. He also helped to found a Pennsylvania forestry association; served as a vice president for a national Forestry Congress; worked in the Law and Order Society of Philadelphia; sat on the Board of Managers for the City Parks Association; and played a key role in the Culture Extension League, an organization created to improve recreational facilities for the poor. He participated in the local Board of Education and in the Universal Peace Union.[69] Common to all these reform organizations was the desire to create a physical and human environment that elite, educated, white, Christian philanthropists felt was most appropriate for U.S. society. And their ideology manifested itself in an approach to Indian policy characterized by dispossession and the spatial, social, political, and economic confinement of Indian people. Welsh and the IRA sought to expand the framework within which they argued about Indian reform, and in doing so, they appealed to like-minded individuals and organizations. Through their efforts and due to a number of contingent factors, their vision of Indian policy and role of the state came to dominate this era.

The Forty-ninth Congress engaged in considerable legislative wrangling leading up to the passage of the Dawes Severalty Bill. The first congressional debate took place on February 19, 1886, during which several senators, such as Henry Teller, Preston Plumb, John Ingalls, Charles Manderson, and Samuel Maxey (many of whom were influenced by the NIDA), expressed their opposition to many of the bill's provisions. According to Bland's account of the debate, Dawes "found himself at his wit's end for arguments" and asserted that the opposing senators simply misunderstood the bill.[70] Interestingly, Bland and the NIDA chose not to raise any objections to the proposed bill during the congressional debates because it contained a clause requiring Indian approval before allotment could be enforced on any reservation. Bland asserted that the NIDA's position, "was pretty well guarded." Before the bill passed the Senate, though, the provision requiring Indian approval was dropped, prompting Bland to express his "hope that it may be either amended, or defeated in the House."[71]

Much to Bland's and the NIDA's delight, the House Indian Committee amended the bill "so as to prevent its enforcement upon tribes of Indians until two-thirds of the men shall have signified their consent." Bland assured the readers of the *Council Fire* that this amendment made the allotment bill "comparatively powerless," and he perhaps believed, following other 1886 NIDA victories, that the hardest battles were behind them.[72] He was wrong.

The new congressional session opened on December 17, 1886, and before Christmas that year, Congress passed a revised version of the allotment bill. The wording of the NIDA amendment had been changed to state that a reservation could not be abolished without Indian consent but that severalty could be implemented without consent. Although Bland noted that the bill had been "so changed that Senator Dawes would hardly recognize it," he concluded that it was "still a most vicious measure, and ought not to become a law."[73] The bill went to committee so that the differences between the Senate and House versions could be rectified, but in the meantime, the NIDA, the IRA, and their prominent leaders sparred in the press.

The *Boston Herald* ran a story that recounted the Philadelphia reformer Huldah H. Bonwill's interview with President Cleveland, which Bland had found so reassuring (described briefly in chapter 6). Fearful of the notion that legislators might be swayed by the interview—in which Cleveland appeared to support the NIDA, its opposition to immediate, forced severalty and its alternative policies—Dawes penned a rebuttal, misrepresenting the president's words so they appeared to support his bill and the IRA's platform. A compromise bill finally passed both houses of Congress—without the NIDA amendment, indicating the rapidly diminishing power Bland's organization wielded. President Cleveland signed the bill into law on February 8, 1887.[74]

The IRA victory provides us with several important insights into Indian policy reform, late-nineteenth-century reform movements more generally, the development of the post–Civil War state, and the significance of historical contingencies. Although debates in the House of Representatives seemed mild compared to the debates between reformers leading up to that moment, the final version of the allotment law in February 1887 represented a wide political alliance and diverse eastern and western political concerns. Some commentators understood allotment as an idealistic yet practical program, while others "saw the law as an opportunity for the Federal government finally to rid itself of its obligations to the Indians."[75] The IRA and the "Friends of the Indian" had been incredibly successful in shaping the terms of the allotment debates and in drawing together diverse interests through their lobbying tactics. By employing a full-time lobbyist, C. C. Painter, they were able to keep Indian issues in the forefront of the minds of congressmen and legislators. This tactic had not yet developed into a mainstay among the broader reform organizations, as it would in the 1890s and after the turn of the twentieth century, and it is significant that this method was used so effectively first in Indian policy reform.

The IRA's ability to control and manipulate newspaper coverage, through letters to the editor and interviews with journalists, helped it to establish the notion that its agenda was the only reasonable approach to solving the "Indian Question." The IRA also drew together several factions of the population and appealed to individuals and organizations that otherwise may not have considered Indian policy among the most pressing issues facing the nation. Though the NIDA often used the *Council Fire* to counter IRA claims, as a narrowly defined reform journal, the paper did not enjoy the same wide readership that larger regional periodicals did.

That the allotment law became a federal policy directive in the late 1880s also provides insight into the mainstream assimilationist ideologies of geographic expansion and the development of the state by the late nineteenth century. The allotment program was in some ways a logical extension of the efforts of William Welsh and the BIC during the peace policy era, at which time the OIA had not yet developed a bureaucracy capable of implementing such a program. Also, federal policy makers were not yet ready to institute such an overt state-sanctioned expansionist policy, even though proposals for such legislation had circulated in Washington, D.C., in the 1870s and before. By the late 1880s, though, the OIA and the Interior Department had developed bureaucratically and, bolstered by an evolving interest in territorial expansion, helped make allotment a political reality. In the post–Civil War era, the settlement of western territories; debates about the potential annexation of Canada, parts of Latin America, and the Caribbean; and the heightened interest in and eventual colonization of Hawaii all took place at the same time as the Indian policy debates described here, and all help to demonstrate the evolution of thought concerning state-structured expansion.[76] This was also a moment when policy makers were increasingly open to accepting new and experimental policy reforms, perhaps more so than at any time in the past.[77] It is significant, then, that it was within this complex social and political milieu that the allotment program became a federal law.

There is one final notable element of this story. The NIDA had gained considerable momentum in 1885 and 1886—recruiting a large number of members and experiencing political victories, including stalling the Dawes Sioux Bill and aiding in the dismissal of Agent McGillycuddy, but at the critical moment that the state began to implement allotment legislation, the NIDA's momentum faltered due to a tragic accident.

Shortly after the passage of the Dawes Act in 1887, Bland and the NIDA, smarting from this devastating political defeat, vowed to challenge the law in the courts and to pursue legal recourse against the congressmen who had supported the bill. In the *Council Fire*, Bland wrote that the bill was "despotic, unjust and unconstitutional," and that "we have protested against its enforcement, and we are vigilantly and anxiously awaiting an opportunity to make our protest before the Supreme Court." He knew that they faced savvy political opponents and noted that the secretary of the interior specifically hindered the NIDA's attempt to test the constitutionality of the program by initially applying it only to small reservations that fell under the jurisdiction of executive order, or to those that had allotment clauses in their individual treaties with the United States.[78] This way, the secretary of the interior did not actually enforce the allotment law, and the NIDA could not field a test case. Bland asserted, "Something besides protest and argument and appeals to public sentiment through the *Council Fire* is needed now." He planned "to go into the lecture field and make a determined effort to correct public opinion on this question, and also to raise a fund sufficient to enable the National Indian Defense Association to meet the expense of defending the legal rights of the Indian tribes in the United States courts."[79] In early May, Thomas and Cora Bland left Washington, D.C., on an East Coast tour of prominent reform centers, including Boston,

Philadelphia, and New York. After their visit to Boston, Bland reported: "[W]e felt quite encouraged with the success attending our efforts to get Boston right on the Indian question."[80]

They left Boston on June 20, encouraged by the positive reception they experienced. The next day, however, tragedy struck. The limited express train from Washington collided with the Blands' homeward bound train at Havre de Grace, Maryland. Their passenger car was "telescoped by the locomotive of the other train." The only other passenger sitting ahead of them was killed instantly, and the Blands "were badly scalded and otherwise injured, but escaped through a window of the car." Bland later noted that he could not remember how they escaped because both he and Cora "had no conscious recollection of the circumstances." They spent the rest of the year and all of 1888 in recovery, suffering from bouts of "brain fever" and "nervous prostration." Although they were able to continue lecturing, their injuries prevented them from writing or editing the *Council Fire*.[81]

The Blands served as the conduit through which the NIDA members communicated and were the main catalysts behind the movement, so their injuries proved a death knell to its alternative reform movement. Although interest in the NIDA seemed to be diminishing following its political defeats in 1887, had it been successful in bringing a case before the United States Supreme Court to test the constitutionality of the allotment law, the implementation of the policy may well have been stalled. Some speculation here seems reasonable. In its 1883 *Ex parte Crow Dog* decision, the Supreme Court had declared that U.S. courts had no jurisdiction on Indian reservations for crimes committed between Native people—a significant recognition of tribal sovereignty. Three years later, however, in *United States v. Kagama*, the Court upheld the constitutionality of the Major Crimes Act of 1885 (Congress's response to *Crow Dog*). With this act, Congress sought to usurp tribal sovereignty by giving the federal courts jurisdiction over certain crimes between Native Americans, even if they occurred on reservations. In essence, the Court gave its stamp of approval to Congress's increasing efforts to assert plenary power over Indian tribes. Based on this evidence, it is unlikely that the Supreme Court would have overturned the Dawes Act in 1887, as Bland and the NIDA hoped. That they tried, though, has an important meaning.

For the student of federal Indian policy, this episode is satisfying in the sense that Bland's and the NIDA's efforts demonstrate that there were individuals who continued to fight against the idea of forced assimilation and dispossession. It is also frustrating, however, to know that the possibility existed for this history to have unfolded differently if not for a tragic accident.

THE GENERATION OF REFORMERS who emerged after the peace policy era adopted and expanded the reform agendas and policy platforms of the previous period. In the debates over Indian policy, Thomas Bland and the NIDA presented viable alternatives that included state protection of Indian communities. Simultaneously, Herbert Welsh and the IRA supported dispossession and coercive assimilation. By connecting their Indian policy agendas to larger issues in state development and social reform, however, this generation of activists fostered and reflected the growth of public interest in Indian affairs. Their actions demonstrate that in order to understand the complexities of this era in U.S. history, scholars must consider the role of the OIA as a meeting ground for ideas about role of the state and its relationship to individuals, and how these ideas served as forbearers of later reform trends.

In his institutional history of the IRA, historian William Hagan writes that while its development provided some variety to the reform movements of the late nineteenth century, the NIDA "never seriously rivaled the IRA."[82] Historian Francis Prucha was slightly more circumspect, suggesting that the NIDA "appeared to have some influence in high places." Prucha, it seems, was on to something, for in the debates leading up to the passage of the general allotment law, the NIDA mounted significant opposition to the IRA. In their rhetoric and reform tactics, Thomas Bland and the NIDA exposed some of the inconsistencies of the IRA platform and its leadership, especially in the persons of Herbert Welsh and Charles C. Painter. Prucha concludes that "Bland's views, if not his methods, look better in the perspective of time than many of those of the united humanitarian reformers [the IRA and the 'Friends']."[83] Perhaps more importantly than anything else, though, Indian policy debates demonstrated that the progression toward land allotment and forced assimilation was contested and contentious.

To end this chapter by focusing on the positive is dangerous, however. To do so would serve an injustice to the pain and suffering caused by the actions of reformers in this era. There should be no doubt that the passage of the Dawes General Allotment Act in 1887 symbolized the IRA victory over the NIDA in this period of Indian policy reform. A program of coercive assimilation coupled with dispossession would guide the OIA for most of the next fifty years. These years were the nadir for tribal nations.

CONCLUSION

>─┤─◆≻─◯─◄◆─┤─◇─┤─◆≻─◯─◄◆─┤─◇─┤─◆≻─◯─◄◆─┤─◄

John Collier's Moment, 1928–1935

A marvelous fruition has come. . . . Every condition favorable
to a large reorganization of Indian affairs now exists. Has the
"century of dishonor" neared its end? The future must tell.
—JOHN COLLIER, "The Coming of Day," *American Indian Life*, 1929

The Indian Rights Association (IRA) and mainstream assimilationists won the policy reform battles of the late nineteenth century, and a policy agenda founded upon Indian confinement moved forward with brash intensity. Though amended several times, in an effort to include additional reservations within its framework, the allotment act profoundly shaped Native history between the late 1880s and the mid 1930s. By the end of this period, the disruption and despair that dispossession caused for tribal nations—results perhaps foreshadowed by the developments Ely Parker witnessed during the Ogden land dispute at the Tonawanda Reservation in the 1840s and 1850s—became painfully apparent in the published findings of a private study on Indian life and governance by the Institute for Government Research in 1928. Known to historians as the Meriam Report (after its editor, Lewis Meriam) and funded by the Rockefeller Foundation, *The Problem of Indian Administration* revealed the outcome of almost fifty years of dispossession and forced assimilation legislation.

The report noted that, in providing education and health care, the Indian Office was failing dramatically. Infant mortality among Indian people was double the national average. It also found that two-thirds of Native people earned less than one hundred dollars per year; that only about one-third of Native people were literate; and that Indians died from tuberculosis at a rate seven times that of the general population and trachoma was commonplace. Finally, the report asserted that many of the problems pervading Indian communities derived from the land allotment policy. "Much loss of land and an enormous increase in the details of administration without a compensating advance in the economic ability of the Indians," the Meriam team argued, had resulted from the Dawes Act. In fact, of the 155,632,312 acres Native people held in 1881, only 52,651,393 remained in Indian hands by 1933.

The report suggested the Office of Indian Affairs (OIA) make significant changes—including greatly minimizing the number of fee patents it issued, ending the practice of leasing Indian land to non-Indians, and regulating the sale of inherited lands to non-Indians—in an effort to reverse harmful trends. In other words, it fell just short of calling for an immediate end to the land allotment program. Although it was not tabulated in *The Problem of Indian Administration*, non-Native people, especially ranchers, homesteaders, land developers, and farmers, profited greatly from the purchase of newly opened reservation lands at a minimum price. In addition, the federal government used these funds to defray some of the costs of Indian governance. Meriam's researchers concluded that the Indian Service needed to establish a fund that could be used to purchase, consolidate, and sell back reservation lands to Indians, giving them permanent and legally recognized title (a program similar to the one Ely Parker helped to negotiate for the Tonawanda Seneca of New York State in 1857).[1]

After the publication of the Meriam Report, interest in Indian policy reform once again intensified—not only as a response to the report itself but also as part of the larger context of Depression-era America. It was within this context that John Collier, President Franklin D. Roosevelt's 1933 appointee as commissioner of Indian affairs, succeeded in institutionalizing elements of his own alternative Indian policies. Under Collier's tutelage, this administration created and implemented a system of legislation for Indian affairs that reflected Roosevelt's broader social and economic policy reform agenda.

Collier first became interested in social policy making through his work with immigrant communities in New York and Los Angeles, but a visit to New Mexico's Taos Pueblo in 1921 sent his career in a new direction. This transformative moment was inspired by what he believed was the ideal premodern human culture among the Indians of the Southwest. Indeed, as historian Flannery Burke suggests in her study of Mabel Dodge Luhan's Taos artist community, Collier "imagined a place with ancient antecedents where artistic production, nature, and everyday life melded into a seamless whole."[2] With the assistance of such women as Stella Atwood of the General Federation of Women's Clubs, Collier began working to improve Indian health care and other social programs. He also became involved in protecting Indian land rights in a campaign against the Bursum Bill, legislation designed to strip Pueblo Indians of their title to approximately 60,000 acres of New Mexico's most valuable lands.

As a part of the campaign against the Bursum Bill, Collier founded a reform organization called the American Indian Defense Association (AIDA) in 1923.[3]

While there is no indication that Collier knew Thomas Bland personally, it is likely that he studied the history of Indian policy reform. The fact that his reform organization's name resembled so closely that of Bland's suggests that Collier might have understood his approach to reform to be, at least in some ways, similar to Bland's earlier work.

It is also unlikely that Collier and Parker ever met (Collier was only eleven when Parker died in 1895), but Parker likely would have supported Collier's fight to repeal allotment legislation and to have backed his reservation government reforms. Although he had supported land allotment proposals during his tenure as commissioner, Parker had changed his opinion considerably by 1885. He wrote to his friend Harriet Maxwell Converse,

> Our wise legislators at Washington . . . are all advocating with a red hot zeal, the allotment and civilization schemes. . . . They say that 6000 Indians already hold allotments of lands in severalty and that not less that 75,000 more are asking for the same privilege. I do not believe in the sanctity or truth of the statement. The Indians, as a body, are deadly opposed to the scheme, for they see in it too plainly the certain and speedy dissolution of their tribal and national organizations. It is very evident to my mind that all schemes, to apparently serve the Indians, are only plausible pleas put out to hoodwink the civilized world that everything possible has been done to save this race from total annihilation, and to wipe out the stain on the American name for its treatment of the aboriginal population.[4]

And though we cannot know whether Collier was influenced by Parker's alternative approach to Indian policy in the late 1860s and early 1870s, there are commonalities in their work.

Both men shared distaste for the Board of Indian Commissioners (BIC); as one of his initial actions as Indian Office head, Collier abolished the BIC via executive order. As historian Francis Prucha has concluded, The "board was a conservative body . . . who clung fast to the assimilationist views that Collier wanted to overturn." While President Roosevelt justified the move as an economic decision, Prucha adds, it "was in fact a symbol of the changing of the guard in the management of Indian affairs."[5] In some ways, this shift reflected both Parker's and Bland's work a generation or two earlier.

It is dangerous to look for too many commonalities, however. Collier's moment was different from Parker's and Bland's in important ways. By the time Collier was appointed commissioner, the Indian Citizenship Act (or Snyder Act) of 1924 had already declared all Native people who were not already

U.S. citizens to have that status. This act affected approximately 125,000 of the 300,000 Indigenous people in the nation. Thus, when Collier challenged land allotment policy, the questions of inclusion and exclusion, or the rights and responsibilities of citizenship, no longer animated the debate as it had for Thomas Bland and the NIDA in the 1880s. Land allotment and concomitant dispossession and forced assimilation were no longer steps in a linear progression toward citizenship; an exigency was gone.[6] In addition, the pressures and the hardships of the Great Depression forced many Americans to embrace the notion that the federal government could, and indeed should, take an active role in leveling the economic playing field and caring for the nation's most needy inhabitants—a large and ever increasing group in the 1930s. The Roosevelt administration's New Deal programs, in many ways, represented a revolution in federal governance, and it was within this context that Collier's long crusade for alternative Indian reform gained traction.

The Indian New Deal—Collier's federal policy agenda in the 1930s—was the culmination of twelve years of firsthand work among Indian people. As commissioner of Indian affairs, he reversed the coercive policies of the allotment era, beginning with the passage of the Wheeler-Howard Act, or Indian Reorganization Act, in 1934. This act "successfully ended land allotment, restored surplus land at various reservations, and provided funds for purchasing new real estate."[7] Collier sought to reshape the colonialist bent of policy makers and reformers by changing the overtly hostile attitude many of them had (as had their predecessors) toward customary Native American cultures and practices. He perceived a beauty and harmony in Native American culture that he believed had been lost in modern society. Consequently, he vowed to protect and foster Indian communities.

While Collier may have possessed an overly romanticized and simplistic view of Native American culture, and while he did not always live up to his own anticoercive ideal, he played a key role in securing the passage of the Johnson-O'Malley Act in 1934, which allowed the secretary of the interior to "provide money for local assistance in the areas of Indian health, education, agriculture, and social welfare."[8] He also created a mechanism by which Indian communities could assert rights of self-government by writing constitutions of their own (following a boilerplate model), electing officers, and adopting laws that the federal government then supported and protected. Through this general program of reform and through specific legislation, Collier's policy alternatives broke contemporary trends and trajectories in Indian affairs and in some ways established a system that resembled the work of both Ely Parker and Thomas Bland from earlier and different political climates.

While Collier's moment represented the institutionalization of at least some genuine policy alternatives, it is important to examine other legacies of nineteenth-century Indian policy reform. Contrary to most interpretations, the period was marked by divergent and competing voices that attempted to speak for Indian people and direct Indian policy. At particular moments—in the immediate aftermath of the Civil War and again in the 1880s—supporters of policies designed to protect Indian communities as distinct entities or to provide Native peoples with opportunities, money, and goods confronted a group of mainstream assimilationists who clung to the status quo, served elitist causes, and found comfort and harmony in a zealous form of Christian belief. While arguing that they understood the best interests of Indigenous communities, these reformers championed Indian confinement and coercive assimilation and supported the ongoing assault on tribal sovereignty within the larger context of U.S. expansion.

This period of contestation and complexity in Indian policy reform was significant in several ways. First, the evolution of Indian policy between the Civil War and the end of the nineteenth century both reflected and shaped larger issues of state development. While the federal government had assaulted external tribal sovereignty prior to the Civil War through dispossession, removal, and geographic confinement—often at the behest of land speculators, mineral and resource extraction industries, and enterprising farmers—after the war, the state became an active force in an intensifying form of westward expansion that evolved into an assault on internal tribal sovereignty. An important and politically powerful group of assimilationists—led in the 1870s by William Welsh and the BIC and in the 1880s and 1890s by Herbert Welsh and the IRA—aided this process by articulating a policy agenda that focused on continued dispossession and replacing customary cultural and political practices within Indian communities with structures and values based on Euro-American models. They also wanted to develop a system of mandatory Christian education for Indian youth, while encouraging their parents to become involved in the market economy. All of these programs operated under the assumption of total Indian confinement. The progression of this policy agenda was not the harmonious, linear development that previous interpretations would have us believe but rather followed a crooked path. A second way this period in Indian reform was significant is that it illustrates the emergence of important constitutive moments, when opposition to the status quo in policy creation and state development gained traction. The first was in the Reconstruction era when an oppositional framework developed within mainstream systems of governance. This framework had previously been apparent in the work of some Native and non-Native political commentators whose positions had kept them outside of the structures of government, but during Reconstruction, they moved into position of prominence. Ely Parker serves as a case study of this phenomenon, and he and like-minded reformers seized their constitutive moment in the late 1860s and early 1870s to suggest viable policy alternatives that included perhaps less disruptive methods designed to provide Native communities with multiple paths to their relationship with an expanding United States. A second constitutive moment in the mid-1880s provided the political space for the reform campaign of Thomas Bland and the National Indian Defense Association. They presented viable alternatives that rejected forced assimilation and focused instead upon using the federal government to provide resources and opportunities for Indigenous nations while simultaneously protecting the integrity of communally held land.

During the Tonawanda Seneca resistance campaign against the Ogden Land Company's removal efforts in the 1840s and 1850s, a young Parker came to understand the profound disruptions that dispossession and confinement could cause for an Indian community. He also understood, though, that as the nineteenth century progressed, that U.S. westward expansion and economic development would likely continue. He and others designed a reform agenda that sought to minimize these disruptions. They attempted to create policies that would provide educational and employment opportunities, as well as money and goods, and protect Indian communities as distinct entities.

Parker's most important ideas differed from those of mainstream assimilationists. He placed a high value on enforcing existing treaties, even if that meant adversely affecting non-Native settlement (or conversely, if it meant enforcing unfair treaties signed under suspected fraudulent circumstances). He saw the military as useful tool in enforcing treaty stipulations and implementing social policy, but he would not support army engagements against Native people except as a last resort. Parker also attempted to slow the process of assimilation and provide opportunities for Indigenous nations to incorporate themselves when and how they chose. He argued that assimilation could be positive and beneficial; but rather than forcing them to assimilate by whatever means necessary, as quickly as possible, he knew a tempered pace would be less disruptive. Finally, Parker, more so than most of his contemporaries, was convinced that if Native people were given the right tools, incentives, and opportunities, not only would they choose to assimilate into mainstream culture and society on their own terms and according to their own timeframe but they would also be productive contributors and rational citizens of the expanding United States. Although Parker's reform campaign ended in disappointment and he no longer worked actively in federal policy making into the 1870s, elements of this framework emerged again in the work of Thomas Bland and the NIDA.

Third, the period is significant in that Ely Parker's career problematizes the existing interpretations that construct Indian leaders who worked within mainstream systems of governance as Indigenous "sellouts." While it is true that Parker served as commissioner of Indian affairs during a period in which notions of Indian confinement evolved, and even that he suggested or supported certain reforms and programs, like the transfer of the Bureau of Indian Affairs from the Interior Department to the Department of War and the movement to end treaty making with Indian nations, he never "abandoned" his heritage. Rather, Parker was an innovative policy maker who wedded an Indigenous worldview to a western intellectual framework. If we understand Parker within this context, an alternate conclusion about him can be surmised.

That Parker's efforts have been construed as detrimental (or at least potentially so) to Native peoples is perhaps unfair. He believed that situating the OIA in the War Department would help insulate Native communities against the corrupting and disruptive influences land speculators and business interests had on federal policy makers. When he sought to officially end treaty making between the federal government and tribal nations, he did so because in his experiences during the Seneca resistance campaign against the Ogden Land Company, he learned how internal political conflicts and individual interests could render community leaders' abilities to negotiate equitable treaties ineffective, or sometimes, potentially destructive to the community interests. Parker, though, underestimated the extent to which the state had shifted toward an assault on internal tribal sovereignty by the early 1870s. Viewed within the context of the evolving nineteenth-century state, his efforts to reform Indian Office corruption, to create policies, and to expand Indigenous educational opportunities can more appropriately be interpreted as a "path not taken" rather than an abandonment of an Indigenous heritage.

Finally and most importantly, an understanding of this period in Indian policy reform suggests that Indian affairs in the nineteenth century were not simply peripheral events in the background of broader and more important developments in U.S. history. Events such as the Seneca resistance campaign against the Ogden Land Company in the early nineteenth century, the postwar peace commissions, Parker's rise to prominence during and after the Civil War in Washington, D.C., and Thomas Bland's public disputes with Valentine

McGillycuddy and Herbert Welsh all reveal the ways local and national leaders and citizens followed events in Indian country intensely and the ways that these events contributed to both state and federal political developments. Later in the century, these connections became even more explicit. The mid- to late-nineteenth-century OIA served as a crucial meeting ground for ideologies of governmental authority and its development. That it served in this capacity not only demonstrates the experimental nature of federal governance in this period, as policy makers allowed the state to take on increasingly active functions; it also shows the evolution of social policy making from the hybrid public and private programs of Reconstruction to the institutionalized federal compensatory programs of the early twentieth century. The most visible reformers and reform organizations of this period, the Indian Rights Association and the National Indian Defense Association, facilitated this development as they connected their notions of Indian policy to broader issues in politics and society in their widely distributed pamphlets and articles in the nation's most important newspapers. They also employed innovative tactics in political lobbying that, within a short period of time, would be adopted by many other social and political reformers. The politicians who came to support these competing organizations were not, as has sometimes been asserted, marginal legislators but some of the most powerful senators, representatives, and jurists in the nation.

While scholars have firmly established that in order to comprehend pre-Revolutionary and late-eighteenth-century North America one must recognize the importance of the Indian experience and the ways Indigenous people shaped this history, scholars have struggled to make similar assertions about the nineteenth-century United States, and most general studies (in particular those of state development) have either disregarded completely or attached little import to events in Indian country. Indian policy reform in this period, though, revealed the ways that ideas about Native people and Indian confinement, as well as actual Indian people themselves, shaped, influenced, and reflected national trends and events. Highlighting the primacy of the OIA in the evolution of the state and recognizing how some state-centered social policy making was modeled first in Indian policy suggests that recognizing the importance of the Native American experience in this era is critical to our broader historical understanding.

Notes

ABBREVIATIONS

APS   American Philosophical Society Library, Philadelphia, Pennsylvania

ARCIA   *Annual Report of the Commissioner of Indian Affairs* (Washington, D.C.: Government Printing Office)

BECHS   Buffalo and Erie County Historical Society Library, Buffalo, New York

HL   Huntington Library, San Marino, California

IRAP   Indian Rights Association Papers (microfilm)

NARA   National Archives and Records Administration, Washington, D.C.

NL   Newberry Library, Chicago, Illinois

NYSA   New York State Archives, Albany, New York

RG   Record Group

RRL-UR   Rush Rhees Library, Rare Books, Special Collections, and Preservation, University of Rochester, Rochester, New York.

INTRODUCTION

1. Parker's biographers often recount this particular event. See Parker, *Life of General Ely S. Parker*, 129–33, and Armstrong, *Warrior in Two Camps*, 108–11. James McPherson interpreted the event a little differently. In his version, the introductions and handshake occurred after the surrender terms had been written and signed and lacked the tension and potential for disaster apparent in the versions recounted by Parker biographers. See McPherson, *Battle Cry of Freedom*, 849.

2. Hannah Rosen, *Terror in the Heart of Freedom*, 4.

3. Richardson, *West from Appomattox*, 343.

4. In his recent book, historian Philip Deloria groups these processes as technologies of power and states that to "be known by name, date and location of baptism, rations drawn, and enrollment number was to be intimately visible to the colonial bureaucracy. It made it easy to locate a particular person in time and in space and to determine the need for education, discipline, containment, and shunning" (*Indians in Unexpected Places*, 26). James C. Scott (*Seeing Like a State*) offers a lengthy examination of these colonial state processes, which he refers to collectively as a project of establishing "legibility." He argues that only when a state can make its citizens and wards legible could it effectively and efficiently conduct its functions, including taxation, conscription, and ration distribution, among others. Ann Laura Stoler (*Race and the Education of Desire*), as well as many other colonization studies scholars address these issues in various regions around the world. Stoler's application of Foucauldian theory to colonization studies has been particularly influential.

5. Philip Deloria argues persuasively that expectations of containment played a significant role in shaping late-nineteenth-century notions of Indian violence and warfare, as well as pacification. While I find his description of "containment" too narrowly defined, and prefer the

more expansive "confinement," my thoughts and analysis have been influenced significantly by his assertion that popular discourse shaped ideas about Indians in this period. See Deloria, *Indians in Unexpected Places*, 20–21.

6. Here and elsewhere I use the term "colonialism" to describe the complex processes and developments that occurred and continue to occur in the United States as non-Indigenous people have displaced, disrupted, and destroyed Indigenous communities. I am fully aware of its inaccuracies, fluidities, and shiftiness. Other scholars, such as Patrick Wolfe, have argued persuasively that "settler colonialism" is a better and more accurate phrase that distinguishes the type of relationships and development I describe. Wolfe asserts that scholars must engage critically with such terms and in particular demonstrates that "settler colonialism" operates with a "logic of elimination" rather than a "logic of genocide." It is both positive and negative; it "destroys to replace"; it is complex, structural, and ongoing, not simply a "one-off" event. I agree with this assessment and argument and use the simpler "colonialism" only as a shorthand term. For more, see Wolfe, *Settler Colonialism and the Transformation of Anthropology*, and Wolfe, "Settler Colonialism and the Elimination of the Native."

7. Although I draw heavily from the foundation they have established, both of the two most prominent scholars of Indian policy development and reform fall into this trap. See Prucha, *American Indian Policy*, and Hoxie, *Final Promise*.

8. Recent work by historians Maureen Flanagan and Glenda Gilmore has indicated the importance in and utility of examining the work of historical actors who lost their political battles in the short term. See Flanagan, *Seeing with Their Hearts*, 10, and Gilmore, *Gender and Jim Crow*, 1–2.

9. For a clear and concise discussion of political entrepreneurs, see Sheingate, "Political Entrepreneurship."

10. Berk, *Alternative Tracks*, 11. Berk provides a useful framework for examining policy alternatives. In his study of railroad consolidation in the late 1800s, Berk makes a "distinction between constitutive politics and politics of power," noting "constitutive eras necessitate experimentation in business strategy, constitutional interpretation, and public policy" (ibid., 11). His work, and therefore mine as well, draws from Roberto Unger's *False Necessity*, a theoretically dense book that demonstrates how dominant social and political institutions are able to repress challenges to their positions. A genuine alternative "may fail," Unger asserts, "because it cannot be grasped and dealt with as an intelligible transformation of remembered sequences or current arrangements" (Unger, *False Necessity*, 170).

11. Orren and Skowronek, *Search for American Political Development*, 19, 20.

12. Ibid., 66. For more on the ways that institutional reconfigurations are interpreted in APD studies, especially the concept of "path dependency," see Pierson, *Politics in Time*. Another way to understand institutional change comes to us from APD scholar Theda Skocpol's *Protecting Soldiers and Mothers*, in which the author suggests that, for a political change to take place, it has to have a recognizable "fit" with the broader goals and capabilities of politically active groups and the changing points of access allowed by political institutions. Her notion of "fit" is one component of her polity-centered approach that also examines the effects of political institutions on identities and goals of social groups that became involved in policy making, and the ways that previous social policies affect subsequent policies.

13. Thomas, *Colonialism's Culture*, 2–3.

14. Rand, *Kiowa Humanity*, 7–8. Simultaneously, though, I take very seriously Jeffery Ostler's recent contention that historians be careful of overemphasizing the power of the colonial state. He asserts that while many reformers framed their notions of assimilation using a language of

altruism and philanthropy, "assimilation functioned in the larger scheme of things as a rationale for the dispossession of Indian lands and the destruction of diversity in the name of national homogeneity" (Ostler, *Plains Sioux and U.S. Colonialism*, 5, 8).

15. Bruyneel, *Third Space of Sovereignty*, xix.

16. Denson, *Demanding the Cherokee Nation*, 116.

17. Richardson suggests that federal power expanded in two ways. First, to conduct its military campaigns, the U.S. Congress implemented a national tax, making every citizen an actual stakeholder in the nation. Then, in the Thirteenth and Fourteenth Amendments, Congress, for the first time "in the history of the American Constitution . . . increased, rather than limited, the power of the national government" (*West from Appomattox*, 3, 7).

18. Literary and film critic Michelle Raheja addresses some of the controversy surrounding Parker's role in Seneca and U.S. history in her recent article, "'I Leave It with the People of the United States to Say.'" For other contemporary opinions concerning Parker's legacy from Iroquois leaders and scholars, see *Ely S. Parker (Seneca): A Warrior in Two Worlds* (Rochester, N.Y.: WXXI Public Broadcasting Council, 2000).

19. Some of the best examples of the classic, "top-down" approach include Priest, *Uncle Sam's Stepchildren*; Prucha, *American Indian Policy*; Danziger, *Indians and the Bureaucrats*; Prucha, *Great Father*; and Hoxie, *Final Promise*. Some of the best examples of the community-based approach include Perdue, *Slavery and the Evolution of Cherokee Society*; Richter, *Ordeal of the Longhouse*; McConnell, *Country Between*; Hatley, *Dividing Paths*; Hoxie, *Parading through History*; Jean O'Brien, *Dispossession by Degrees*; Kugel, *To Be the Main Leaders of Our People*; Saunt, *New Order of Things*; and Greg O'Brien, *Choctaws in a Revolutionary Age*.

20. Scholars of American political development suggest that reevaluating the evolution of the state in the nineteenth century is of critical scholarly importance. See Leuchtenburg, "Pertinence of Political History." For a good overview of the history and current direction of the APD school, see Orren and Skowronek, *Search for American Political Development*. For some of the best examples of APD scholarship, see Skowronek, *Building a New American State*; Bensel, *Yankee Leviathan*; Skocpol, *Protecting Soldiers and Mothers*; Novak, *People's Welfare*; and Clemens, *People's Lobby*.

21. At this point there is only one monograph-length study of the development of the Office of Indian Affairs, Paul Stuart's *Indian Office*, which is primarily an institutional history that does not thoroughly contextualize its subject. A second, more interesting, monograph, Cathleen Cahill's *Federal Fathers and Mothers*, addresses the ways that the federal government used Euro-American gender roles and familial structures to disrupt tribal notions of kinship. In this way, she argues, intimate colonialism shaped federal assimilation policies and employment strategies in the Indian Service. Her introduction situates the OIA within these broader federal developments very clearly and has been influential in my thinking.

22. The notion of "dropping" the Gilded Age and instead understanding the period from the end of the Civil War through the Great Depression as the "Long Progressive Era" has gained considerable scholarly traction, and it is a schematic that makes the most sense in thinking about Indian policy development. For a concise articulation of this periodization argument, see Edwards, "Politics."

CHAPTER ONE

1. Harriet Maxwell Converse, "A Prophesy Fulfilled," *Buffalo Express*, January 24, 1897, Box 6: 1886–1946 and (n.d.), Parker Papers, APS. The story of this prophetic dream is recounted

in both Parker biographies. See Armstrong, *Warrior in Two Worlds*, 14–15, and Parker, *Life of General Ely S. Parker*, 47–49. Neither author, though, questioned this story critically, nor did either author mention Parker's own skepticism concerning the dream. On the significance of dreams among the Seneca, see Wallace, *Death and Rebirth of the Seneca*, 59–75.

2. Ely S. Parker to Harriet Maxwell Converse, January 11, 1887, Parker Papers, 1803–1894, MSS PA 1–126, HL.

3. Harriet Maxwell Converse, "A Prophesy Fulfilled," *Buffalo Express*, January 24, 1897, Box 6: 1886–1946 and (n.d.), Parker Papers, APS.

4. The literature on the "vanishing Indian" trope is well established. For a good example, see Dippie, *Vanishing American*. The New York State context within which Converse wrote had a deep investment in this trope. For a clear example, see Philip Deloria's characterization of Lewis Henry Morgan's creation of the New Confederacy of the Iroquois in *Playing Indian*, 77–79, 83–85.

5. For an excellent examination of the relationship between Indian nations and states, see Deborah Rosen, *American Indians and State Law*.

6. For an excellent and concise encapsulation of this contradiction, see Denson, *Demanding the Cherokee Nation*, 5. For more on contradictions in Indian policy and law, see Deloria and Lytle, *American Indians*, 33; Wilkinson, *American Indians, Time, and the Law*; Pommersheim, *Braid of Feathers*; and David Wilkins, *American Indian Sovereignty*.

7. Wunder, "Retained by the People," 17.

8. Prucha, *American Indian Treaties*, 21.

9. For a clear discussion of the commerce clause, see Deloria and Wilkins, *Tribes, Treaties*, 25–26; Pommersheim, *Braid of Feathers*, 121; and Wilkins and Lomawaima, *Uneven Ground*, 9.

10. Prucha, *American Indian Treaties*, 32–33.

11. Deloria and Wilkins, *Tribes, Treaties*, 7.

12. Ibid., 2.

13. Ibid., 81–82; Wright, "Creek-American Treaty of 1790"; Roberts, "Chief of State."

14. Knox articulated his ideas in three reports to George Washington on May 23, 1789, June 15, 1789, and July 6–7, 1789. See Lowrite, *American State Papers*, 7–8, 12–14, 15–54. For an excellent discussion of Knox's policy ideas, see Buss, *Winning the West with Words*, 17–19.

15. See Buss, *Winning the West with Words*. For more on the Treaty of Greenville, see Cayton, "'Noble Actors,'" and Owens, *Mr. Jefferson's Hammer*.

16. Deloria and Wilkins (*Tribes, Treaties*, 72) referred to this as reflective of "the humanitarian impulse of the United States" and noted its beginning with the passage of a congressional act "making provision for the civilization of the Indian tribes adjoining the frontier settlements."

17. Prucha, *American Indian Treaties*, 129–44. Significantly, Richard White (*Middle Ground*, 523) acknowledges the shift in military and economic power between the United States and Great Lakes Indian nations in the aftermath of the War of 1812 by ending his study at that point. In his epilogue he wrote, the "American arrived and dictated."

18. Wilkins and Lomawaima, *Uneven Ground*, 65. Francis Prucha asserts that the trust responsibility is a recent development, while Vine Deloria argues that it was part and parcel of the doctrine of discovery. If the government claimed Indian lands through the doctrine of discovery, Deloria notes, it assumed the role of protector for the Indians. See Prucha, *Indian in American Society*. Wilkins and Lomawaima argue that they and "the majority of political and legal scholars, jurists, and federal policymakers assert that the federal trust responsibility is an ancient and entrenched (although ambiguous) legal doctrine that permeates the tribal-federal relationship" (*Uneven Groud*, 67). See also Bruyneel, *Third Space of Sovereignty*, 18.

19. For a fuller historical account of the doctrine of discovery, see Miller, *Native America*. Wilkins and Lomawaima (*Uneven Ground*, 19–63) offer a sharp repudiation of the concept as "a clear legal fiction that needs to be explicitly stricken from the federal government's political and legal vocabulary" (63). See also David Wilkins, *American Indian Sovereignty*, 27–38. For more on John Marshall, see Jean Smith, *John Marshall*. Legal scholar Robert A. Williams summarizes the tragedy of justice embodied in *Johnson v. M'Intosh* as "a case involving two white litigants, [that] effectively denied American Indian tribes recognizable full legal title to their ancestral homelands under the Doctrine of Discovery, which had been adopted by Marshall and the Court as the domestic law of the United States" (Williams, *American Indian in Western Legal Thought*, 313).

20. In fact, legal historian Lindsay G. Robertson (*Conquest by Law*, xii) concludes that "the United States has inherited a legal regime dependent on . . . a wrongly decided, collusive case." His book was based on previously unused documents from the land speculators involved in the case. His research has greatly enriched our understanding of the *Johnson* case.

21. Quoted in Prucha, *American Indian Treaties*, 166, 167.

22. Ibid., 156–68; Robertson, *Conquest by Law*, 138–39; David Wilkins, *American Indian Sovereignty*, 21–22, 275–76. For a full discussion of the Cherokee cases, see Norgren, *Cherokee Cases*.

23. Perdue and Green, *Cherokee Removal*, 167–68.

24. A few notable examples include Perdue and Green, *Cherokee Removal*; Thurman Wilkins, *Cherokee Tragedy*; Wallace, *Long, Bitter Trail*; Remini, *Andrew Jackson and His Indian Wars*; and McLoughlin, *After the Trail*.

25. *ARCIA*, 1856, serial 875, p. 571, quoted in Prucha, *American Indian Treaties*, 236.

26. Prucha, *American Indian Treaties*, 260. See also Prucha, *Great Father*, 315–410.

27. See Prucha, *American Indian Treaties*, 261–85; Abel, *American Indian as Participant in the Civil War*; Abel, *American Indian and the End of the Confederacy*; and Bailey, *Reconstruction in Indian Territory*.

28. In his book *Demanding the Cherokee Nation*, Andrew Denson argues that Cherokee leaders used the post–Civil War reform era as an opportunity to improve their conditions in Indian Territory.

29. Deloria, *Indians in Unexpected Places*, 25–26. Ann Stoler has masterfully described in much of her work these processes in the context of Dutch colonialism in Indonesia. For an example that includes discussion of the U.S. context, see her "Tense and Tender Ties." On the concept of "legibility" and its use in colonial state projects, see Scott, *Seeing Like a State*. Scott asserts that arranging a population to make it legible "simplified the classic state functions of taxation, conscription, and prevention of rebellion" (2).

30. Deloria, "Self-Determination," 25.

31. Bruyneel, *Third Space of Sovereignty*, 23.

32. Wilkins and Deloria argue that from the commerce clause "springs the massive edifice of legislation, court decisions, and administrative rules and regulations that compose the structure and substance of the federal relationship with Indians and Indian tribes" (*Tribes, Treaties*, 25).

33. Wilkins and Lomawaima, *Uneven Ground*, 9. They refer to this concept powerfully as the doctrine of inherent sovereignty.

34. David Wilkins, *American Indian Sovereignty*, 22.

35. New work in APD is pushing scholars to rethink nineteenth-century political development in important ways. One example that has influenced my thinking is Brian Balogh's *Government Out of Sight*. Without developing bureaucratic machinery, Balogh argues, "national

governance remained hidden in plain sight because many of its activities were directed at the margins of society." One of the "margins" to which he refers was most definitely Indian country, and though many standard narratives of state development in the United States overlook Indian history, at least indirectly, his work indicates that shifting our lens to more centrally locate this experience can reveal important insights of interest to historians beyond the subfield of Native American and indigenous history. See Balogh, *Government Out of Sight*, 11.

36. Aleinikoff, *Semblances of Sovereignty*, 7; Bruyneel, *Third Space of Sovereignty*, 17.

37. Quoted in Prucha, *American Indian Treaties*, 211.

38. Ibid., 212–13.

39. *U.S. Statutes at Large*, 4:729–35. See also David Wilkins, *American Indian Sovereignty*, 36–37, and Harring, *Crow Dog's Case*, 40.

40. David Wilkins, *American Indian Sovereignty*, 37–38.

41. In fact, Wilkins argues that this case "was every bit as traumatic for tribes as his infamous *Dred Scott* decision . . . would be for African Americans" (*American Indian Sovereignty*, 42).

42. Harring, *Crow Dog's Case*, 60–61; David Wilkins, *American Indian Sovereignty*, 42–44 (for Taney's quote, see 43).

43. For the definitive account of this case, see Harring, *Crow Dog's Case*.

44. David Wilkins, *American Indian Sovereignty*, 68–69.

45. Harring, *Crow Dog's Case*, 137.

46. Quoted in Prucha, *American Indian Treaties*, 349.

47. Quoted in David Wilkins, *American Indian Sovereignty*, 79.

48. *U.S. Statutes at Large*, 16:566, excerpted in Prucha, *Documents of United States Indian Policy*, 135.

49. Deloria and DeMallie, *Documents of American Indian Diplomacy*, 233.

50. See also Wunder, "No More Treaties."

51. Bruyneel, *Third Space of Sovereignty*, 71, 75. For Bruyneel's full discussion, see chap. 3. Maureen Konkle, working within the framework of literary critique, refers to this same concept as "Indian difference." See Konkle, *Writing Indian Nations*, 15.

52. Colonialism is never monolithic but provides space for "creation" as well as "destruction." See Thomas, *Colonialism's Culture*.

53. Wilkins and Lomawaima, *Uneven Ground*, 8–9.

54. Denson (*Demanding the Cherokee Nation*, 116) asserts that by "replacing wardship with tribal autonomy," the Cherokee "radically altered the meaning of the peace policy as it applied to the Indian Territory."

55. For an excellent examination of this history, see Bowes, *Exiles and Pioneers*.

56. Rand, *Kiowa Humanity*, 8.

57. Ibid., 61–92.

58. Ibid., 133–35.

59. Ibid., 7–8.

60. Williams, *Linking Arms Together*, 132.

61. Ibid., 133.

CHAPTER TWO

1. George Cooper to Ely S. Parker, May 22, 1852, Box 3: 1849–1852, Parker Papers, APS.

2. For more on the Iroquois matrilineal system and kinship relationships, see Fenton, *Great Law and the Longhouse*, 28–29.

3. Ely S. Parker to "Sir Isaac" Newton Parker, June 22, 1852, Box 3: 1849–1852, Parker Papers, APS. See also Conable, "Steady Enemy," 318.

4. Much has been made about the "Iroquois mystique" in the scholarly literature. The notion that the Iroquois maintained a vast inland empire was first developed by the British to facilitate treaty making. After the American Revolution, it seems that the idea of a coercively powerful Iroquois empire slowly but certainly dwindled. For more, see Jones, *License for Empire*; Jennings, *Ambiguous Iroquois Empire*; Richter and Merrell, *Beyond the Covenant Chain*; Lehman, "End of the Iroquois Mystique"; and Richter, *Ordeal of the Longhouse*.

5. Campisi, "From Stanwix to Canandaigua," 64. For the fullest account of the Treaty of Fort Stanwix, see Manley, *Treaty of Fort Stanwix*.

6. Conable, "Steady Enemy," chap. 1. For more on the Holland Land Company, see Chazanof, *Joseph Ellicott and the Holland Land Company*, and Wyckoff, *Developer's Frontier*.

7. For more on this event, see Dennis, *Seneca Possessed*, esp. the introduction.

8. For more on Handsome Lake, see Wallace, *Death and Rebirth*. For New York State legal codes, see Hauptman, *Conspiracy of Interests*, 115.

9. For more on Quaker efforts to create schools, see Nicholas, "Little School"; Swalzer, *Friend among the Senecas*; and Barton, *Quaker Promise Kept*.

10. The Allegany Reservation was the second smallest of the four major western New York reserves, covering roughly 30,500 acres. Cattaraugus was the smallest, at 28,000 acres, while Tonawanda, at 46,200 acres, and Buffalo Creek, consisting of 83,500 acres, were the largest. See Conable, "Steady Enemy," 9–10.

11. See Conable, "Steady Enemy," chap. 2. See also Hauptman, *Conspiracy of Interests*, esp. pt. 2.

12. In New York Seneca factionalism, see Abler, "Seneca Moieties"; Abler, "Friends, Factions"; and Abler, "Factional Dispute and Party Conflict."

13. The total land base reduction was 86,887 acres. See Hauptman, *Conspiracy of Interests*, 155.

14. For more on the campaign against the 1826 treaty, see Manley, "Red Jacket's Last Campaign," and Hauptman, *Conspiracy of Interests*, 154–61. See also Conable, "Steady Enemy," chap. 3.

15. Hauptman, *Conspiracy of Interests*, 176. For a thorough discussion of Jacksonian Indian policy, see Satz, *American Indian Policy*. For a more apologetic examination of Jackson and his legacy in Indian history, see Remini, *Andrew Jackson and His Indian Wars*.

16. Stryker, a U.S. Indian subagent, defrauded New York Indians, mostly the Seneca, of approximately $30,000 worth of annuity payments between the late 1830s and 1850. Schermerhorn aided Andrew Jackson's removal policies more than any other man, notably in regard to the Cherokee of Georgia and Iroquois of New York. Gillet, a onetime Democratic congressman from Ogdenburg, secured the treaty, but when later allegations of fraud emerged, he escaped blame. For more, see Goldstein, "Albany Regency"; Van Hoeven, "Salvation and Indian Removal"; and Garraty, *Silas Wright*.

17. Hauptman, *Conspiracy of Interests*, 178–90. See also Conable, "Steady Enemy," chap. 5, and Manley, "Buying Buffalo from the Indians." For more on the city of Buffalo, see Gerber, *Making of an American Pluralism*, and Goldman, *High Hopes*.

18. The 1842 treaty is most often referred to as the supplemental treaty or the compromise treaty. Throughout this chapter, I use the latter term.

19. Hauptman, *Conspiracy of Interests*, 212.

20. See Conable, "Steady Enemy," chap. 8, and Mark Nicholas, chap. 4, "The Full Emergence of the Seneca New Order," of his Lehigh University 2006 dissertation (of which I have been

unable to acquire a complete copy). See also "Petition from the Tonawanda Women to President John Tyler," n.d., Box 2: Correspondence, December 1817–August 1845, Isaac and Amy Post Family Papers, RRL-UR. Removal efforts, as Nicholas asserts in his recent dissertation, shaped Indian governance in significant ways that scholars have not yet fully recognized. Most of the scholarship in this direction has focused on Indians in the Southeast. See Greg O'Brien, *Choctaws in a Revolutionary Age*; Saunt, *New Order of Things*; and McLoughlin, *Cherokee Renascence in the New Republic*.

21. For more on the political impact of the Panic of 1837, see Huston, *Land and Freedom*; McCurdy, *Anti-Rent Era*; and Summerhill, *Harvest of Dissent*. See also Hauptman, *Conspiracy of Interests*, 189–90.

22. Hauptman, *Conspiracy of Interests*, 210–12.

23. In his newest book, historian Laurence Hauptman argues that Parker was just one in a long line of Seneca leaders in this resistance campaign. In fact, he suggests that Parker was far less significant than John Blacksmith, Jimmy Johnson, or even the non-Native lawyer, John Martindale. At various points in his text, Hauptman makes statements to minimize Parker's importance but states it most clearly in a brief chapter titled "The Runner." He argues, "Parker's role has been misconstrued. He was never the sole leader of his people's struggles" (76). While there is certainly validity to Hauptman's point, and I understand his willingness to critically question the existing historiography, it is difficult to make this argument about Parker, especially considering the significant inroads he made with negotiations and the compromises he brokered after being raised to his position as condoled chief in 1851. For more, see Hauptman, *Tonawanda Senecas' Heroic Battle*.

24. Two Guns (Seneca) to Henry Clay, 1838(?), Box 1: 1794–1845, Parker Papers, APS.

25. T. Hartley Crawford to Messrs. Cook and Love, January 4, 1844, and Ely S. Parker to William Parker, January 29, 1844, both Box 1: 1794–1845, Parker Papers, APS.

26. W. C. Bouck to Chiefs Blacksmith and Jimmy Johnson, June 17, 1844, and John G. Paerpery [Palfrey] to John Blacksmith and others, October 12, 1844, both Box 1: 1794–1845, Parker Papers, APS. Although Massachusetts sold its preemptive rights to the Seneca lands, it maintained a right to employ a commissioner to witness any proceedings between the Indians and future preemptors, such as the Ogden Company, to ensure the legality and fairness of the transactions. In the Buffalo Creek Treaty period, General Henry Dearborn filled this role. For more, see "Journals of Henry A. S. Dearborn."

27. Hauptman, *Conspiracy of Interests*, 178.

28. Tonawanda Chiefs to Governor Wright, February 22, 1845, Box 1: 1794–1845; Silas Wright to Tonawanda Chiefs, April 4, 1846, Box 2: 1846–1848; and Joseph Fellows to Ely S. Parker, November 7, 1845, Box 1: 1794–1845, all Parker Papers, APS.

29. Petition from Tonawanda Leaders to the Governor of New York, 1846, Folder 12842, Ely S. Parker Papers, NYSA; Hauptman, *Tonawanda Senecas' Heroic Battle*, 20.

30. Kappler, *Indian Affairs*, 539–40.

31. Ely S. Parker to William Parker, January 29, 1844, Box 1: 1794–1845, Parker Papers, APS.

32. Isaac Shanks, Isaac Doctor, and Nicholson Parker to Ely S. Parker, May 19, 1846, Box 2: 1846–1848, Parker Papers, APS.

33. R. B. Warren to Ely S. Parker, February 21, 1849, and Tonawanda Chiefs to William L. Marcy, Secretary of War, March 12, 1849, both Box 3: 1849–1852, Parker Papers, APS. It is important to note that this line of reasoning was very similar to that employed by squatters and other non-Native settlers in the Ohio Valley and farther west. They argued that the federal government should not remove them because they had improved the land. In the early nineteenth

century, the federal government had passed several retroactive preemption acts allowing settlers who already improved the land the first right of purchase. The most significant of these was the Preemption Act of 1841. However, this legislation always pertained to federal public lands, not Indian reservations. For more, see Gates, *Farmer's Age*, and Taylor, *Liberty Men and Great Proprietors*.

34. Nicholson Parker, "Memo on conference at Batavia and Albany with attorney Martindale, State Senator Clark, and the Governor, on course of legal action for removing white settlers," June 12, 1846, and W. P. Angel to Ely S. Parker, February 20, 1848, both Box 2: 1846–1848, Parker Papers, APS.

35. *Blacksmith v. Fellows*, 7 N.Y. 401 (1852); *Fellows v. Blacksmith*, 19 How. U.S., 761 (1857). See also Conable, "Steady Enemy," 381–85.

36. For example, see U.S. Congress, Senate, Committee on Indian Affairs, *Memorial of Tonawanda*, 113.

37. *Buffalo Courier*, July [?], 1851, Box 3: 1849–1852, Parker Papers, APS; *Spirit of the Times*, September 30, 1851; Armstrong, *Warrior in Two Camps*, 49. For more on the rights and responsibilities of Seneca sachems, see Fenton, *Parker on the Iroquois*, bk. 3, 34–40.

38. Spencer Cone to Ely S. Parker, July 31, 1851, Box 3: 1849–1852, Parker Papers, APS. In this letter, Cone revealed that there was some question as to whether Parker would actually be raised to the position; Isaac Shanks and Jimmy Johnson may not have approved of it.

39. Ely S. Parker to Nicholson Parker, June 21, 1846, Box 2: 1846–1848, Parker Papers, APS.

40. Ibid., July 15, 1846.

41. Tonawanda Chiefs to Ely S. Parker, July 15, 1846, Box 2: 1846–1848, Parker Papers, APS.

42. Armstrong, *Warrior in Two Camps*, 8, 11, and 51.

43. Arthur C. Parker, "Note Describing Cone," in William Parker to Spencer H. Cone, October 13, 1846, Box 2: 1846–1848, Parker Papers, APS.

44. William Parker and James Williams to Spencer H. Cone, August 30, 1845, Box 1: 1794–1845; Ely S. Parker to Spencer H. Cone, June 8, 1846, Box 2: 1846–1848; and Spencer H. Cone to A. H. H. Stuart, Secretary of the Interior, April 3, 1851, Box 3: 1849–1852, all Parker Papers, APS.

45. Even though he ultimately returned and reintegrated himself, the rift caused by the Ogden dispute lasted for almost a decade and influenced Ely Parker's political education. See Armstrong, *Warrior in Two Camps*, 51.

46. Perdue and Green, *Cherokee Removal*; Thurman Wilkins, *Cherokee Tragedy*; Wallace, *Long, Bitter Trail*; Remini, *Andrew Jackson and his Indian Wars*; McLoughlin, *After the Trail*.

47. Ely S. Parker to Tonawanda Chiefs, March 2, 1861, reproduced as an appendix in Parker, *Life of General Ely S. Parker*, 292.

48. Armstrong, *Warrior in Two Camps*, 1–3. The quotation is from "Copy of an Address Read by Scenandoah [Morgan] at the Monthly Council of the Cayugas April 17, 1844," Morgan Papers, RRL-UR.

49. Morgan frequently asked Parker to take notes at Seneca council meetings or spiritual rituals. See Lewis Henry Morgan to Ely S. Parker, September 26, 1848, Folder 12: Morgan Correspondence, 1848; Morgan to Parker, January 29, 1850, Folder 15: Morgan Correspondence; and Morgan to Parker, August 2, 1850, Folder 15: Morgan Correspondence, all Box 1: Correspondence, 1839–1854, Morgan Papers, RRL-UR. Parker usually responded with notes that Morgan included in *The League*. See "A translation of the speech made by Jimmy Johnson at the Grand Council of the Confederacy of Iroquois held at the Indian village of Tonawanda . . . translated by Ely S. Parker," October 1845, Ayer MS 451, Ayer Collection, NL; "Notes," n.d., Folder 65:

Writings, [An Account of an Indian Council by Ely S. Parker], Box 2, Arthur C. Parker Papers, NYSA; and "Separation of the Senecas and Wyandottes," Folder 12843, Ely S. Parker Papers, NYSA. In his chapter titled "The Purloined Indian," Ox Frankel (*States of Inquiry*, 291–98) suggests that the Parker/Morgan relationship had both practical and symbolic power for each man. Unfortunately, his discussion of this relationship is brief.

50. Ely S. Parker to Lewis Henry Morgan, April 2, 1846, Folder 7: Morgan Correspondence, January to April 1846, Box 1: Correspondence, 1839–1854, Morgan Papers, RRL-UR.

51. "Albany or Rochester Newspaper Article," March 29, 1847, Box 2: 1846–1848, Parker Papers, APS.

52. For more on the life of Henry Rowe Schoolcraft, see Bremer, *Indian Agent and Wilderness Scholar*. Hauptman (*Tonawanda Senecas' Heroic Battle*) suggests that leaders at Tonawanda before Parker viewed Schoolcraft skeptically. "The Tonawanda chiefs," he wrote, "refused to cooperate, viewing him as a spy or agent for the Ogden Land Company and the state" (65).

53. Henry Rowe Schoolcraft to Ely S. Parker, August 8, 1845, Box 1: 1794–1845, Parker Papers, APS.

54. Ely S. Parker to Henry Rowe Schoolcraft, May 2, 1846, and Schoolcraft to Parker, May 7, 1846, Folder 8: Morgan Correspondence, May 1846, Box 1: Correspondence, 1839–1854, Morgan Papers, RRL-UR.

55. U.S. Senate, Committee on Indian Affairs, *Petition of the Tonawanda Band of Seneca Indians*, 2–3.

56. Schoolcraft's study resulted in a six-volume work published between 1851 and 1857 titled *Historical and Statistical Information Respecting the History, Condition, and Prospects on the Indian Tribes of the United States*.

57. Ely S. Parker to Henry Rowe Schoolcraft, January 23, 1848, Folder 12: Morgan Correspondence, May 1848, Box 1: Correspondence, 1839–1854, Morgan Papers, RRL-UR; Parker to Schoolcraft, March 11, 1849, Box 3: 1849–1852, Parker Papers, APS.

58. Ely S. Parker to Lewis Henry Morgan, February 13, 1847, Folder 11: Morgan Correspondence, 1847, Box 1: Correspondence, 1839–1854, Morgan Papers, RRL-UR.

59. I am deeply indebted to Thomas Summerhill for his insights into the landholder/tenant relationship in early-nineteenth-century New York. For more on the Revolutionary generation of New York farmers and landholders, as well as their sons and the antirent wars, see Summerhill, *Harvest of Dissent*, 7–88. For more on the farmers' use of Indian imagery, see ibid., 64–65; Summerhill, "Farmer's Republic," 38–70; and Christman, *Tin Horns and Calico*, 91–93. For more on the significance of non-Natives using Indian symbolism in their political protests, see Deloria, *Playing Indian*.

60. Petition to the Senate of the United States, Folder 109: Seneca Indians at Tonawanda, Box 24: Mss of Articles, etc., Morgan Papers, RRL-UR.

61. Petition to the Senate of the United States, Folder 110: Seneca Indians at Tonawanda, Petitions on their behalf, Box 24: Mss of Articles, etc., Morgan Papers, RRL-UR.

62. See Nathaniel Strong, *Appeal to the Christian Community*.

63. Littlefield, "'They Ought to Enjoy the Home of their Fathers,'" 94.

64. Susan Gray examined a similar situation in Michigan and found that settlers there benefited from their interactions with Indians in a variety of ways, including from the specie they provided. See Gray, "Limits and Possibilities: Indian-White Relations in Western Michigan in the Era of Removal." In his recent book, *Sovereign Selves*, critic David Carlson defends Strong's actions and offers a different reading of *Appeal*. He suggests that Strong saw no problem with

the Ogden purchase and the Buffalo Creek Treaty because it was "neither a subversion of the trust responsibilities of the federal government nor a threat to the long-term welfare of the Seneca" (52). This interpretation, however, ignores the unique and significant history of landholding patterns in New York State.

65. U.S. Senate, Committee on Indian Affairs, *Mass Meeting for the Indians*, 119, 121.

66. Ibid., 122–25. Thirty-three non-Native men signed these documents, although many more may have been involved in their creation.

67. Marcus Johnson to President Franklin Pierce, October 8, 1856; N. E. Paine to President Franklin Pierce, October 10, 1856; I. A. Verplanck to William L. Marcy, October 10, 1856; Frederick Follett to President Franklin Pierce, October 13, 1856; and Frederick Follett to Robert McClelland, October 13, 1856, all Box 4: 1853–1858, Parker Papers, APS.

68. Ely S. Parker to George Manypenny, Commissioner of Indian Affairs, September 25, 1856, and Manypenny to Parker, September 29, 1856, both Box 4: 1853–1858, Parker Papers, APS.

69. Tonawanda Chiefs to John H. Martindale, November 9, 1852, Box 3: 1849–1852, Parker Papers, APS.

70. Nicholson Parker to Ely S. Parker, June 11, 1846, Box 2: 1846–1848; Memo by Nicholson Parker, June 12, 1846, Box 2: 1846–1848; W. P. Angel to Ely S. Parker, February 20, 1848, Box 2: 1846–1848; Ely S. Parker to William Parker, April 14, 1852, Box 3: 1849–1852; and Ely S. Parker to Tonawanda Chiefs, February 23, 1853, Box 4: 1853–1858, all Parker Papers, APS. See also Armstrong, *Warrior in Two Camps*, 21, 42–43.

71. Armstrong, *Warrior in Two Camps*, 35, 58.

72. Tonawanda Chiefs, "Power of Attorney for John H. Martindale and Others," June 16, 1857, and Ely S. Parker, John H. Martindale, William G. Bryan, and Frederick Follett to J. W. Dever, Commissioner of Indian Affairs, June 30, 1857, both Box 4: 1853–1858, Parker Papers, APS; *New York Herald*, July 6, 1857; Ely S. Parker, Nicholson H. Parker, J. H. Martindale, William G. Bryan, and Frederick Follett to Charles E. Mix, November 1, 1857, Box 4: 1853–1858, and Nicholson Parker to Ely S. Parker, 17 May, 1860, Box 5: 1859–1885, both Parker Papers, APS. See also Armstrong, *Warrior in Two Camps*, 64–66.

73. William Parker to Ely S. Parker, January 11, 1860, Box 5: 1859–1885, Parker Papers, APS.

74. Ely S. Parker to Lewis H. Morgan, February 13, 1847, Folder 11: Morgan Correspondence, 1847, Box 1: Correspondence, 1839–1854, Morgan Papers, RRL-UR.

75. "Diary Entry Written by Ely Parker," January 16, 1848, Box 2: 1846–1848, Parker Papers, APS.

76. Ely S. Parker to Lewis H. Morgan, February 13, 1847, Folder 11: Morgan Correspondence, 1847, Box 1: Correspondence, 1839–1854, Morgan Papers, RRL-UR.

77. From the late 1700s through 1822, Indian affairs were managed at the federal level by the secretary of war's office and the Office of Indian Trade. Congress abolished the Office of Indian Trade in 1822, and in 1824, Secretary of War John Calhoun established the Office of Indian Affairs in the War Department. Congress informally recognized the OIA in 1832, when it authorized the president to appoint a commissioner. In 1849, Congress moved the OIA to the Department of the Interior, where it currently remains. For most of the nineteenth century, it was referred to as the Indian Office or the Office of Indian Affairs. The name Bureau of Indian Affairs was adopted officially in 1947. For more, see Kvasnicka and Viola, *Commissioners of Indian Affairs*, and Paul Stuart, *Indian Office*.

78. Armstrong, *Warrior in Two Camps*, 64–66. See also "Notes regarding a meeting with the Commissioner of Indian Affairs about Ogden Co.," June 26, 1857; "Notes regarding a meeting with the Commissioner of Indian Affairs about Ogden Co.," June 29, 1857; and "Notes

regarding a meeting with the Commissioner of Indian Affairs about Ogden Co.," June 30, 1857, all Folder 4: Non-Correspondence Legal and Financial Business, Ely S. Parker Papers, UR-RRL.

79. Conable, "Steady Enemy," 324.

80. Nicholas, dissertation, 248–49.

81. Despite his effort to deal with this episode in Seneca history in greater detail than other scholars, Hauptman devotes little more than a page to the postremoval campaign reforms and offers very little analysis, choosing instead to emphasize state intrusions into tribal governance. Although he is correct in his emphasis, by thinking more broadly and connecting the Tonawanda story to the Peace Policy through Parker, these developments take on greater significance. See Hauptman, *Tonawanda Senecas' Heroic Battle*, 120–21.

82. William Parker to Ely S. Parker, January 11, 1860, Box 5: 1859–1885, Parker Papers, APS.

83. Tonawanda Chiefs to Ely S. Parker, February 15, 1860, Folder 1: 1860–1909, Box 1: Correspondence, 1860–1952, Arthur C. Parker Papers, RRL-UR.

84. Abler, "Friends, Factions," 75–78.

85. See "Declaration of the Seneca Nation of Indian Changing Their Form of Government and Adopting a Constitutional Character," December 4, 1848, in Wilkins, *Documents of Native American Political Development*, 75–80. The Seneca Nation's political revolution and installation of a new governmental structure resembled similar events among the Cherokee as they fought against removal. See Nicholas, dissertation, 222, and Mary Young, "Cherokee Nation."

86. Sheingate, "Political Entrepreneurship," 188, 192.

87. Ely S. Parker to Tonawanda Chiefs, March 2, 1861, reproduced as an appendix in Parker, *Life of General Ely S. Parker*, 287–88.

88. Ibid., 289–90, 292.

89. Ibid., 292.

90. Ibid.

91. Abler, "Friends, Factions," 75–78. Nicholas (dissertation, 222) suggests that the men most closely associated with the Seneca declaration were not significant property holders in any way.

92. Abler, "Friends, Factions," 78–79.

93. Ely S. Parker to "The President of the Seneca Nation of N.Y.," September 13, 1858, Box 6: Seneca Indian Papers, 1836–1858, Parker Family Papers, BECHS.

94. Ely S. Parker to Henry Rowe Schoolcraft, March 25, 1853, Box 4: 1853–1858, Parker Papers, APS.

95. Ely S. Parker to Tonawanda Chiefs, March 2, 1861, reproduced as an appendix in Parker, *Life of General Ely S. Parker*, 292.

96. Ely S. Parker, John Martindale, William G. Bryan, and Frederick Follett to J. W. Denver, Commissioner of Indian Affairs, June 30, 1857, Box 4: 1853–1858, Parker Papers, APS; Conable, "Steady Enemy," 315–16. See also "The Tonawanda Indians of New York," *New York Herald*, July 6, 1857; "Draft of an agreement between the Tonawanda Band of Senecas and the Ogden Land Company," November 1, 1857, Box 4: 1853–1858, Parker Papers, APS; "New Treaty with the Senecas," *New York Evening Express*, November 5, 1857; and Ely S. Parker to N. B. Matthews, August 20, 1858, Box 4: 1853–1858, Parker Papers, APS.

97. See Hauptman, *Conspiracy of Interests*, 147, 155; and Conable, "Steady Enemy," 316.

CHAPTER THREE

1. Report by Commissioners Alfred Sully and Ely S. Parker, September 6, 1867, Records concerning an investigation of the Fort Phil Kearney (or Fetterman) massacre, 1867, Records of the Civilization Division, 25, RG 75, NARA.

2. For an example of this kind of scholarship, see Levine, "Indian Fighters and Indian Reformers."

3. Historian David Nichols (*Lincoln and the Indians*) contends that the Bureau of Indian Affairs was already a corrupt agency when Lincoln took office and that the Civil War, differences of opinion between congressmen, and the president's focus on white western settlement impeded any efforts at reform. Edmund Danziger, in his book *Indians and Bureaucrats*, argues that the OIA's problems in the 1860s were directly related to larger developments in the 1850s, including "accelerated territorial expansion, the nation's preoccupation with the slavery question, the 'Indian Ring,' whiskey hucksters, fraudulent records, disagreements with the war department, cultural clash, race hatreds and the political power of frontiersmen in Indian matters" (12). Danziger also excuses Lincoln from any kind of blame because of his devotion to Civil War issues. For an alternate and more nuanced study of Lincoln and his efforts to reform political institutions and practices, see Greenstone, *Lincoln Persuasion.*

4. Beeson, *Plea for the Indians*, 110.

5. Quoted in Fritz, *Movement for Indian Assimilation*, 37. For more on Beeson, see Prucha, *American Indian Policy*, 4–6; Mardock, *Reformers and the American Indian*, 10–14; and Fritz, *Movement for Indian Assimilation*, 34–38.

6. For more on Whipple, see Prucha, *American Indian Policy*, 4–10; Mardock, *Reformers and the American Indian*, 10–14; and Fritz, *Movement for Indian Assimilation*, 38–45.

7. The majority of the Sisseton and Wahpeton Bands opposed the war, but some members did participate. See Hasian, "Cultural Amnesia and Legal Rhetoric," 99.

8. At the time, there were rumors that the Indians had been whipped into a frenzy by "rebel emissaries," although there is little evidence to support this claim. See Hasian, "Cultural Amnesia and Legal Rhetoric," 95.

9. For more, see Oehler, *Great Sioux Uprising*; Schultz, *Over the Earth I Come*; Namias, *Six Weeks in the Sioux Tepees*; Clodfelter, *Dakota War*; Keenan, *Great Sioux Uprising*; and Bergemann, *Brackett's Battalion.*

10. Namias, *Six Weeks in the Sioux Tepees*, 110.

11. For more on Sand Creek, see Hoig, *Sand Creek Massacre*; Svaldi, *Sand Creek and the Rhetoric of Extermination*; Hatch, *Black Kettle*; and Greene and Scott, *Finding Sand Creek.*

12. Prucha, *American Indian Policy*, 13.

13. "Indian Troubles," *New York Times*, July 29, 1865, 4. See also Curtin, "From Pity to Necessity," 7.

14. *Frank Leslie's Illustrated Newspaper*, February 1, 1868, 306, in Curtin, "From Pity to Necessity," 10.

15. "The Indian Massacre," *New York Times*, January 19, 1867, 3. See also Curtin, "From Pity to Necessity," 10.

16. *New York Times*, January 10, 1867. See also *New York Times*, April 23 and April 28, 1867.

17. Prucha, *American Indian Policy*, 14–19.

18. Quoted in Summers, *Era of Good Stealings*, 21.

19. Ibid.

20. See Foner, *Reconstruction*. See also Cimbala and Miller, *Freedmen's Bureau and Reconstruction*, in particular Randall Miller's introduction and Michael Fitzgerald's essay titled "Emancipation and Military Pacification." For recent historiographical essays, see Thomas Brown, *Reconstructions.*

21. Finley, *From Slavery to Uncertain Freedom*, 8, 9–10, 23. For more on Oliver O. Howard, see McFeely, *Yankee Stepfather.*

22. For more on this goal, see Simpson, *Let Us Have Peace*.

23. Denson, *Demanding the Cherokee Nation*, 69–70.

24. Foner, *Reconstruction*, xv–xvi. See also Nelson, *Roots of American Bureaucracy*; Bensel, *Yankee Leviathan*; and Carpenter, *Forging of Bureaucratic Autonomy*.

25. Armstrong, *Warrior in Two Camps*, 66.

26. Ibid., 41–43; Parker, *Life of General Ely S. Parker*, 91–98. See also "Alumni Notes," 11.

27. Armstrong, *Warrior in Two Camps*, 71–107; Parker, *Life of General Ely S. Parker*, 99–116. Although there has been very little written about Native military service during the Civil War in general, the best treatment of an individual group's involvement is Hauptman, *Iroquois in the Civil War*. Hauptman devotes one brief chapter to a discussion of Parker's Civil War experience and asserts that after the war, he abandoned his people and sought fame and fortune in mainstream society.

28. Armstrong, *Warrior in Two Camps*, 107.

29. Prucha, *American Indian Policy*, 26; Armstrong, *Warrior in Two Camps*, 113.

30. Andrew Denson (*Demanding the Cherokee Nation*, 92), for example, refers to the report of the 1867–68 Peace Commission as "a blueprint for the peace policy." See also Oman, "Beginning of the End."

31. Armstrong, *Warrior in Two Camps*, 115. For a lengthy description of the daily activities of this commission, see Abel, *American Indian and the End of the Confederacy*, chap. 6.

32. Bruyneel, *Third Space of Sovereignty*, 36.

33. Abel, *American Indian and the End of the Confederacy*, 176.

34. For the official reports of council, see *ARCIA*, 1865, 202–5, 480–537

35. Documents relating to the negotiations of ratified and unratified treaties with various tribes of Indians, 1801–69, General Records of the Bureau of Indian Affairs,?1801–1952, RG 75, NARA.

36. Minutes of Meetings of the Special Commission, March 4–June 12, 1867, Records concerning an investigation of the Fort Phil Kearney (or Fetterman) massacre, 1867, Records of the Civilization Division, 28–30, RG 75, NARA.

37. Proceedings of Commissioners Alfred Sully and Ely S. Parker, May 21–July 31, 1867, Records concerning an investigation of the Fort Phil Kearney (or Fetterman) massacre, 1867, Records of the Civilization Division, 99, RG 75, NARA.

38. Report by Commissioners Alfred Sully and Ely S. Parker, September 6, 1867, Records concerning an investigation of the Fort Phil Kearney (or Fetterman) massacre, 1867, Records of the Civilization Division, 26, RG 75, NARA.

39. Ibid., 29.

40. Ibid., 26.

41. For all of these recommendations, see ibid., 26–35. The final point is especially interesting because, during the Fort Smith council, Parker seemingly supported Commissioner Cooley's effort to discredit John Ross, the erstwhile Cherokee leader, and place in his stead men more supportive of the government's policies. It would appear, based on this suggestion, that Parker did not actually agree with Cooley's position, or had changed his perspective in the intervening months.

42. U.S. Congress, House, *Letter from the Secretary of War*, 1.

43. Ibid., 4–5.

44. Ibid., 5–7.

45. Ibid., 4.

46. Ibid., 7.

47. Ibid.

48. Ibid., 5.

49. Ibid., 7.

50. Ibid., 1, 2.

51. Ibid., 2.

52. Armstrong, *Warrior in Two Camps*, 123.

53. Ibid., 123 (emphasis added).

54. Skocpol, *Protecting Soldiers and Mothers*, 103. See also Murdock, *One Million Men*, and Geary, *We Need Men*. For more on the expansion of the military bureaucracy, see Angevine, *Railroad and the State*.

55. For more on the significance of the development of the War Department during the Civil War, see Bensel, *Yankee Leviathan*, esp. chap. 3.

56. Fitzgerald, "Emancipation and Military Pacification," 53.

57. For the classic study of the Freedmen's Bureau, see Bentley, *History of the Freedmen's Bureau*.

58. Henry Wilson to Ely S. Parker, January 28, 1867, Ayer MS 1009, Ayer Collection, NL.

59. Denson, *Demanding the Cherokee Nation*, 93. For a description of the peace commission, see Prucha, *American Indian Policy*, 18–25.

60. U.S. Congress, House, *Report of the Peace Commissioners*, 10.

61. Ibid., 17.

62. Ibid., 18.

63. Deloria and DeMallie, *Proceedings of the Great Peace Commission*, 163.

64. U.S. Congress, House, *Report of the Peace Commissioners*, 20.

65. Ibid., 7.

66. Deloria and DeMallie, *Proceedings of the Great Peace Commission*, 170–71.

67. Ibid., 165.

68. U.S. Congress, House, *Report of the Peace Commissioners*, 18.

69. Ibid., 21.

70. Ibid.

71. William T. Sherman to Senator E. G. Ross, January 7, 1869, quoted in Waltmann, "Interior Department," 149.

72. Deloria and DeMallie, *Proceedings of the Great Peace Commission*, 165–70.

73. U.S. Congress, House, *Report of the Peace Commissioners*, 7.

74. Deloria and DeMallie, *Proceedings of the Great Peace Commission*, 169.

CHAPTER FOUR

1. Inaugural Addresses of the Presidents of the United States, http://www.bartleby.com/124/, October 7, 2010.

2. This congressional infighting was very significant for Indian affairs in this period and is discussed later in this book. For a good, brief discussion of the events described here, see Jean Smith, *Grant*, 524–25.

3. *ARCIA*, 1869, 446–47.

4. Parker's appointment as commissioner of Indian affairs was covered in many newspapers; see, for example, "Nominations Sent to the Senate," *New York Herald*, April 14, 1869, 5; and "Nominations Confirmed," *New York Herald*, April 17, 1869, 3. For the quotes, see Ely S. Parker to Felix Reville Brunot, July 14, 1869, Records of the Bureau of Indian Affairs, Letters Sent, vol. 90, July 8–October 10, 1869, RG 75, NARA.

5. Prucha, *American Indian Policy*, 30–31.

6. In his masterful two-volume study of federal Indian policy, *Great Father*, Francis Prucha asserts that "governmental structures that marked the peace policy were a remarkable manifestation of reliance of the 'Christian nation' on professedly Christian men and principles" (1:501). His interpretations have defined much of the literature on the peace policy. For examples of work influenced by or responding to Prucha, see Higham, *Noble, Wretched, and Redeemable*; Milner, *With Good Intentions*; Trennert, "John H. Stout and the Grant Peace Policy"; Keller, *American Protestantism*; Keller, "Episcopal Reformers"; Illick, "'Some of Our Best Indians Are Friends'"; Bender, *New Hope for the Indians*; Cary Collins, "Fall from Grace"; and Stamm, "Peace Policy at Wind River." Andrew Denson (*Demanding the Cherokee Nation*, 90–98) offers a brief but very well defined sketch of the major elements of the peace policy.

For studies of the policy administrators, see Zwink, "On the White Man's Road"; Bunin, "Quaker Agents"; Cutler, "Lawrie Tatum and the Kiowa Agency"; and Waltmann, "John C. Lowrie."

For the non-Native reformers, see Priest, *Uncle Sam's Stepchildren*, 252; Utley, "Celebrated Peace Policy"; Fritz, *Movement for Indian Assimilation*; Fritz, "Making of Grant's Peace Policy"; Mardock, *Reformers and the American Indian*; and Mardock, "Anti-Slavery Humanitarians."

For the military during the peace policy era, see Wooster, *Military and United States Indian Policy*, and St. Pierre, "General O. O. Howard."

For Grant and Indian policy reform, see Rushmore, *Indian Policy*; McFeely, *Grant*; Jean Smith, *Grant*; and Waltmann, "Circumstantial Reformer." In *Cigars, Whiskey, and Winning*, Al Kaltman, in an effort to celebrate all of Grant's accomplishments, lists his appointment of a Native American as the commissioner of Indian affairs as one of his top ten positive actions as president.

7. Levine, "Indian Fighters and Indian Reformers," 330. The disparate elements Levine refers to include the creation of the Board of Indian Commissioners, the attempt to transfer the Bureau of Indian Affairs from the Department of the Interior back to the War Department (it was housed in the War Department before 1849), the experiment of allowing religious organizations to staff specific Indian agencies, the increased concentration of Native communities on reservations, and an expanded program of government appropriations for subsistence, agriculture, and educational staff/facilities.

8. "Condition of the Indian Tribes: Report of the Joint Special Committee, Appointed under Joint Resolution of March 3, 1865, with an Appendix," *Senate Report*, no. 156, 39th Cong., 2nd sess., serial 1279, 7–8.

9. Ely S. Parker to Sec. of the Interior Jacob D. Cox, May 25, 1869, Report Books of the Bureau of Indian Affairs, 1838–1881, vol. 18, 358–59, RG 75, NARA.

10. Ely S. Parker to Sec. of the Interior Jacob D. Cox, July 8, 1869, Report Books of the Bureau of Indian Affairs, 1838–1881, vol. 18, 426, RG 75, NARA.

11. Ely S. Parker to Sec. of the Interior Jacob D. Cox, June 7, 1869, Report Books of the Bureau of Indian Affairs, 1838–1881, vol. 18, 386, RG 75, NARA.

12. Ely S. Parker to Indian Superintendent Alfred Sully, June 1, 1869, Records of the Office of Indian Affairs, Letters Sent, vol. 90, April 30–August 7, 1869, 257–58, RG 75, NARA.

13. Ely S. Parker to Indian Superintendent Alfred Sully, August 17, 1869, Records of the Office of Indian Affairs, Letters Sent, vol. 91, July 8–October 14, 1869, 257–58, RG 75, NARA.

14. Ely S. Parker to Indian Superintendent A. B. Meacham and all other Superintendents, Independent Agents, and Agents in the Southern Superintendency, April 4, 1870, Records of

the Office of Indian Affairs, Letters Sent, vol. 94, December 15, 1869–April 14, 1870, 496–98, RG 75, NARA.

15. Ely S. Parker to Sec. of the Interior Jacob D. Cox, July 30, 1869, Report Books of the Bureau of Indian Affairs, 1838–1881, vol. 18, 479, RG 75, NARA.

16. Wooster, *Military and United States Indian Policy*, 88–89.

17. Ely S. Parker to Sec. of the Interior Jacob D. Cox, June 8, 1869, Report Books of the Bureau of Indian Affairs, 1838–1881, vol. 18, 390–91, RG 75, NARA.

18. *ARCIA*, 1869, 447.

19. Ibid., 448.

20. U.S. Congress, House, *Memorial of Yearly Meetings of the Society of Friends Relative to the Treatment of the Indians*, 40th Cong., 3rd sess., H. Misc. Doc. 29, 1869, 2.

21. Hutton, *Phil Sheridan and His Army*, 189–91.

22. U.S. Congress, Senate, *Message of the President of the United States*, 90. See also Hutton, "Phil Sheridan's Pyrrhic Victory."

23. Wooster, *Military and United States Indian Policy*, 89.

24. Ely S. Parker to Sec. of the Interior Jacob D. Cox, April 26, 1870, Report Books of the Bureau of Indian Affairs, 1838–1881, vol. 19, 327–28, RG 75, NARA.

25. Report by Commissioners Alfred Sully and Ely S. Parker, September 6, 1867, Records Relating to the Investigation of the Fort Philip Kearney (or Fetterman) Massacre, 27, RG 75, NARA. The second chapter of Mardock's *Reformers and the American Indian* is titled "Feed Them or Fight Them," but he does not reference Parker and Sully's recommendation. He instead focuses upon the Peace Commission of 1868.

26. See U.S. Congress, House, *Letter from the Secretary of War*, 8.

27. Ely S. Parker to Sec. of the Interior Jacob D. Cox, August 14, 1869, Report Books of the Bureau of Indian Affairs, 1838–1881, vol. 18, 492, RG 75, NARA.

28. Ely S. Parker to Sec. of the Interior Jacob D. Cox, November 3, 1869, Report Books of the Bureau of Indian Affairs, 1838–1881, vol. 19, 77, RG 75, NARA.

29. Ely S. Parker to Sec. of the Interior Jacob D. Cox, February 26, 1870, Report Books of the Bureau of Indian Affairs, 1838–1881, vol. 19, 211, RG 75, NARA.

30. Armstrong, *Warrior in Two Camps*, 149–50.

31. Ely S. Parker to Sec. of the Interior Jacob D. Cox, May 22, 1869, Report Books of the Bureau of Indian Affairs, 1838–1881, vol. 18, 355, RG 75, NARA.

32. Ely S. Parker to Sec. of the Interior Jacob D. Cox, July 19, 1869, Report Books of the Bureau of Indian Affairs, 1838–1881, vol. 18, 453, RG 75, NARA.

33. Ely S. Parker to Sec. of the Interior Jacob D. Cox, April 23, 1870, Report Books of the Bureau of Indian Affairs, 1838–1881, vol. 19, 319–20, RG 75, NARA.

34. U.S. Department of the Interior, *Report of Honorable E. S. Parker*, 2.

35. Foner, *Short History of Reconstruction*, 43.

36. Ely S. Parker to Cousin Gayaneshaoh (Harriet Maxwell Converse), ca. 1885, MS 674, Folder 5, Parker Papers, NL.

37. Armstrong, *Warrior in Two Camps*, 21–22.

38. Lewis Henry Morgan to Ely S. Parker, Gah-sah-nah 14, 1848, Box 1, Folder 4: Lewis Henry Morgan to Ely S. Parker and his sister Caroline Parker, Photostats, 1844–1868, Arthur C. Parker Papers, SC13604, NYSA.

39. *ARCIA*, 1869, 445.

40. Ibid.

41. Ibid., 480.

42. Ibid., 488.

43. Ely S. Parker to Cousin Gayaneshaoh (Harriet Maxwell Converse), ca. 1885, MS 674, Folder 5, Parker Papers, NL.

44. Ely S. Parker to Sec. of the Interior Jacob D. Cox, March 9, 1870, Report Books of the Bureau of Indian Affairs, 1838–1881, vol. 19, 237, RG 75, NARA.

45. Ely S. Parker to Sec. of the Interior Jacob D. Cox, April 8, 1870, Report Books of the Bureau of Indian Affairs, 1838–1881, vol. 19, 297–98, RG 75, NARA.

46. *ARCIA*, 1869, 448.

47. Bruyneel, *Third Space of Sovereignty*, 69.

48. *ARCIA*, 1869, 448.

49. Ely S. Parker to William Welsh, June 19, 1869, Records of the Office of Indian Affairs, Letters Sent, vol. 90, April 30–August 7, 1869, 406, RG 75, NARA.

50. Ely S. Parker to Sec. of the Interior Columbus Delano, February 15, 1871, Report Books of the Bureau of Indian Affairs, 1838–1881, vol. 20, 199–203, RG 75, NARA.

51. Ely S. Parker to Henry Rowe Schoolcraft, March 25, 1853, Box 4: 1853–1858, Parker Papers, APS.

52. Ely S. Parker to Nicholson Parker, June 21, 1846, Box 2: 1846–1848, Parker Papers, APS.

53. *ARCIA*, 1869, 448 (emphasis added). Note the similarity in Parker's thought to historian Andrew Denson's identification of the nineteenth-century "Indian problem" as the need to resolve the contradiction in which the federal government recognized Native American people as autonomous communities that predated the Constitution while simultaneously identifying them as subjects of the federal government. See Denson, *Demanding the Cherokee Nation*.

54. Ely S. Parker, "Draft for lecture containing autobiographical notes, notes on the history of Indian-White relations and on religion," ca. 1878, MS 674, Folder 2, Parker Papers, NL.

55. Deloria and DeMallie, *Documents of American Indian Diplomacy*, 233.

56. U.S. Congress, *Congressional Globe*, 41st Cong., 3rd sess., pt. 3, 1811.

57. Ibid., 1824.

58. Ibid., 1822.

59. Ibid., 1823.

60. Ibid., 1824.

61. Ibid., 445.

62. Ibid., 450–51.

63. Ely S. Parker to Columbus Delano, January 4, 1871, *Senate Report*, 41st Cong., 3rd sess., S. Doc. 26, serial 1440, 3.

64. Historian Andrew Denson offers the best and most thorough interpretation of the Okmulgee Council in *Demanding the Cherokee Nation*, chap. 4.

65. U.S. Congress, House, *Letter from the Secretary of War*, 4, 8.

66. Ely S. Parker to William Welsh, June 17, 1869, Records of the Office of Indian Affairs, Letters Sent, vol. 90, April 30–July 8, 1869, 394–95, RG 75, NARA.

67. Ely S. Parker to Sec. of the Interior Columbus Delano, November 12, 1870, Report Books of the Bureau of Indian Affairs, 1838–1881, vol. 20, 50–52, RG 75, NARA.

68. Ely S. Parker to Choctaw Delegate Peter Pitchlynn, October 24, 1870, Records of the Office of Indian Affairs, Letters Sent, vol. 98, August 28–December 21, 1870, 245–46, RG 75, NARA.

69. *ARCIA*, 1870, 473.

70. The Doolittle Commission of 1867 also recommended inspection boards to oversee the work of the OIA. The work of the New York Indian Board in the 1820s and 1830s also served

as motivation. There is no consensus in the literature as to which, if any, of these recommendations was most significant in the establishment of the BIC; it appears that the idea emerged and evolved organically through the series of recommendations. See Prucha, *American Indian Policy*, 32–34, and Keller, *American Protestantism*, 20–21.

71. Keller, *American Protestantism*, 20–21.

72. Historian Robert Keller persuasively argues that both William Welsh and second BIC chairman Felix Reville Brunot "believed that government and politics must involve the Church." See Keller, *American Protestantism*, 77. Undoubtedly, there would have been Native people who fit Welsh's Christian mold, including many Native clergy in the Plains and Northwest, but it is clear that he did not consider Native people as proper candidates for policymaking responsibilities. For more on Native clergy members, see Lewis, *Creating Christian Indians*.

73. Prucha, *American Indian Policy*, 26–28.

74. Inaugural Addresses of the Presidents of the United States, http://www.bartleby.com/124/, October 7, 2010.

75. Stuart, *Life of George H. Stuart*, 20.

76. 16 *U.S. Statutes at Large* 40. Several scholars have suggested that the early peace policy era was characterized by significant tensions between executive and legislative branch officials. The establishment of the BIC has been seen as part of a larger congressional campaign to resist Grant's efforts to control patronage appointments. In the late 1860s and early 1870s, Congress also passed legislation prohibiting army officers from accepting civilian appointments and the president from negotiating any additional treaties with Native nations. It is clear that members of Congress and President Grant differed in their notions of Indian policy reform, and while party politics certainly played a role in these tensions, I am most interested in the debates between Parker, Welsh, and the Board of Indian Commissioners, as well as the intentionality of their actions. For more on the tensions between Congress and Grant in regard to Indian Affairs, see Milner, *With Good Intentions*, 1–4; Prucha, *Great Father*, 1:527–33; and Cahill, "'Only the Home Can Found a State,'" 6.

77. For more on Brunot, see Slattery, *Felix Reville Brunot*. See also Allen Johnson, *Dictionary of American Biography*, 5:352–53 and 3:462–63.

78. Johnson, *Dictionary of American Biography*, 6:295; *National Cyclopaedia of American Biography*, 7:541 and 13:270–71; Keller, *American Protestantism*, 73; Johnson, *Dictionary of American Biography*, 3:206–7; Slattery, *Felix Reville Brunot*, 143.

79. Ely S. Parker to George Stuart, May 25, 1869, Records of the Office of Indian Affairs, Letters Sent, vol. 91, July 8–October 14, 1869, 339–40, RG 75, NARA.

80. Ely S. Parker to George Stuart, May 16, 1869, Records of the Office of Indian Affairs, Letters Sent, vol. 90, April 30–July 8, 1869, 115–17, RG 75, NARA; Ely S. Parker to George Stuart, May 25, 1869, Records of the Office of Indian Affairs, Letters Sent, vol. 90, April 30–July 8, 1869, 123–24, RG 75, NARA.

81. William Welsh, *Indian Office*, 2.

82. Minutes of November 17, 1869, Records of the BIC, Minutes, vol. 1, 40–41, MS 907, Ayer Collection, NL.

83. Keller, *American Protestantism*, 77.

84. William Welsh, *Indian Office*, 2

85. For examples of Cox's effort to appease Welsh, see Secretary of the Interior Jacob Cox to William Welsh, June 2, 1869, Letters Sent by the Indian Division of the Office of the Secretary of the Interior, vol. 8: Miscellaneous, January 3, 1868–April 30, 1870, 310–13 and 313–16, RG 75, NARA.

86. Ely S. Parker to William Welsh, May 25, 1869, Records of the Office of Indian Affairs, Letters Sent, vol. 90, April 30–July 8, 1869, 500–501, RG 75, NARA.

87. Secretary of the Interior Jacob Cox to Felix R. Brunot, July 5, 1869, Letters Sent by the Indian Division of the Office of the Secretary of the Interior, vol. 8: Miscellaneous, January 3, 1868–April 30, 1870, 327–30, RG 75, NARA.

CHAPTER FIVE

1. "Affairs in the Indian Department," *House Report*, no. 39, 41st Cong., 3rd sess., serial 1464, ii.

2. Francis Prucha (*American Indian Policy*, 45) notes that prior to the 1873 mass resignation of many of its initial members, the BIC held some authority but that its position within the federal government was ambiguous.

3. Prucha, *Great Father*, 502.

4. Keller, *American Protestantism*, 73–75.

5. Ibid., 74.

6. William Welsh, *Taopi and His Friends*, xii–xiii.

7. Ibid., xiv–xvi.

8. William Welsh wrote many other pamphlets and reports on Indian issues, but they did not tend to deviate from his assertions in *Taopi and His Friends*. For other examples, see *Journal of the Rev. S. D. Hinman* and *Reports to the Missionary Organizations*.

9. William Welsh, *Report of a Visit to the Sioux*, 28.

10. William Welsh, *Taopi and his Friends*, xiii.

11. Keller, *American Protestantism*, 74.

12. Summers, *Era of Good Stealings*, x.

13. William Welsh, *Indian Office*, 2; E. P. Smith to George Whipple, December 15, 1870, American Missionary Association Archives, Amistad Research Center, Tulane University, New Orleans, La., quoted in Armstrong, *Warrior in Two Camps*, 154.

14. Minutes of November 17, 1869, Records of the BIC, Minutes, vol. 1, 40–41, MS 907, Ayer Collection, NL.

15. *ARCIA*, Accompanying Papers, 1870, 491–92.

16. Minutes of May 15, 1871, Records of the BIC, Minutes, vol. 1, 40–41, MS 907, Ayer Collection, NL.

17. Prucha, *American Indian Policy*, 45.

18. "The Indians: Great Council at Okmulgee: Proposed Confederation of the Tribes in the Indian Territory: A New State Looming Up in the Southwest," *New York Herald*, December 19, 1870, 7.

19. U.S. Department of the Interior, *Report of Honorable E. S. Parker, Commissioner of Indian Affairs, to the Honorable Secretary of the Interior, on the Communication of William Welsh, Esq., Relative to the Management of Indian Affairs*, 1, Ayer Collection, NL.

20. "Affairs in the Indian Department," *House Report*, no. 39, 41st Cong., 3rd sess., serial 1464, i. Appropriations Committee members deemed it necessary to aid Welsh in the "rigid examination of witnesses" because he was "not a lawyer." See ibid, ii.

21. "Indian Bureau," *New York Herald*, December 30, 1870, 8.

22. William Welsh to J. D. Cox, March 26, 1869, Records of the Department of the Interior, Letters Received, 1849–1880, Miscellaneous, Box 72, RG 48, NARA.

23. Armstrong, *Warrior in Two Camps*, 150.

24. Ibid., 154.

25. Keller, *American Protestantism*, 74.

26. Parker, *Report of Hon. E. S. Parker*, 4.

27. Keller, *American Protestantism*, 81–83; Mardock, *Reformers and the American Indian*, 105.

28. William Welsh, *Summing Up of Evidence*, 4–5.

29. Ibid., 9.

30. William Welsh to Vincent Colyer, December 17, 1870, Records of the Board of Indian Commissioners, Letters Received, 1870–1872, Box 1, RG 75, NARA.

31. William Welsh to Vincent Colyer, January 2, 1871, Records of the Board of Indian Commissioners, Letters Received, 1870–1872, Box 1, RG 75, NARA.

32. U.S. Congress, House, *Affairs in the Indian Department*, 12–14.

33. Armstrong, *Warrior in Two Camps*, 157–58.

34. However, since it appears Kountz was trying to make an argument that he had been unjustly denied a contract, his comment should be read with some skepticism. See U.S. Congress, House, *Testimony Taken before the Committee on Indian Affairs*, 23.

35. U.S. Congress, House, Committee on Appropriations, *Investigation into Indian Affairs*, 14.

36. Ibid., 240.

37. U.S. Congress, House, *Affairs in the Indian Department*, ii.

38. Ibid., 62.

39. "Indian Affairs," *New York Times*, August 13, 1875.

40. U.S. Congress, House, *Affairs in the Indian Department*, 62.

41. William Welsh to Lewis Henry Morgan, March 20, 1873, Morgan Papers, RRL-UR. For more on Parker's marriage, see Genetin-Pilawa, "'All Intent on Seeing the White Woman Married to the Red Man.'"

42. John D. Lang to Vincent Colyer, April 12, 1870, Records of the Board of Indian Commissioners, Letters Received, 1870–1872, Box 1, RG 75, NARA.

43. Nathan Bishop to Vincent Colyer, January 18, 1872, Records of the Board of Indian Commissioners, Letters Received, 1870–1872, Box 2, RG 75, NARA.

44. U.S. Census Bureau, "Population Schedules, 1870," Philadelphia, Ward 7, District 18, Philadelphia, Pennsylvania, NARA Microfilm Publication M593, Roll 1392, p. 239A, NARA, http://search.ancestrylibrary.com/cgibin/sse.dll?h=2877828&db=1870usfedcen&indiv=try (accessed July 20, 2011). The history of domestic labor in the United States is a fascinating topic and the subject of an ever-growing literature. For an overview, see Sutherland, *Americans and their Servants*. For a recent study of Irish domestic workers in the United States, see Lynch-Brennan, *Irish Bridget*. For a similar issue in the South, see Sharpless, *Cooking in Other Women's Kitchens*. For more on racial/ethnic prejudices against Irish immigrants, see Ignatiev, *How the Irish Became White*.

45. U.S. Congress, House, Committee on Appropriations, *Investigation into Indian Affairs*, 114.

46. *Congressional Globe*, 41st Cong., 2nd sess., 1870, 4080.

47. Ibid., 4079, 4082.

48. See Skocpol, *Protecting Soldiers and Mothers*.

49. *Congressional Globe*, 41st Cong., 2nd sess., 1870, 4087–88.

50. Ibid., 4083–84.

51. William Welsh to Vincent Colyer, April 29, 1871, Records of the Board of Indian Commissioners, Letters Received, 1870–1872, Box 1, RG 75, NARA.

52. Robert Campbell to Felix Brunot, May 21, 1871, Records of the Board of Indian Commissioners, Letters Received, 1870–1872, Box 2, RG 75, NARA.

53. George Stuart to Ely S. Parker, May 26, 1871, Records of the Board of Indian Commissioners, Letters Received, 1870–1872, Box 2, RG 75, NARA.

54. Ely S. Parker to Vincent Colyer, April 22, 1871, Letters Sent by the Office of Indian Affairs, January 3–March 23, 1871, vol. 99, 423, RG 75, NARA.

55. Armstrong, *Warrior in Two Camps*, 160.

56. U.S. Congress, House, Committee on Appropriations, *Investigation into Indian Affairs*, vi–vii.

57. "The Recent Change in the Indian Bureau," *Nation*, August 17, 1871, 100–101.

58. "Resignation of Gen. Parker as Indian Commissioner," *New York Times*, July 18, 1871.

59. The editors at the *Nation* and William Welsh both supported Brunot as the replacement candidate. See Keller, *American Protestantism*, 84.

60. Interior Secretary Columbus Delano to Felix Brunot, January 12, 1872, Letters Sent by the Indian Division of the Office of the Secretary of the Interior, vol. 10: Miscellaneous, May 3, 1870–April 8, 1872, 371–72, RG 75, NARA. See also Keller, *American Protestantism*, 84–86.

61. Keller, "Episcopal Reformers," 116–26, 122–25. See also Keller, *American Protestantism*, 86–93. The Department of the Interior published numerous reports related to the BIC's efforts to repress policy alternatives in the 1870s. In particular see U.S. Department of the Interior, *Documents Relating to the Charges of Professor O. C. Marsh, Statement of Affairs at the Red Cloud Agency*, and *Report of Commission Appointed by the Secretary of the Interior*.

62. U.S. Congress, House, *Letter from the Secretary of War*, 2.

63. In his study of global colonial state development, *Seeing Like a State* (2–7, 343), James C. Scott describes the components of state projects that ultimately failed to help the people for whom they were designed. His observations have influenced my understanding of the allotment program in important ways. First, Scott states that all of these failed projects began with the process of finding "legibility," that is, "a state's attempt to make a society legible, to arrange the population in ways that simplified the classic state functions of taxation, conscription, and prevention of rebellion." He noted that problems arose in states where the population became legible and the state valued a "high modernist" ideology, one that demonstrated a "version of self-confidence about scientific and technical progress . . . the mastery of nature (including human nature), and, above all, the rational design of social order commensurate with the scientific understanding of natural laws." If such a state was "willing and able to use the full weight of its coercive power to bring these high-modernist designs into being," and if the society under scrutiny lacked "the capacity to resist these plans," then the state-run project was likely to fail. One would be hard-pressed to find a more accurate description of the coercive assimilation reformers in the late 1860s and 1870s. The history of Indian affairs demonstrates that the work these men carried out during the peace policy era effectively drew to a close a moment when alternate frameworks for Indian policymaking were possible and that the program they established instead led to decades of suffering among Indian communities.

64. Keller, *American Protestantism*, 15.

65. Letter from Christopher Columbus Andrews, Minister to Sweden, to E. B. Washburne Minister of the United States in Paris, May 25, 1870, forwarded to Ely S. Parker, Miscellaneous Letters, Ayer MS 22, Ayer Collection, NL.

66. "The Recent Change in the Indian Bureau," *Nation*, August 17, 1871, 100.

CHAPTER SIX

1. "To Churchmen," *Council Fire* 1 (January 1878): 3.

2. The act itself was the result of a lengthy legislative evolution that began much earlier. An earlier version of the allotment program was embodied in the Coke Bill, legislation introduced

by Senator Richard Coke in 1880, 1882, and 1884. Dawes revised the bill and reintroduced the legislation in 1886, and it passed in 1887. At several points after 1887 the program was amended, significantly in 1891 and 1906. These amendments applied the program to additional reservations previously excluded from its jurisdiction and allowed Indian people to legally lease their allotments to non-Native people. The latter development seemingly undercut the law's ability to encourage Native farming.

3. Richardson, *West from Appomattox*, 2–3.

4. Ibid., 4–5.

5. Senier, "Allotment Protest," 422. See also Senier's *Voices of American Indian Assimilation*, in which he asserts that some of the most significant critics of coercive assimilation were Native women writers.

6. In his seminal study *American Indian Policy*, Francis Prucha argues that the "harmony that marked the Lake Mohonk conferences was based on a common philanthropic and humanitarian outlook expressed in Christian terms, for the reform organizations represented there had a strong religious orientation." Prucha frames this movement within the larger context of nineteenth-century evangelism, asserting that the "decades at the end of the century in which Indian reform flourished were marked by an intensification of the desire on the part of zealous evangelicals to create a 'righteous empire' in America, and the Indians were caught up in that thrust." He adds, "Only a few men spoke out [against these organizations] . . . and they were quickly overwhelmed" (147). See also Prucha, *Great Father*, and Prucha, *Americanizing the American Indian*, 8. The idea that the reformers were "well-intentioned" runs throughout this literature. In the 1930s, two books began this trend. In the first, D. S. Otis (*Dawes Act*) asserts that it was not private interests that motivated the development of the allotment program, but rather that it came out of the idealism of Congress and the reformers who wished to protect and "civilize" Indians. J. P. Kinney (*Continent Lost*) argues that the late-nineteenth-century reform policy represented the culmination of two hundred years of efforts to assimilate and "civilize" the Indians. Henry Fritz (*Movement for Indian Assimilation*) suggests that there were some conflicts during that Lake Mohonk Conference, but these involved the timetable and intensity of coercive assimilation plans, not the coercive/assimilative ideology itself. In his book *Assault on Indian Tribalism*, Wilcomb Washburn is not as kind to the humanitarians, arguing that when the allotment program failed, they focused blame on the settlers who pressured the government to divest Indians of their land base and OIA officials who were unable to oversee the allotment process carefully. He concludes that it was actually the overzealous reformers and policymakers who should be blamed for the choices and judgments they made.

7. In his organizational history of the Indian Rights Association, William Hagan writes that once the allotment campaign began in earnest, it "was only a matter of time until some sort of severalty bill would be enacted into law" (*Indian Rights Association*, 37, 66).

8. Benjamin Johnson, "Red Populism?," 15–37, 18.

9. Ibid., 20.

10. Historian Frederick Hoxie represents an exception to this interpretation. He notes that the reformers of the 1880s "bore a surface similarity to the antislavery groups of the 1840s and 1850s and to the previous decade's peace policy advocates." He asserts that like "their predecessors they campaigned for 'equal rights' for Native Americans and declared that they were driven by a sense of Christian mission." He also argues that many of the reformers framed their ideas within an almost "proto-progressive" framework that recognized that society was becoming increasingly interdependent and Indians would no longer be able to remain isolated. However, like Prucha, Hoxie also suggests that the reformers "were marked by a minimum of

factionalism and a general willingness to shape contrasting interests into common proposals." See Hoxie, *Final Promise*, 11–13. In his study of Indian policy reform, Robert Mardock (*Reformers and the American Indian*) also focuses on the similarities between these reformers and the antislavery advocates before them. Like Prucha, he also asserts that a kind of social gospel motivated their actions and shaped their philosophies. Hoxie is clearly influenced by Robert Wiebe's modernization thesis that posits that the development of the United States in this period as an evolution from "island communities" to a coherent nation. For more, see Wiebe, *Search for Order*. Additionally, Alan Trachtenberg, who suggests that the process of "incorporation" was broader than industrial and business organization, influences my thinking here. The reformers who debated one another in this period were part of "the emergence of a changed, more tightly structured society with new hierarchies of control, and also changed conceptions of that society, of America itself" (Trachtenberg, *Incorporation of America*, 3–4).

11. My assertion here fits well with Heather Cox Richardson's recent work. She argues that the emerging middle-class ideologues of the late nineteenth century "deliberately repressed anyone who called for government action to level the American economic, social, or political playing field" (Richardson, *West from Appomattox*, 7).

12. Haller, *Medical Protestants*, xv. See also Haller, *Profile in Alternative Medicine*.

13. For a very brief sketch of Cora Bland's life, see Pollack, *Woman Walking Ahead*, 67–68. She was most often referred to as "M. Cora" or simply "Cora."

14. Advertisements for these products ran in issues of the *Council Fire* throughout the 1880s.

15. Benjamin Johnson, "Red Populism?," 18. My analysis of Bland's reform interests owes a considerable debt to Johnson's article. He persuasively argues that it is important to understand Indian policy reformers within a larger context, and I agree wholeheartedly.

16. Bland, *Farming as a Profession*, *How to Grow Rich*, and *Life of Benjamin Butler*. See also Behrens, "In Defense of 'Poor Lo,'" 79. He also published a short biography of the Greenback Party members of Congress in 1879 titled *The Spartan Band*.

17. Bland, *Reign of Monopoly*, 10. Darby also published the *Council Fire*.

18. For more on the National Greenback Party, see Irwin Unger, *Greenback Era*, and Ritter, *Goldbugs and Greenbacks*.

19. See also Behrens, "In Defense of 'Poor Lo,'" 80. For more on the significance of railroads in U.S. history, see Stover, *American Railroads*; Kolko, *Railroads and Regulations*; Sarah Gordon, *Passage to Union*; Welke, *Recasting American Liberty*; and White, *Railroaded*.

20. See Behrens, "In Defense of 'Poor Lo,'" 80. See also Bland, *People's Party Shot and Shell*.

21. For more on populism, see Goodwyn, *Democratic Promise*.

22. Unfortunately there is no extant collection of Thomas or Cora Bland papers. There is a brief biography in the introduction to his edited volume titled *Pioneers of Progress* (1906), penned by Rev. H. W. Thomas, D.D. (pp. 10–15). There is also some biographical information in Behrens, "In Defense of 'Poor Lo,'" 78–81. See also Cowger, "Dr. Thomas A. Bland."

23. Meacham described the attack in his lecture "The Tragedy of the Lava Beds," reprinted in Bland, *Life of Alfred B. Meacham*.

24. Memo, September 21, 1873, Meacham Papers, quoted in Phinney, "Alfred B. Meacham," 228. See also Behrens, "In Defense of 'Poor Lo,'" 63–65, and Bland, *Life of Alfred B. Meacham*, 42. Meacham wanted to serve as legal counsel for his attackers because he believed that the government had put them in a position where there was no other option than violence.

25. Behrens, "In Defense of 'Poor Lo,'" 59. See also Phinney, "Alfred B. Meacham," 109–10.

26. Phinney, "Alfred B. Meacham," 221.

27. Cowger, "Dr. Thomas A. Bland," 78.

28. Behrens, "In Defense of 'Poor Lo,'" 80.

29. Ibid., 69–77. For more on the Ponca issue, see Mathes and Lowitt, *Standing Bear Controversy*. In it the authors argued that it was this event that helped to spark the intensified movement for Indian reform in the late nineteenth century and that rather than the eastern humanitarians, who are usually interpreted as the leaders of this movement, it was the western lawyers and policymakers who provided much of the early leadership and ideas.

30. M. Cora Bland, "From Savage Life to Civilization," *Council Fire* 2 (October 1878): 150.

31. "Indian Rights Associations," *Council Fire* 6 (June 1883): 84. See also Cowger, "Dr. Thomas A. Bland," 79.

32. "Indian Rights Associations," *Council Fire* 6 (June 1883): 84

33. For more on McGillycuddy, see the biography written by his second wife, McGillycuddy, *McGillycuddy Agent*.

34. Ostler, *Plains Sioux*, 203.

35. Herbert Welsh to William F. Vilas, July 3, 1888, IRAP, Series 1-C, Reel 69, January 25, 1888–June 8, 1889.

36. Hagan, *Indian Rights Association*, 28. See also Herbert Welsh, *Report of a Visit to the Sioux Reserve*, IRAP, Series 2, Subseries A, Reel 102.

37. Pollack, *Woman Walking Ahead*, 71.

38. Thomas A. Bland, "Our Visit to Red Cloud and His People," *Council Fire* 7 (July–August 1884): 97.

39. Ostler, *Plains Sioux*, 207.

40. Ibid.

41. McGillycuddy, *McGillycuddy Agent*, 222.

42. "The Dakota Sioux," newspaper article, Special File 264: Ejection of T. A. Bland from the Pine Ridge Reservation by V. T. McGillycuddy, 1882–1885, Special Files of the Office of Indian Affairs, 1807–1904, Roll 73, RG 75, NARA.

43. Ibid. In McGillycuddy, *McGillycuddy Agent*, he is quoted him as saying that they "were talking about the Indian country where affairs had to be handled according to a code of their own" (223).

44. Ibid., 224. Bland's wife, Cora, played a crucial role in the development of Thomas's and the NIDA's ideas about reform. Unfortunately, the historical record provides even less insight into her life and contributions than it does for her husband.

45. McGillycuddy, *McGillycuddy Agent*, 224.

46. Several scholars have also written about this confrontation. See Hyde, *Sioux Chronicle*, 96–99; Olson, *Red Cloud and the Sioux Problem*, 294–95; McGillycuddy, *McGillycuddy Agent*, 221–25; and Cowger, "Dr. Thomas A. Bland," 80–81. There is an extensive file in the National Archives containing documents related to a hearing about these events as well; see Special File 264: Ejection of T. A. Bland from the Pine Ridge Reservation by V. T. McGillycuddy, 1882–1885, Special Files of the Office of Indian Affairs, 1807–1904, Roll 73, RG 75, NARA. Bland's quote comes from a newspaper article in the file.

47. Ostler, *Plains Sioux*, 208–9.

48. *Springfield Republican*, September 7, 1884, reprinted as a pamphlet, Dawes, *Case of McGillycuddy*.

49. "The Indian Rights Association: Is The Name A Misnomer?," *Council Fire* 8 (April 1885): 49.

50. "The National Indian Defense Association," *Council Fire* 8 (December 1885): 174.

51. Ibid., 173; "Truth and Justice Must Triumph," *Council Fire* 9 (February 1886): 21.

52. "The National Indian Defense Association," *Council Fire* 8 (December 1885): 175.

53. "Constitution of the National Indian Defense Association," *Council Fire* 8 (December 1885): 176.

54. "Why Not Profit by Experience?," *Council Fire* 8 (January 1885): 1.

55. "Shall We Now Adopt a Wise Indian Policy?," *Council Fire* 9 (July 1886): 102.

56. "Why Not Profit by Experience?," *Council Fire* 8 (January 1885): 1.

57. George Manypenny, "How the Delawares Were Disinherited," *Council Fire* 9 (January 1886): 1–5.

58. Ibid.

59. "Intemperate and Ill-Directed Zeal," *Council Fire* 8 (September 1885): 122.

60. "Meeting of the Indian Commissioners," *Council Fire* 8 (February 1885): 20.

61. "Then and Now: A Review of Indian Policies," *Council Fire* 12 (December 1889): 100.

62. "The Mohonk Platform," *Council Fire* 8 (November 1885): 157. See also "Status of the Indians, Political and Proprietary," *Council Fire* 9 (October 1886), in which Bland stated, "Our first duty toward the Indian is to do what we have engaged to perform towards him. Having done this we may do him all the good in our power. To disregard the right of another in order to force upon him that which we regard for his good and against his inclinations is of the worst form of tyranny, usually blended with hypocrisy" (136).

63. A. J. Willard, "A Brief of Objections to the Sioux Bill," *Council Fire* 9 (June 1886): 90.

64. Ibid., 94.

65. Ibid. See also Behrens, "Forgotten Challengers to Severalty," 135.

66. "The Mohonk Platform," *Council Fire* 8 (November 1885): 157.

67. A. J. Willard, "A Brief of Objections to the Sioux Bill," *Council Fire* 9 (June 1886).

68. "Discussing the Dawes Sioux Bill," *Council Fire* 9 (March 1886): 38–39.

69. Ibid.

70. Ibid.

71. Ostler, *Plains Sioux*, 209.

72. "Agent McGillycuddy Removed from Office," *Council Fire* 9 (June 1886): 86.

73. Ostler, *Plains Sioux*, 210–11.

74. Alexander Kent, "An Address to the Friends of Justice," *Council Fire* 10 (March 1887): 37.

75. Ibid., 38.

76. "Discussing the Dawes Sioux Bill," *Council Fire* 9 (March 1886): 39. See also Benjamin Johnson, "Red Populism?," 22.

77. "An Indian on the Allotment Bill," *Council Fire* 9 (June 1886): 96.

78. See also (among others), "Chief Brant's View of Civilization," *Council Fire* 9 (June 1886): 97; "Speech of Col. G. W. Harkins of the Chickasaws," *Council Fire* 9 (February 1886): 23; and "Speech of Chief John Jumper of the Seminoles," *Council Fire* 9 (February 1886): 24.

79. "Annual Conference of Indian Commissioners," *Council Fire* 10 (February 1887): 21.

80. W. C. Lykins, Peoria Chief, to Herbert Welsh, October 18, 1886, IRAP, Series 1-A, Reel 2. See also C. C. Painter to Herbert Welsh, February 16, 1887, IRAP, Series I-C, Reel 68: March 1886–January 25, 1888.

81. "Names of Members," *Council Fire* 9 (November–December 1886): 157–58.

82. Benjamin Johnson, "Red Populism?," 22–23.

83. "Misrepresenting the President's Policy," *Council Fire* 10 (January 1887): 10.

84. Behrens, "Forgotten Challengers to Severalty," 153 n. 5. See also "Annual Meeting of the N.I.D.A.," *Council Fire* 10 (February 1887): 18.

85. For IRA numbers, see Hagan, *Indian Rights Association*, 45, 47. See also Prucha, *American Indian Policy*, 142. Prucha states that even by 1892 the IRA had only 1,300 members nationwide, but he also notes that even though the membership numbers were low, IRA founder Herbert Welsh was able to appeal to a wide audience through the media.

86. "The Sinews of War Are Needed," *Council Fire* 10 (February 1887): 27.

87. "Agent McGillycuddy Removed from Office," *Council Fire* 9 (June 1886): 86.

88. "Conference of Indian Commissioners," *Council Fire* 9 (February 1886): 28.

89. Behrens, "In Defense of 'Poor Lo,'" 187–88.

90. "The General Severalty Bill . . .," *Council Fire* 9 (May 1886): 74. See also Behrens, "In Defense of 'Poor Lo,'" 188; "Senator Dawes' Bill to Allot Lands . . .," *Council Fire* 9 (March 1886): 48–49, "There Is at This Date . . .," *Council Fire* 9 (July 1886): 110; "A History of the Policy of Coercion," *Council Fire* 10 (December 1887): 92; and Hagan, *Indian Rights Association*, 65.

91. Behrens, "In Defense of 'Poor Lo,'" 189. See also "Opposing the Dawes Bill," *Council Fire* 9 (April 1886): 55–60, and "There Is at This Date . . .," *Council Fire* 9 (July 1886): 110.

92. "Miss Bonwill's Talk with the President," *Council Fire* 9 (December 1886): 160.

CHAPTER SEVEN

1. The reform ideology of the Indian Rights Association can best be understood as a combination of traditional internal colonialism that involved economic exploitation and political domination with elements of a "social control" mind-set. For an excellent discussion of the viability of internal colonialism as an analytic concept in studying Indigenous history in the United States, see Linda Gordon, "Internal Colonialism and Gender." For two recent examples of scholarship that use the social control concept to explain social reform in the late nineteenth and early twentieth centuries, see McGerr, *Fierce Discontent*, and Stromquist, *Reinventing "The People."* Earlier scholarship has also portrayed progressives as social conservatives or "corporate liberals," including Hayes, "Politics of Reform," and Kolko, *Triumph of Conservatism*. Other scholarship has presented many of the shortcomings of Progressives, including their racist, imperialist, and sexist orientations. See Bederman, *Manliness and Civilization*, and Matthew Jacobson, *Barbarian Virtues*.

2. Thinking about Welsh and the IRA as part of a longer, broader continuum of progressive thought is one of the ways that this project helps contribute to a larger historiographic reconsideration. In particular, I find arguments against distinctly demarcating the Gilded Age from the Progressive Era to be compelling and prefer to think about a Long Progressive Era. For more, see Edwards, "Politics."

3. For more on the history of interest-group lobbying, see Clemens, *People's Lobby*. Clemens's work typifies some of the most interesting work being done in the American political development school of political science and she has been heavily influenced by the work of Theda Skocpol and Stephen Skowronek. Clemens argues that in the late nineteenth century, interests were able to assert more influence because they changed their "organizational repertoires." They became less radical in their demands and more willing to compromise. They advocated specific policy reforms, monitored the behaviors of policymakers, and educated their membership on how to vote. The Indian Rights Association fit this description; however, it made these innovations prior to the agricultural, labor, and women's lobbyist groups that Clemens discusses in her study.

4. Hagan, *Indian Rights Association*, 2–3.

5. Ibid., 4–5. For more on the significance of the Centennial Exhibition, see Rydell, *All the World's a Fair*. Rydell argues that world's fairs and expositions serve as clear representations of America's imperial interests. It is interesting to note that Herbert's father served a leading role in the creation of the Philadelphia exposition, as it was the first in this tradition. It is not surprising that, between his father's influence and the influence of his uncle William, Herbert approached Indian policy from a perspective that supported settler colonialism and coercive assimilation.

6. Hagan, *Indian Rights Association*, 6–7; Prucha, *American Indian Policy*, 138–39.

7. Herbert Welsh, *Four Weeks*, 29.

8. Welsh, *Four Weeks*, 30–31.

9. Pancoast, *Impressions of the Sioux Tribes*, 6. The following year, Pancoast published a second pamphlet espousing very similar ideas, although he added that making Indians full and immediate citizens of the United States would help to terminate the different legal status that he believed was such a hindrance. See Pancoast, *Indian Before the Law*, 8–9 and 21.

10. Prucha, *American Indian Policy*, 139. See also *Constitution and By-Laws of the Indian Rights Association*, IRAP, Series 2, Subseries A, Reel 102, 3.

11. Hagan, *Indian Rights Association*, 17.

12. Ibid., 18–19; Prucha, *American Indian Policy*, 139–40.

13. Painter to Armstrong, April 25, 1883, in Armstrong Papers, quoted in Hagan, *Indian Rights Association*, 21. Eileen Pollack mentions this anecdote in her biography as well. See *Woman Walking Ahead*, 67.

14. Hagan, *Indian Rights Association*, 23. At this time the IRA also hired Matthew Sniffen, a seventeen-year-old Philadelphian, to serve as clerk at its main office. Sniffen was a very talented organizational manager, and it is because of his painstaking work that scholars today have access to a complete file of the organization's records (which comprises 136 reels of microfilm).

15. *Constitution and By-Laws of the Indian Rights Association*, IRAP, Series 2, Subseries A, Reel 102, 4, 7.

16. *What the Indian Rights Association Is Doing*, IRAP, Series 2, Subseries A, Reel 102, 2.

17. *Second Annual Address to the Public of the Lake Mohonk Conference . . . In Behalf of the Civilization and Legal Protection of the Indians of the United States* (1884), IRAP, Series 2, Subseries A, Reel 102, 6, 3.

18. *What the Indian Rights Association Is Doing*, IRAP, Series 2, Subseries A, Reel 102, 2; *The First Annual Report of the Executive Committee of the Indian Rights Association*, IRAP, Series 2, Subseries A, Reel 102, and Subseries C, Reel 103, 6.

19. *What the Indian Rights Association Is Doing*, IRAP, Series 2, Subseries A, Reel 102, 2. See also Hagan, *Indian Rights Association*, 83–87.

20. *What the Indian Rights Association Is Doing*, IRAP, Series 2, Subseries A, Reel 102, 2.

21. David Wilkins, *American Indian Sovereignty*, 68–69.

22. For more on sovereignty issues, see Wilkins and Lomawaima, *Uneven Ground*, in which the authors argue that tribal sovereignty had been firmly established in legislative, juridical, and constitutional precedents. See also Norgren, *Cherokee Cases*, and Harring, *Crow Dog's Case*. Harring argues that in the late nineteenth century, Indian communities experienced a comprehensive assault on tribal sovereignty and self-government that included the passage of the Major Crimes Act of 1885, the establishment of Indian police by reservation agents, the creation of courts and codes of offenses by the OIA, and the Dawes Act itself.

23. As in chapter 5, my thinking is influenced by Heather Cox Richardson's recent work, *West from Appomattox*, 344–45.

24. *The Indian Rights Association* (1884), IRAP, Series 2, Subseries A, Reel 102, 1.

25. *Synopsis of Three Bills Advocated* (1886), IRAP, Series 2, Subseries A, Reel 102, 1.

26. Indian Rights Association to President of the United States, Grover Cleveland, June 14, 1885, IRAP, Series 1-A, Reel 1.

27. Economic interest and political domination are the key elements of internal colonialism, and the IRA's program, as well as its supporters, demonstrated this quite clearly. In a recent article, "Internal Colonialism and Gender," historian Linda Gordon describes internal colonialism as an analytical concept first developed by Lenin and Gramsci. For these theorists, "it came to characterize intersecting economic exploitation and political exclusion of a subordinated group that differed racially or ethnically from the dominant group: and all this within a polity rather than across oceans or borders" (427–28). Gordon adds that this concept is a metaphor that focuses on the "similarities between classical colonialism[,] in which countries of the global north occupied and exploited 'Third World' developing regions and peoples[,] and international relations of domination in which exploitation coincided with racism and national chauvinism" (428). This concept draws attention to the role racism played in the creation of cheap labor, or in this case, cheap and easy access to natural resources (i.e., land, oil reserves, minerals, etc.). In other words, it demonstrates the ways in which racism is at its most basic level an economic phenomenon. While many scholars abandoned this concept in the face of newer trends in social and cultural analysis, more recently a literature has emerged that attempts to revive and refashion these ideas to incorporate newer interpretive schema. For a broader discussion of the history and development of this concept, see ibid. and Hind, "Internal Colonial Concept." For a discussion of how this concept can be applied to Native American history, see Cardell Jacobson, "Internal Colonialism and Native Americans." For a more recent effort to apply this concept to Native American history in a comparative framework, see Strobel, "Contested Grounds."

28. B. J. Templeton, President of the Pierre Board of Trade (Dakota) to Herbert Welsh, October 20, 1886, IRAP, Series 4, Reel 133, August 1877–July 1900.

29. See *Synopsis of Three Bills Advocated* (1886), IRAP, Series 2, Subseries A, Reel 102.

30. For more on Lake Mohonk, see Prucha, *American Indian Policy*, 143–44. See also Prucha, *Americanizing the American Indians*; Burgess, "We'll Discuss It at Mohonk"; Hoxie, *Final Promise*, 12; and Prucha, *Great Father*, chap. 24.

31. These organizations often held joint conferences in addition to attending the Lake Mohonk affairs. See Circular, *Resolutions Passed at a Joint Conference of the Board of Indian Commissioners, Indian Rights Association, Woman's National Indian Association . . .* (1885), IRAP, Series 2, Subseries A, Reel 102. The WNIA, founded by Amelia Stone Quinton and Mary Bonney, played a significant role in the intensification of Indian policy reform efforts in the 1870s and 1880s. For more, see Mathes and Lowitt, *Standing Bear Controversy*. For a brief history of the organization, see Mathes, "Nineteenth-Century Women and Reform," and Wanken, "Woman's Sphere and Indian Reform."

32. For more, see Hagan, *Indian Rights Association*, 36–37. The IRA often republished in pamphlet form newspaper articles written by Elaine Goodale Eastman and distributed them to other reformers and legislators. See, for example, Eastman, *The Senator and the School-House*, IRAP, Series 2, Subseries A, Reel 102 (originally published in the *New York Independent*, March 4, 1886). Pratt occasionally vacillated in his support of the organization because he did not agree with the IRA's stance on reservation schools.

33. In his article "The End of the Savage," historian Frederick Hoxie writes that between "1880 and 1900 the Senate was probably the most influential branch of American government, and its members among the most accomplished politicians of their day" (158).

34. *The Second Annual Report of the Executive Committee of the Indian Rights Association* (Philadelphia, 1885), IRAP, Series 2, Subseries A, Reel 102, and Subseries C, Reel 103, 12. The IRA frequently published and circulated pamphlets that either summarized or reprinted full articles from several prominent newspapers. See, for example, *The Opinions of the Press on the Need of Legislation for Indians by the Present Congress*, IRAP, Series 2, Subseries A, Reel 102.

35. *The First Annual Report of the Executive Committee of the Indian Rights Association*, IRAP, Series 2, Subseries A, Reel 102, and Subseries C, Reel 103, 9.

36. Henry Dawes, *The Case of McGillycuddy*, IRAP, Series 2, Subseries A, Reel 102, and Subseries C, Reel 103 (originally published in the *Springfield Republican*, August 7, 1884).

37. Herbert Welsh, *The Indian Problem*, IRAP, Series 2, Subseries A, Reel 102, and Subseries C, Reel 103 (originally published in the *Boston Herald*, December 27, 1886).

38. Herbert Welsh, *Friendship That Asks for Pay*, IRAP, Series 2, Subseries A, Reel 102, and Subseries C, Reel 103 (originally published in the *New York Tribune*, March 13, 1887). See also "Allotment of Lands. Defense of the Dawes Indian Severalty Bill," IRAP, Series 2, Subseries A, Reel 102, and Subseries C, Reel 103 (originally published in the *Boston Post*, April 6, 1887).

39. C. C. Painter, *The Dawes Land in Severalty Bill and Indian Emancipation*, IRAP, Series 2, Subseries A, Reel 102, and Subseries C, Reel 103.

40. Behrens, "In Defense of 'Poor Lo,'" 76.

41. IRA, *Allotment of Lands*, 4.

42. Thomas Bland, "Injustice Sustained by Falsehood," *Council Fire* 10 (April–May 1887): 59.

43. Ibid, 60.

44. For more on the IRA's manipulations of the press in an effort to frame its opponents as unreasonable or otherwise dangerous, see Behrens, "In Defense of 'Poor Lo,'" 199.

45. Thomas Bland, "Injustice Sustained by Falsehood," *Council Fire* 10 (April–May 1887): 57.

46. C. C. Painter to Herbert Welsh, December 11, 1885, IRAP, Series 1-A, Reel 1. A "grip sack" was a small piece of luggage or a handbag. For more on Sarah Winnemucca and her criticism of coercive assimilation, see Senier, *Voices of American Indian Assimilation and Resistance*, and Zanjani, *Sarah Winnemucca*. For more on Painter's characterization of Sarah Winnemucca, see Hagan, *Indian Rights Association*, 85–86.

47. Hiram Chase to Herbert Welsh, May 27, 1886, IRAP, Series 4, Reel 133, August 1877–July 1900. For more on Alice Fletcher, see Mark, *Stranger in Her Native Land*, and Tong, *Susan La Flesche Picotte*.

48. J. D. C. Atkins, Commissioner of Indian Affairs, to James McLaughlin, Indian Agent, Standing Rock Agency, September 27, 1886, IRAP, Series 1-A, Reel 2.

49. Secretary of the Interior Lamar to Herbert Welsh, February 25, 1886, IRAP, Series 1-A, Reel 1. For a similar exchange, see Frank Wood to Herbert Welsh, March 10, 1887, ibid.

50. Hoxie, "End of the Savage," 165.

51. Prucha, *American Indian Policy*, 167–68.

52. "How Shall the Indians Hold Their Lands?," *Council Fire* 8 (October 1885): 139.

53. A. J. Willard, "The Dawes Land-in-Severalty Bill," *Council Fire* 10 (January 1887): 13.

54. A. J. Willard, "Indian Jurisdiction After Division in Severalty," *Council Fire* 12 (March 1889): 46–47.

55. *Constitution and By-Laws of the Indian Rights Association*, IRAP, Series 2, Subseries A, Reel 102, 3.

56. The Pendleton Act established the U.S. Civil Service Commission and is understood to be the official end of patronage politics. The impetus for this legislation was Garfield's assassination by Charles Guiteau, a disgruntled office-seeker. However, it is also important to note that many politicians initially criticized the law.

57. For more, see Hagan, *Indian Rights Association*, 81–82, 113–14. That Welsh sought out allies among editors is significant in that it fit nicely with the IRA's tactic of using and controlling the media.

58. Ibid., 81.

59. *Address of Herbert Welsh, Corresponding Secretary of the Indian Rights Association, Delivered before the Mohonk Indian Conference, October 14th, 1886*, IRAP, Series 2, Subseries A, Reel 102, 2–4.

60. General R. H. Milroy to Herbert Welsh, September 17, 1885, IRAP, Series 1-A, Reel 1.

61. Hagan, *Indian Rights Association*, 88–89.

62. Welsh, *A Sketch of the History of Civil Service Reform in England and in the United States*, IRAP, Series 2, Subseries A, Reel 102, 6. Welsh also supported V. T. McGillycuddy wholeheartedly. Prior to his removal, McGillycuddy sent a letter to Welsh outlining some of the actions the OIA had taken at his agency, including removing his school superintendent and matron. He stated that they were "New Englanders," seemingly a compliment that Welsh would have understood. The replacement superintendent, he stated, was "a single man" and "a good democrat," seemingly questioning his background; similarly, he asserted that the new matron was from the "solid south" and the daughter of an "ex-guerilla." He also mentioned that he had been sent a new assistant teacher who, "half-demented," wandered "around the building talking to herself." See V. T. McGillycuddy to Herbert Welsh, September 17, 1886, IRAP, Series 1-A, Reel 2.

63. For more on the civil service in U.S. history and civil service reform, see Ronald Johnson, *Federal Civil Service System*; Ingraham, *Foundation of Merit*; and Schultz and Moranto, *Politics of Civil Service Reform*.

64. Herbert Welsh, "The Meaning of the Dakota Outbreak," *Scribner's Magazine* 9 (1891): 439–52, 440, 441.

65. Ibid., 452. See also Benjamin Johnson, "Red Populism?," 29–30.

66. Painter, *Proceedings of the Seventh Annual Meeting of the Lake Mohonk Conference of Friends of the Indian* (1889), 84–89. This source is part of an edited collection of documents of the Friends. See Prucha, *Americanizing the American Indian*, 114–21.

67. Painter, *Dawes Land in Severalty Bill*.

68. See Leonard Carlson, *Indians, Bureaucrats, and Lands*, and Greenwald, *Reconfiguring the Reservation*.

69. For more on Welsh's other reform interests, see Hagan, *Indian Rights Association*, 49, 98.

70. "The Bill to Allot Lands," *Council Fire* 9 (March 1886): 48.

71. "Senator Dawes' Bill," *Council Fire* 9 (March 1886): 49.

72. "The General Severalty Bill," *Council Fire* 9 (May 1886): 74; "The Mohonk Platform for 1886," *Council Fire* 9 (November–December 1886): 158.

73. "The Indian Severalty Bill," *Council Fire* 10 (January 1887): 6.

74. For a clear and concise account of these events, see Behrens, "Forgotten Challengers," 142–46.

75. Hoxie, "End of the Savage," 169.

76. For more on the military campaigns against western Indian nations and the settlement of the western territories, see Utley, *Indian Frontier*; Utley, *Frontier Regulars*; Wooster, *Military and*

United States Indian Policy; Wooster, *Nelson A. Miles*; Buecker, *Fort Robinson*; and McChristian, *Fort Bowie*. In 1865–66, the plan to annex Canada played a key role in the development of the confederation movement in Canada. In 1866, an annexation bill even passed the House of Representatives. For more on Canadian confederation, see Martin, *Britain and the Origins of Canadian Confederation*; Moore, *1867*; and Vaughan, *Canadian Federalist Experiment*. For more on U.S. involvement in Latin America and the Caribbean in the post–Civil War era, see Nelson, *Almost a Territory*; Topik, *Trade and Gunboats*; Webb, *Impassioned Brothers*; Healy, *James G. Blaine*; John Johnson, *Hemisphere Apart*; and Holden and Zolov, *Latin America and the United States*. For more on the colonization of Hawaii, see Coffman, *Nation Within*, and Silva, *Aloha Betrayed*. For more general studies of American imperialism in this time period, see Paolino, *Foundations of American Empire*, and LaFeber, *New Empire*.

77. For more on this idea of openness to experimental policy reforms, see Rodgers, *Atlantic Crossings*.

78. "A History of the Policy of Coercion," *Council Fire* 10 (December 1887): 92.

79. "A Special Word to Our Readers," *Council Fire* 10 (April–May 1887): 66.

80. "Report of Work during the Summer," *Council Fire* 10 (November 1887): 74. See also Behrens, "In Defense of 'Poor Lo,'" 200, and Behrens, "Forgotten Challengers," 151.

81. "Homeward Bound: A Railroad Collision," *Council Fire* 10 (November 1887): 77.

82. Hagan, *Indian Rights Association*, 37.

83. Prucha, *American Indian Policy*, 166, 167.

CONCLUSION

1. For more, see The Brookings Institution, Institute for Government Research, *Problem of Indian Administration*. See also Philip, *John Collier's Crusade*, 90–91; Hoxie, *Final Promise*, 242; and Greenwald, *Reconfiguring the Reservation*, 146. The Dawes Act itself was only one of the methods by which Indians were dispossessed in this period, but the land cessions that also occurred were part of the general framework of dispossession and coercive assimilation.

2. Burke, *From Greenwich Village to Taos*, 46.

3. Kelly, *Assault on Assimilation*, 124–29.

4. Ely S. Parker to Cousin Gayaneshaoh (Harriet Maxwell Converse), ca. 1885, MS 674, Folder 5, Parker Papers, NL.

5. Prucha, *Great Father*, 319–20.

6. For an excellent concise discussion of the Indian Citizenship Act that focuses on the ways it functioned within the larger movement chipping away at tribal sovereignty, see Bruyneel, "Challenging American Boundaries."

7. Philip, *John Collier's Crusade*, 186.

8. Ibid., 133. For more on Collier's background and reform agenda, see Kelly, *Assault on Assimilation*, and Swartz, "Red Atlantis Revisited."

Bibliography

ARCHIVAL MATERIALS

Albany, New York
  New York State Archives
    William Beauchamp Papers
    Ogden Record Book
    Arthur C. Parker Papers
    Ely S. Parker Papers
    Henry Randall Papers
    Alfred B. Street Letters
Buffalo, New York
  Buffalo and Erie County Historical Society Library
    Miscellaneous Folders
    Parker Family Papers
    Seneca Indian Papers
    Writings of Ely S. Parker
Chicago, Illinois
  Newberry Library
    Edward E. Ayer Manuscript Collection (Vault Boxes)
    Miscellaneous Letters (Ayer Collection)
    Ely Samuel Parker Papers
    Ely S. Parker Scrapbooks
    Records of the Board of Indian Commissioners
Philadelphia, Pennsylvania
  American Philosophical Society Library
    Ely S. Parker Papers
Rochester, New York
  Rush Rhees Library, Rare Books, Special Collections, and Preservation,
      University of Rochester
    Lewis Henry Morgan Papers
    Arthur C. Parker Papers
    Ely S. Parker Papers
    Isaac and Amy Post Family Papers
    Post Family Papers
San Marino, California
  Huntington Library
    Ely S. Parker Papers
Springfield, Illinois
  Abraham Lincoln Presidential Library (previously known as the Illinois State
      Historical Library)

Orville H. Browning Papers
William R. Rowley Papers
Washington, D.C.
National Archives and Records Administration
Record Group 48: Records of the Office of the Secretary of the Interior
Record Group 75: Records of the Bureau of Indian Affairs
Record Group 94: Records of the Army Adjutant General
Record Group 107: Records of the Office of the Secretary of War
Record Group 108: Records of the Headquarters of the Army
Record Group 159: Records of the Office of the Inspector General

MICROFILM

Indian Rights Association Papers, 1864–1973 (136 Reels)
Series 1-A, Incoming Correspondence, 1864–1968
Series 1-C, Letterpress Copy Books, 1886–1943
Series 2, Organizational Records, 1882–1968, Subseries A, IRA Pamphlets, 1883–92
Series 2, Organizational Records, 1882–1968, Subseries C, IRA Printed Matter,
    Miscellaneous, 1885–1973
Series 2, Organizational Records, 1882–1968, Subseries D, IRA Annual Reports, 1883–90
Series 2-C, IRA Office Diary, 1884–87
Series 3-B, Printed Matter, 1867–1961
Series 3-C, Indian Organizations, 1879–1967
Series 4, Herbert Welsh Papers, 1877–1934

GOVERNMENT DOCUMENTS

Annual Report of the Commissioner of Indian Affairs. Washington, D.C.: Government
    Printing Office, 1865–1900.
Kappler, Charles J., comp. *Indian Affairs: Laws and Treaties.* 5 vols. Washington, D.C.:
    Government Printing Office, 1903–41.
New York State Legislature. *Laws (Statutes) of the State of New York.* 1777–1851.
U.S. Congress. *Congressional Globe.* 1865–77.
U.S. Congress. House. *Affairs in the Indian Department.* 41st Cong., 3rd sess., 1871, H. Misc.
    Doc. 39.
———. *Letter from the Secretary of War, Addressed to Mr. Schenck, Chairman of the Committee
    on Military Affairs, Transmitting a Report by Colonel Parker on Indian Affairs.* 39th Cong.,
    2nd sess., 1867, H. Misc. Doc. 37.
———. *Memorial of Yearly Meetings of the Society of Friends Relative to the Treatment of the
    Indians.* 40th Cong., 3rd sess., 1869, H. Misc. Doc. 29.
———. *Report of the Peace Commissioners.* 40th Cong., 2nd sess., January 7, 1868, H. Doc. 97
    (Serial 1337).
———. *Testimony Taken Before the Committee on Indian Affairs Concerning the Management of
    the Indian Department.* 44th Cong., 1st sess., 1876, H. Misc. Doc. 167.
U.S. Congress. House. Committee on Appropriations. *Investigation into Indian Affairs, before
    the Committee on Appropriations of the House of Representatives, Argument of N. P.
    Chipman, on Behalf of Hon. E. S. Parker, Commissioner of Indian Affairs.* Washington, D.C.:
    Powell, Ginck, 1871.

U.S. Congress. Senate. *Message of the President of the United States Communicating the Second Annual Report of the Board of Indian Commissioners.* 41st Cong., 3rd sess., 1871, S. Ex. Doc. 39.

U.S. Congress. Senate. Committee on Indian Affairs. *Mass Meeting for the Indians.* 29th Cong., 2nd sess., 1847, S. Doc. 156.

————. *Memorial of Tonawanda.* 29th Cong., 2nd sess., 1847. S. Doc. 156.

————. *Petition of the Tonawanda Band of Seneca Indians.* 29th Cong., 1st sess., April 2, 1846, S. Doc. 273.

U.S. Department of the Interior. *Documents Relating to the Charges of Professor O. C. Marsh on Fraud and Mismanagement at the Red Cloud Agency.* Washington, D.C., 1875.

————. *Report of Commission Appointed by the Secretary of the Interior to Investigate the Charges against Hon. E. P. Smith, the Commissioner of Indian Affairs.* Washington, D.C., 1875.

————. *Report of Honorable E. S. Parker, Commissioner of Indian Affairs, to the Honorable Secretary of the Interior, on the Communication of William Welsh, Esq., Relative to the Management of Indian Affairs.* Washington, D.C.: Joseph L Pearson, Printer, 1870.

————. *A Statement of Affairs at the Red Cloud Agency Made to the President of the United States, by Professor O. C. Marsh.* Washington, D.C.: 1875.

U.S. Statutes at Large.

PERIODICALS

American Indian Life
Boston Herald
Boston Post
Buffalo Courier (Buffalo, N.Y.)
Buffalo Express (Buffalo, N.Y.)
The Congressional Globe
The Council Fire (Washington, D.C.)
Daily News (Batavia, N.Y.)
Frank Leslie's Illustrated Newspaper
  (New York, N.Y.)
The Nation
New York Daily Tribune

New York Evening Express
New York Herald
New York Independent
New York Times
New York Tribune
Scribner's Magazine
Spirit of the Times (Batavia, N.Y.)
Springfield Republican (Springfield, Ill.)
Washington, D.C. Daily Morning Chronicle
Washington, D.C. Evening Star
Washington, D.C. National Republican

JOURNAL ARTICLES AND ESSAYS IN EDITED VOLUMES

Abler, Thomas S. "Friends, Factions, and the Seneca Revolution of 1848." *Niagara Frontier* 21 (1974): 74–79.

————. "Seneca Moieties and Heredity Chieftainships: The Early-Nineteenth-Century Political Organization of an Iroquois Nation." *Ethnohistory* 51, no. 3 (2004): 459–88.

"Alumni Notes." *The Polytechnic* 12, no. 1 (1895): 11.

Anderson, Gary. "Joseph Renville and the Ethos of Biculturalism." In *Being and Becoming Indian: Biographical Studies of North American Frontiers*, edited by James A. Clifton, 59–81. Chicago: Dorsey Press, 1989.

Annella, Sister M. "Some Aspects of Interracial Marriage in Washington, D.C." *Journal of Negro Education* 25, no. 4 (1956): 380–91.

Behrens, Jo Lea Wetherilt. "Forgotten Challengers to Severalty: The National Indian Defense Association and *Council Fire.*" *Chronicles of Oklahoma* 75, no. 2 (1997): 128–59.

Bledstein, Burton. "Introduction: Storytellers of the Middle Class." In *The Middling Sorts: Explorations in the History of the American Middle Class,* edited by Burton Bledstein and Robert Johnston, 1–27. New York: Routledge, 2001.

Briggs, Charles, and Richard Bauman. "'The Foundation of All Future Researches': Franz Boas, George Hunt, Native American Texts, and the Construction of Modernity." *American Quarterly* 51, no. 3 (1999): 479–528.

Brown, D. A. "'One Real American.'" *American History Illustrated* 4, no. 7 (1969): 12–21.

Bruyneel, Kevin. "Challenging American Boundaries: Indigenous People and the 'Gift of U.S. Citizenship.'" *Studies in American Political Development* 18, no. 1 (Spring 2004): 30–43.

Bunin, Martha. "The Quaker Agents of the Kiowa, Comanche, and Wichita Indian Reservation." *Chronicles of Oklahoma* 10, no. 2 (1932): 204–18.

Burgess, Larry. "We'll Discuss It at Mohonk." *Quaker History: The Bulletin of Friends Historical Association* 40 (Spring 1971): 14–28.

Campisi, Jack. "From Stanwix to Canandaigua: National Policy, States' Rights and Indian Land." In *Iroquois Land Claims,* edited by Christopher Vecsey and William A. Sterna, 49–66. Syracuse: Syracuse University Press, 1988.

Carnes, Mark. "Middle-Class Men and the Solace of Fraternal Ritual." In *Meanings for Manhood: Constructions of Masculinity in Victorian America,* edited by Mark C. Carnes and Clyde Griffen, 37–60. Chicago: University of Chicago Press, 1990.

Cayton, Andrew R. L. "'Noble Actors' upon 'the Theatre of Honour': Power and Civility in the Treaty of Greenville." In *Contact Points: American Frontiers from the Mohawk Valley to the Mississippi, 1750–1830,* edited by Andrew R. L. Cayton and Fredricka Teute. Chapel Hill: University of North Carolina Press, 1998.

Collins, Cary. "A Fall from Grace: Sectarianism and the Grant Peace Policy in Western Washington Territory, 1869–1882." *Pacific Northwest Forum* 8, no. 2 (1995): 55–77.

Collins, Patricia. "It's All in the Family: Intersections of Gender, Race, and Nation." *Hypatia* 13, no. 3 (1998): 62–82.

Cooper, Frederick, and Ann Laura Stoler. "Tensions of Empire: Colonial Control and Visions of Rule." *American Ethnologist* 16, no. 4 (November 1989): 609–21.

Cowger, Thomas C. "Dr. Thomas A. Bland, Critic of Forced Assimilation." *American Indian Culture and Research Journal* 16, no. 4 (1992): 77–97.

Curtin, Patricia. "From Pity to Necessity: How National Events Shaped Coverage of the Plains Indian War." *American Journalism* 12, no. 1 (Winter 1995): 3–21.

Cutler, Lee. "Lawrie Tatum and the Kiowa Agency, 1869–1873." *Arizona and the West* 13, no. 3 (1971): 221–44.

Davis, Robert. "Introduction: Lacan and Narration." *Comparative Literature* 98, no. 5 (1983): 848–59.

Deloria, Vine, Jr. "Self-Determination and the Concept of Sovereignty." In *Economic Development in American Indian Reservations,* edited by Roxanne Dunbar Ortiz, 22–28. Albuquerque: University of New Mexico Press, 1979.

Dexter, Ralph W. "Putnam's Problems Popularizing Anthropology." *American Scientist* 54, no. 3 (September 1966): 315–32.

Edwards, Rebecca. "Politics, Social Movements, and the Periodization of U.S. History." *Journal of the Gilded Age and Progressive Era* 8, no. 4 (October 2009): 463–73.

"Ely Samuel Parker: From Sachem to Brigadier General." *New York State and the Civil War* 1, no. 4 (1961): 1–5.

Fenton, William. "Harriet Maxwell Converse." In *Notable American Women, 1607–1950: A Biographical Dictionary*. Vol. 1. Cambridge: Harvard University Press, 1971.

———. "Tonawanda Longhouse Ceremonies: Ninety Years After Lewis Henry Morgan." In *Smithsonian Institution, Bureau of American Ethnology Bulletin 128*. Washington, D.C.: Government Printing Office, 1941.

Fitzgerald, Michael W. "Emancipation and Military Pacification: The Freedmen's Bureau and Social Control in Alabama." In *The Freedmen's Bureau and Reconstruction: Reconsiderations*, edited by Paul Cimbala and Randall M. Miller, 46–62. New York: Fordham University Press, 1999.

Fritz, Henry. "The Making of Grant's Peace Policy." *Chronicles of Oklahoma* 37 (1959–60): 411–32.

Genetin-Pilawa, C. Joseph. "'All Intent on Seeing the White Woman Married to the Red Man': The Parker/Sackett Affair and the Public Spectacle of Intermarriage." *Journal of Women's History* 20, no. 2 (Summer 2008): 57–85.

Gordon, Linda. "Internal Colonialism and Gender." In *Haunted by Empire: Geographies on Intimacy in North American History*, edited by Ann Laura Stoler, 427–51. Durham: Duke University Press, 2006.

Gray, Susan E. "Limits and Possibilities: Indian-White Relations in Western Michigan in the Era of Removal." *Michigan Historical Review* 20, no. 2 (Fall 1994): 71–191.

Grossberg, Michael. "Institutionalizing Masculinity: The Law as a Masculine Profession." In *Meanings for Manhood: Constructions of Masculinity in Victorian America*, edited by Mark C. Carnes and Clyde Griffen, 133–51. Chicago: University of Chicago Press, 1990.

Hahn, Steven. "'Extravagant Expectations' of Freedom: Rumour, Political Struggle, and the Christmas Insurrection Scare of 1865 in the American South." *Past & Present* 157 (1997): 122–58.

Hasian, Marhouf. "Cultural Amnesia and Legal Rhetoric: Remembering the 1862 United States–Dakota War and the Need for Military Commissions." *American Indian Culture and Research Journal* 27, no. 1 (2003): 91–117.

Hayes, Samuel P. "The Politics of Reform in Municipal Government in the Progressive Era." *Pacific Northwest Quarterly* 55 (1964): 157–69.

Hind, Robert J. "The Internal Colonial Concept." *Comparative Studies in Society and History* 26 (1984): 543–68.

Hoxie, Frederick. "The End of the Savage: Indian Policy in the United States Senate, 1880–1900." *Chronicles of Oklahoma* 55, no. 2 (1977): 157–79.

Hutton, Paul. "Phil Sheridan's Pyrrhic Victory: The Piegan Massacre, Army Politics, and the Transfer Debate." *Montana* 32, no. 2 (1982): 32–43.

Illick, Joseph E. "'Some of Our Best Indians Are Friends . . .': Quaker Attitudes and Actions Regarding the Western Indians during the Grant Administration." *Western Historical Quarterly* 2, no. 3 (1971): 283–94.

"An Indian Craftsman." *Masonic Review* 19 (1858): 364.

"The Indian Craftsman." *Masonic Review* 23, no. 1 (1860): 16–17.

Jacobson, Cardell. "Internal Colonialism and Native Americans: Indian Labor in the United States from 1871 to World War II." *Social Science Quarterly* 65 (1984): 158–71.

Johnson, Benjamin Heber. "Red Populism? T. A. Bland, Agrarian Radicalism, and the Debate over the Dawes Act." In *The Countryside in the Age of the Modern State: Political Histories of Rural America*, edited by Catherine McNicol Stock and Robert D. Johnson, 15–37. Ithaca: Cornell University Press, 2001.

"Journals of Henry A. S. Dearborn." *Proceedings of the Buffalo Historical Society* 7 (1904): 35–228.

Kaplan, Amy. "'Left Alone with America': The Absence of Empire in the Study of American Culture." In *Cultures of United States Imperialism*, edited by Amy Kaplan and Donald Pease, 3–21. Durham: Duke University Press, 1993.

Keller, Robert. "Episcopal Reformers and Affairs at Red Cloud Agency, 1870–1876." *Nebraska History* 68, no. 3 (1987): 116–26.

Lehman, J. David. "The End of the Iroquois Mystique: The Oneida Land Cession Treaties of the 1780s." *William and Mary Quarterly* 47, no. 4 (October 1990): 523–47.

Leuchtenburg, William. "The Pertinence of Political History: Reflections on the Significance of the State in America." *Journal of American History* 73, no. 3 (1986): 585–600.

Levine, Richard. "Indian Fighters and Indian Reformers: Grant's Indian Peace Policy and the Conservative Consensus." *Civil War History* 31, no. 4 (1985): 329–52.

Liberty, Margot. "Francis La Flesche: The Osage Odyssey." In *American Indian Intellectuals*, edited by Margot Liberty, 45–60. St. Paul, Minn.: West, 1978.

Littlefield, Daniel F., Jr. "'They Ought to Enjoy the Home of their Fathers': The Treaty of 1838, Seneca Intellectuals, and Literary Genesis." In *Early Native American Writing: New Critical Essays*, edited by Helen Jaskoski, 83–103. New York: Cambridge University Press, 1996.

Manley, Henry. "Buying Buffalo from the Indians." *New York History* 28 (1947): 313–29.

———. "Red Jacket's Last Campaign." *New York History* 31 (1950): 149–68.

Mardock, Robert. "The Anti-Slavery Humanitarians and Indian Policy Reform." *Western Humanities Review* 7 (Spring 1958): 131–46.

"Marking the Grave of Do-Ne-Ho-Geh-Weh." *Proceedings of the Buffalo Historical Society* 8 (1905): 511–19.

Mathes, Victoria. "Nineteenth-Century Women and Reform: The Women's National Indian Association." *American Indian Quarterly* 14, no. 1 (1990): 1–18.

McClurken, James M. "Augustin Hamlin, Jr.: Ottawa Identity and Politics of Ottawa Persistence." In *Being and Becoming Indian: Biographical Studies of North American Frontiers*, edited by James A. Clifton, 82–111. Chicago: Dorsey Press, 1989.

Mehta, Uday. "Liberal Strategies of Exclusion." In *Tensions of Empire: Colonial Cultures in a Bourgeois World*, edited by Frederick Cooper and Ann Laura Stoler, 59–86. Berkeley: University of California Press, 1997.

Merrill, Karen. "In Search of the 'Federal Presence' in the American West." *Western Historical Quarterly* 30 (Winter 1999): 449–74.

Nicholas, Mark A. "A Little School, a Reservation Divided: Quaker Education and the Allegany Seneca Leadership in the Early American Republic." *American Indian Culture and Research Journal* 30, no. 3 (2006): 1–21.

Oman, Kerry. "The Beginning of the End: The Indian Peace Commission of 1867–1868." *Great Plains Quarterly* 22 (Winter 2002): 35–51.

Parker, Arthur C. "Ely S. Parker: Last Grand Sachem." *American Indian* 1 (1944): 11–15

———. "Ely S. Parker—Man and Mason." *Transactions–American Lodge of Research* 8, no. 2 (1961): 229–47.

Pascoe, Peggy. "Race, Gender, and Intercultural Relations: The Case of Interracial Marriage." *Frontiers* 12, no. 1 (1991): 5–18.

Raheja, Michelle. "'I Leave It with the People of the United States to Say': Autobiographical Disruption in the Personal Narratives of Black Hawk and Ely S. Parker." *American Indian Culture and Research Journal* 30, no. 1 (2006): 87–108.

Reinhardt, Akim. "A Crude Replacement: The Indian New Deal, Indirect Colonialism, and Pine Ridge Reservation." *Journal of Colonialism and Colonial History* 6, no. 1 (2005): 1–56.

Roberts, Gary L. "The Chief of State and the Chief." *American Heritage* 26 (October 1975): 28–33, 86–89.

Senier, Siobhan. "Allotment Protest and Tribal Discourse: Reading Wynema's Successes and Shortcomings." *American Indian Quarterly* 24, no. 3 (2000): 420–40.

Sheingate, Adam. "Political Entrepreneurship, Institutional Change, and American Political Development." *Studies in American Political Development* 17 (Fall 2003): 185–203.

Spivak, Gayatri. "The Letter as Cutting Edge." *Yale French Studies* 55/56 (1977): 208–26.

Stamm, Henry. "The Peace Policy at Wind River: The James Irwin Years, 1871–1877." *Montana* 41, no. 3 (Summer 1991): 56–69.

Stoler, Ann Laura. "Carnal Knowledge and Imperial Power: Gender and Morality in the Making of Race." In *Carnal Knowledge and Imperial Power: Race and the Intimate in Colonial Rule*, edited by Ann Laura Stoler, 41–78. Berkeley: University of California Press, 2002.

———. "Intimidations of Empire: Predicaments of the Tactile and Unseen." In *Haunted by Empire: Geographies of Intimacy in North American History*, edited Ann Laura Stoler, 1–23. Durham: Duke University Press, 2006.

———. "Tense and Tender Ties: The Politics of Comparison in North American History and (Post) Colonial Studies." *Journal of American History* 88, no. 3 (December 2001): 829–65.

———. "Sexual Affronts and Racial Frontiers: Cultural Competence and the Dangers of Metissage." In *Carnal Knowledge and Imperial Power: Race and the Intimate in Colonial Rule*, edited by Ann Laura Stoler, 79–111. Berkeley: University of California Press, 2002.

Strong, Pauline T. "Representational Practices." In *A Companion to the Anthropology of American Indians*, edited by Thomas Biolsi, 341–60. Malden, Mass.: Blackwell Publishers, 2004.

Sturtevant, William. "First Visual Images of Native America." In *First Images of America*. Vol. 1, edited by F. Chiapelli, M. J. Allen, and R. L. Benson, 417–54. Lincoln: University of Nebraska Press, 1976.

Swartz, E. A. "Red Atlantis Revisited: Community and Culture in the Writings of John Collier." *American Indian Quarterly* 18 (1994): 507–31.

Tooker, Elisabeth. "Ely S. Parker." In *American Indian Intellectuals*, edited by Margot Liberty, 15–30. St. Paul, Minn.: West, 1978.

Trennert, Robert. "John H. Stout and the Grant Peace Policy Among the Pimas." *Arizona and the West* 28, no. 1 (1986): 45–68.

Utley, Robert. "The Celebrated Peace Policy of General Grant." *North Dakota History* 20 (1953): 121–42.

Waltmann, Henry. "Circumstantial Reformer: President Grant and the Indian Problem." *Arizona and the West* 13, no. 4 (1971): 323–42.

———. "John C. Lowrie and Presbyterian Indian Administration, 1870–1882." *Journal of Presbyterian History* 54, no. 2 (1976): 259–77.

Wolfe, Patrick. "Settler Colonialism and the Elimination of the Native." *Journal of Genocide Research* 8, no. 4 (2006): 287–409.

Wright, J. Leitch, Jr. "Creek-American Treaty of 1790: Alexander McGillivray and the Diplomacy of the Old Southwest." *Georgia Historical Quarterly* 51 (December 1967): 379–400.

"Writings of General Parker." *Proceedings of the Buffalo Historical Society* 8 (1905): 520–36.

Wunder, John. "No More Treaties: The Resolution of 1871 and the Alteration of Indian Rights to their Homelands." In *Working the Range: Essays on the History of Western Land*

Management and the Environment. Edited by John Wunder. Westport, Conn.: Greenwood Press, 1985.

Young, Mary E. "The Cherokee Nation: Mirror of the Republic." *American Quarterly* 33 (1981): 502–24.

Zwink, T. Ashley. "On the White Man's Road: Lawrie Tatum and the Formative Years of the Kiowa Agency, 1869–1873." *Chronicles of Oklahoma* 56, no. 4 (1978–79): 431–41.

BOOKS, PAMPHLETS, AND DISSERTATIONS

Abel, Annie H. *The American Indian and the End of the Confederacy, 1863–1866.* 1925. Lincoln: University of Nebraska Press, 1993.

———. *The American Indian as Participant in the Civil War.* Cleveland: Arthur H. Clark Company, 1919.

Abler, Thomas S. "Factional Dispute and Party Conflict in the Political System of the Seneca Nation (1845–1895): An Ethnohistorical Analysis." Ph.D. diss., University of Toronto, 1969.

Adas, Michael. *Dominance by Design: Technological Imperative and America's Civilizing Mission.* Cambridge: Belknap Press of Harvard University Press, 2006.

Aleinikoff, T. Alexander. *Semblances of Sovereignty: The Constitution, the State, and American Citizenship.* Cambridge: Harvard University Press, 2002.

Angevine, Robert. *The Railroad and the State: War, Politics, and Technology in Nineteenth-Century America.* Stanford: Stanford University Press, 2004.

Armstrong, William H. *Warrior in Two Camps: Ely S. Parker, Union General and Seneca Chief.* Syracuse: Syracuse University Press, 1978.

Bailey, Minnie T. *Reconstruction in Indian Territory: A Story of Avarice, Discrimination, and Opportunism.* Port Washington, N.Y.: Kennikat Press, 1972.

Balogh, Brian. *A Government Out of Sight: The Mystery of National Authority in Nineteenth-Century America.* New York: Cambridge University Press, 2009.

Barton, Lois. *A Quaker Promise Kept: Philadelphia Friends' Work with the Allegany Senecas.* Eugene, Oreg.: Spencer Butte Press, 1990.

Basch, Norma. *Framing American Divorce: From the Revolutionary Generation to the Victorians.* Berkeley: University of California Press, 1999.

Bederman, Gail. *Manliness and Civilization: A Cultural History of Gender and Race in the United States, 1880–1917.* Chicago: University of Chicago Press, 1995.

Beeson, John. *A Plea for the Indians, with Fact and Features of the Late War in Oregon.* New York: John Beeson, 1858.

Behrens, Jo Lea Wetherilt. "In Defense of 'Poor Lo': *The Council Fire's* Advocacy of Native American Civil Rights, 1878–1889." Master's thesis, University of Nebraska, Omaha, 1992.

Bender, Norman. *New Hope for the Indians: The Grant Peace Policy and the Navajos in the 1870s.* Albuquerque: University of New Mexico Press, 1989.

Bensel, Richard. *Yankee Leviathan: The Origins of Central State Authority in America, 1859–1877.* New York: Cambridge University Press, 1990.

Bentley, George. *A History of the Freedmen's Bureau.* Philadelphia: University of Pennsylvania Press, 1955.

Bergemann, Kurt D. *Brackett's Battalion: Minnesota Cavalry in the Civil War and Dakota War.* St. Paul, Minn.: Borealis Books, 2004.

Berk, Gerald. *Alternative Tracks: The Constitution of American Industrial Order, 1865–1917.* Baltimore: Johns Hopkins University Press, 1994.

Berkhofer, Robert. *The White Man's Indian: Images of the American Indian from Columbus to the Present.* New York: Vintage Books, 1979.

Bieder, Robert. *Science Encounters the Indian, 1820–1880: The Early Years of American Ethnology.* Norman: University of Oklahoma Press, 1986.

Bland, Thomas A. *Farming as a Profession.* Boston: Loring, 1870.

———. *How to Grow Rich.* Washington, D.C.: R. H. Darby, 1881.

———. *The Life of Alfred B. Meacham.* Washington, D.C.: T. A. and M. C. Bland, 1883.

———. *The Life of Benjamin Butler.* Boston: Lee and Shepard, 1879.

———. *People's Party Shot and Shell.* Chicago: Charles M. Kerr and Co., 1892.

———. *Reign of Monopoly.* Washington, D.C.: Rufus H. Darby, 1881.

———, ed. *Pioneers of Progress.* Chicago: Blakely Printing Company, 1906.

Bledstein, Burton. *The Culture of Professionalism: The Middle Class and the Development of Higher Education in America.* New York: Norton, 1976.

Blumin, Stuart. *The Emergence of the Middle Class: Social Experience in the American City, 1760–1900.* New York: Cambridge University Press, 1989.

Bowes, John P. *Exiles and Pioneers: Eastern Indians in the Trans-Mississippi West.* New York: Cambridge University Press, 2007.

Boyer, Paul. *Urban Masses and Moral Order in America, 1820–1920.* Cambridge: Harvard University Press, 1978.

Bremer, Richard. *Indian Agent and Wilderness Scholar: The Life of Henry Rowe Schoolcraft.* Mount Pleasant, Mich.: Clarke Historical Library, Central Michigan University, 1987.

The Brookings Institution. Institute for Government Research. *The Problem of Indian Administration.* Baltimore: Johns Hopkins University Press, 1928.

Brown, Thomas J., ed. *Reconstructions: New Perspectives on the Postbellum United States.* New York: Oxford University Press, 2006.

Bruyneel, Kevin. *The Third Space of Sovereignty: The Postcolonial Politics of U.S. Indigenous Relations.* Minneapolis: University of Minnesota Press, 2007.

Buecker, Thomas. *Fort Robinson and the American West, 1874–1899.* Norman: University of Oklahoma Press, 2003.

Burke, Flannery. *From Greenwich Village to Taos: Primitivism and Place at Mabel Dodge Luhan's.* Lawrence: University Press of Kansas, 2008.

Buss, James Joseph. *Winning the West with Words: Language and Conquest in the Lower Great Lakes.* Norman: University of Oklahoma Press, 2011.

Cahill, Cathleen. *Federal Fathers and Mothers: A Social History of the United States Indian Service, 1869–1933.* Chapel Hill: University of North Carolina Press, 2011.

———. "'Only the Home Can Found a State': Gender, Labor, and the Federal Indian Service, 1869–1928." Ph.D. diss., University of Chicago, 2004.

Carlson, David. *Sovereign Selves: American Indian Autobiography and the Law.* Urbana: University of Illinois Press, 2006.

Carlson, Leonard. *Indians, Bureaucrats, and Lands: The Dawes Act and the Decline of Indian Farming.* Westport, Conn.: Greenwood Press, 1981.

Carnes, Mark. *Secret Ritual and Manhood in Victorian America.* New Haven: Yale University Press, 1989.

Carpenter, Daniel. *The Forging of Bureaucratic Autonomy: Reputations, Networks, and Policy Innovation in Executive Agencies, 1862–1928.* Princeton, N.J.: Princeton University Press, 2001.

Chazanof, William. *Joseph Ellicott and the Holland Land Company: The Opening of Western New York.* Syracuse: Syracuse University Press, 1970.

Christman, Henry. *Tin Horns and Calico: A Decisive Episode in the Emergence of Democracy.* New York: Henry Holt, 1945.

Cimbala, Paul. *Under the Guardianship of the Nation: The Freedmen's Bureau and the Reconstruction of Georgia, 1865–1870.* Athens: University of Georgia Press, 1997.

Cimbala, Paul, and Randall Miller, eds. *The Freedmen's Bureau and Reconstruction.* New York: Fordham Press, 1999.

Clemens, Elisabeth. *The People's Lobby: Organizational Innovation and the Rise of Interest Group Politics in the United States, 1890–1925.* Chicago: University of Chicago Press, 1997.

Clifton, James A., ed. *Being and Becoming Indian: Biographical Studies of North American Frontiers.* Chicago: Dorsey Press, 1989.

Clodfelter, Michael. *The Dakota War: The United States Army versus the Sioux, 1862–1865.* Jefferson, N.C.: McFarland, 1998.

Coffman, Tom. *A Nation Within: The Story of America's Annexation of Hawai'i.* Kane'oha: EPI Center, 1998.

Comaroff, Jean, and John Comaroff. *Revelation and Revolution: Christianity, Colonialism, and Consciousness in South Africa.* 2 vols. Chicago: University of Chicago Press, 1991.

Conable, Mary H. "A Steady Enemy: The Ogden Land Company and the Seneca Indians." Ph.D. diss., University of Rochester, 1994.

Converse, Harriet Maxwell. *Sheaves: A Collection of Poems.* New York: G. P. Putnam and Sons, Knickerbocker Press, 1885.

Cooper, Frederick. *Colonialism in Question: Theory, Knowledge, Power.* Berkeley: University of California Press, 2005.

Cooper, Frederick, and Ann Laura Stoler, eds. *Tensions of Empire: Colonial Cultures in a Bourgeois World.* Berkeley: University of California Press, 1997.

Coward, John. *The Newspaper Indian: Native American Identity in the Press, 1820–1890.* Urbana: University of Illinois Press, 1999.

Danziger, Edmund J., Jr. *The Indians and the Bureaucrats: Administering the Reservation Policy during the Civil War.* Urbana: University of Illinois Press, 1974.

Darnell, Regna. *Invisible Genealogies: A History of Americanist Anthropology.* Lincoln: University of Nebraska Press, 2001.

Dawes, Henry L. *The Case of McGillycuddy.* Philadelphia: Indian Rights Association, 1884.

Deloria, Philip. *Indians in Unexpected Places.* Lawrence: University Press of Kansas, 2005.

———. *Playing Indian.* New Haven: Yale University Press, 2001.

Deloria, Vine, Jr., and Clyde Lytle. *American Indians, American Justice.* Austin: University of Texas Press, 1984.

Deloria, Vine, Jr., and David E. Wilkins. *Tribes, Treaties, and Constitutional Tribulations.* Austin: University of Texas Press, 1999.

Deloria, Vine, Jr., and Raymond DeMallie, eds. *Documents of American Indian Diplomacy: Treaties, Agreements, and Conventions, 1775–1979.* Vol. 1. Norman: University of Oklahoma Press, 1999.

———. *Proceedings of the Great Peace Commission of 1867–1868.* Washington, D.C.: Institute for the Development of Indian Law, 1975.

Dennis, Matthew. *Seneca Possessed: Indians, Witchcraft, and Power in the Early American Republic.* Philadelphia: University of Pennsylvania Press, 2010.

Denson, Andrew. *Demanding the Cherokee Nation: Indian Autonomy and American Culture, 1830–1900.* Lincoln: University of Nebraska Press, 2004.

Dilworth, Leah. *Imagining Indians in the Southwest: Persistent Visions of a Primitive Past.* Washington, D.C.: Smithsonian Institution Press, 1996.

Dippie, Brian. *The Vanishing American: White Attitudes and U.S. Indian Policy.* Middletown, Conn.: Wesleyan University Press, 1982.

Dominguez, Susan Rose. "The Gertrude Bonnin Story: From Yankton Destiny into American History, 1804–1938." Ph.D. diss., Michigan State University, 2005.

Doolen, Andy. *Fugitive Empire: Locating Early American Imperialism.* Minneapolis: University of Minnesota Press, 2005.

Dowd, Gregory. *A Spirited Resistance: The North American Indian Struggle for Unity, 1740–1815.* Baltimore: Johns Hopkins University Press, 1991.

Eastman, Elaine G. *The Senator and the School-House.* Philadelphia: Indian Rights Association, 1886.

Fenton, William. *The Great Law and the Longhouse: A Political History of the Iroquois Confederacy.* Norman: University of Oklahoma Press, 1998.

———, ed. *Parker on the Iroquois.* Syracuse: Syracuse University Press, 1968.

Finley, Randy. *From Slavery to Uncertain Freedom: The Freedmen's Bureau in Arkansas, 1865–1869.* Fayetteville: University of Arkansas Press, 1996.

Flanagan, Maureen A. *Seeing with Their Hearts: Chicago Women and the Vision of the Good City, 1871–1933.* Princeton, N.J.: Princeton University Press, 2002.

Frankel, Oz. *States of Inquiry: Social Investigations and Print Culture in Nineteenth Century Britain and the United States.* Baltimore: Johns Hopkins University Press, 2006.

Fritz, Henry. *The Movement for Indian Assimilation, 1860–1890.* Philadelphia: University of Pennsylvania Press, 1963.

Fogelson, Raymond, and Richard Adams, eds. *The Anthropology of Power: Ethnographic Studies from Asia, Oceania, and the New World.* New York: Cambridge University Press, 1977.

Foner, Eric. *Reconstruction: America's Unfinished Revolution, 1863–1877.* New York: Harper and Row, 1988.

———. *A Short History of Reconstruction.* New York: Harper and Row, 1990.

Fowler, David. *Northern Attitudes Towards Interracial Marriage: Legislation and Public Opinion in the Middle Atlantic and the States of the Old Northwest, 1780–1930.* New York: Garland Publishing, 1987.

Fulford, Tim. *Romantic Indians: Native Americans, British Literature, and Transatlantic Culture, 1756–1830.* New York: Oxford University Press, 2006.

Gabriel, Ralph. *Elias Boudinot, Cherokee and His America.* Norman: University of Oklahoma Press, 1941.

Garraty, John. *Silas Wright.* New York: Columbia University Press, 1949.

Gates, Paul W. *The Farmer's Age: Agriculture, 1815–1860.* New York: Holt, Rinehart, and Winston, 1960.

Gidley, Mick. *Edward S. Curtis and the North American Indian, Incorporated.* New York: Cambridge University Press, 1998.

Gilmore, Glenda Elizabeth. *Gender and Jim Crow: Women and the Politics of White Supremacy in North Carolina, 1896-1920.* Chapel Hill: University of North Carolina Press, 1996.

Gilmore, Paul. *The Genuine Article: Race, Mass Culture, and American Literary Manhood.* Durham: Duke University Press, 2001.

Gerber, David A. *The Making of an American Pluralism: Buffalo, New York, 1825–1860.* Urbana: University of Illinois Press, 1989.

Goldman, Mark. *High Hopes: The Rise and Decline of Buffalo.* Albany: State University of New York Press, 1983.

Goldstein, Kalman. "The Albany Regency: The Failure of Practical Politics." Ph.D. diss., Columbia University, 1969.

Goodwyn, Lawrence. *Democratic Promise: The Populist Moment in America.* New York: Oxford University Press, 1976.

Gordon, Sarah. *Passage to Union: How the Railroads Transformed American Life, 1829–1929.* Chicago: Ivan R. Dee, 1997.

Geary, James. *We Need Men: The Union Draft in the Civil War.* Dekalb: Northern Illinois University Press, 1991.

Greene, Jerome, and Douglas Scott. *Finding Sand Creek: History, Archeology, and the 1864 Massacre Site.* Norman: University of Oklahoma Press, 2004.

Greenstone, J. David. *The Lincoln Persuasion: Remaking American Liberalism.* Princeton, N.J.: Princeton University Press, 1993.

Greenwald, Emily. *Reconfiguring the Reservation: The Nez Perces, Jicarilla Apaches, and the Dawes Act.* Albuquerque: University of New Mexico Press, 2002.

Hagan, William T. *The Indian Rights Association: The Herbert Welsh Years, 1882–1904.* Tucson: University of Arizona Press, 1985.

Haller, John S. *Medical Protestants: The Eclectics in American Medicine, 1825–1939.* Carbondale: Southern Illinois University Press, 1994.

———. *Outcasts from Evolution: Scientific Attitudes of Racial Inferiority, 1859–1900.* Carbondale: University of Southern Illinois Press, 1995.

———. *A Profile in Alternative Medicine: The Eclectic Medical College of Cincinnati, 1845–1942.* Kent, Ohio: Kent State University Press, 1999.

Halttunen, Karen. *Confidence Men and Painted Women: A Study of Middle-Class Culture in America, 1830–1870.* New Haven: Yale University Press, 1982.

Harring, Sidney. *Crow Dog's Case: American Indian Sovereignty, Tribal Law, and United States Law in the Nineteenth Century.* New York: Cambridge University Press, 1994.

Hartz, Louis. *The Liberal Tradition in America: An Interpretation of American Political Thought since the Revolution.* New York: Harcourt, Brace, 1955.

Hatch, Thom. *Black Kettle: The Cheyenne Chief who sought Peace but Found War.* Hoboken, N.J.: John Wiley and Sons, 2004.

Hatley, Tom. *The Dividing Paths: Cherokees and South Carolinians through the Era of Revolution.* New York: Oxford University Press, 1995.

Hauptman, Laurence M. *A Conspiracy of Interests: Iroquois Dispossession and the Rise of New York State.* Syracuse: Syracuse University Press, 1999.

———. *The Iroquois in the Civil War: From Battlefield to Reservation.* Syracuse: Syracuse University Press, 1993.

———. *The Tonawanda Senecas' Heroic Battle against Removal: Conservative Activist Indians.* Albany: State University of New York Press, 2011.

Healy, David. *James G. Blaine and Latin America.* Columbia: University of Missouri Press, 2001.

Helms, Mary W. *Ulysses' Sail: An Ethnographic Odyssey of Power, Knowledge, and Geographic Distance.* Princeton, N.J.: Princeton University Press, 1988.

Higham, Carol. *Noble, Wretched, and Redeemable: Protestant Missionaries to the Indian in Canada and the United States, 1820–1900.* Albuquerque: University of New Mexico Press, 2000.

Hinsley, Curtis. *Savages and Scientists: The Smithsonian Institution and the Development of American Anthropology, 1846–1910.* Washington, D.C.: Smithsonian Institution Press, 1981.

———. *The Smithsonian and the American Indian: Making a Moral Anthropology of in Victorian American.* Washington, D.C.: Smithsonian Institution Press, 1994.

Hodes, Martha, ed. *Sex, Love, and Race: Crossing Boundaries in North American History.* New York: New York University Press, 1999.

Hoig, Stan. *The Sand Creek Massacre.* Norman: University of Oklahoma Press, 1961.

Holden, Robert, and Eric Zolov, eds. *Latin America and the United States: A Documentary History.* New York: Oxford University Press, 2000.

Holm, Tom. *The Great Confusion in Indian Affairs: Native Americans and Whites in the Progressive Era.* Austin: University of Texas Press, 2005.

Honour, Hugh. *The New Golden Land: European Images of America from the Discoveries to the Present Time.* New York: Pantheon, 1975.

Hoxie, Frederick. *A Final Promise: The Campaign to Assimilate the Indians, 1880–1920.* Lincoln: University of Nebraska Press, 1984. Reprinted with new preface by the author. Lincoln: University of Nebraska Press, 2001.

———. *Parading through History: The Making of the Crow Nation in America, 1805–1935.* New York: Cambridge University Press, 1995.

Huston, Reeve. *Land and Freedom: Rural Society, Popular Protest, and Party Politics in Antebellum New York.* New York: Oxford University Press, 2000.

Hutton, Paul. *Phil Sheridan and His Army.* Lincoln: University of Nebraska Press, 1985.

Hyde, George E. *A Sioux Chronicle.* Norman: University of Oklahoma Press, 1956.

Ignatiev, Noel. *How the Irish Became White.* New York: Routledge, 1995.

Indian Rights Association. *Allotment of Lands. Defense of the Dawes Indian Severalty Bill.* Philadelphia: Indian Rights Association, 1887.

———. *Constitution and By-Laws of the Indian Rights Association.* Philadelphia: Indian Rights Association, 1884.

———. *First Annual Report of the Executive Committee of the Indian Rights Association.* Philadelphia: Indian Rights Association, 1884.

———. *Opinions of the Press on the Need of Legislation for Indians by the Present Congress.* Philadelphia: Indian Rights Association, 1885.

———. *Resolutions Passed at a Joint Conference of the Board of Indian Commissioners, Indian Rights Association, Woman's National Indian Association . . . .* Philadelphia: Indian Rights Association, 1885.

———. *Second Annual Address to the Public of the Lake Mohonk Conference . . . In Behalf of the Civilization and Legal Protection of the Indians of the United States.* Philadelphia: Indian Rights Association, 1884.

———. *Second Annual Report of the Executive Committee of the Indian Rights Association.* Philadelphia: Indian Rights Association, 1885.

———. *Synopsis of Three Bills Advocated.* Philadelphia: Indian Rights Association, 1886.

———. *What the Indian Rights Association Is Doing.* Philadelphia: Indian Rights Association, 1885.

Ingraham, Patricia. *The Foundation of Merit: Public Service in American Democracy.* Baltimore: Johns Hopkins University Press, 1995.

Iverson, Peter. *Carlos Montezuma and the Changing World of American Indians.* Albuquerque: University of New Mexico Press, 1982.

Jacobs, Kathryn A. *Capital Elites: High Society in Washington, D.C., after the Civil War.* Washington, D.C.: Smithsonian Institution Press, 1995.

Jacobson, Matthew Frye. *Barbarian Virtues: The United States Encounters Foreign Peoples at Home and Abroad, 1876–1917.* New York: Hill and Wang, 2000.

———. *Whiteness of a Different Color: European Immigrants and the Alchemy of Race.* Cambridge: Harvard University Press, 1999.

Jennings, Francis. *The Ambiguous Iroquois Empire: The Covenant Chain Confederation of Tribes with English Colonies from Its Beginning to the Lancaster Treaty of 1744.* New York: Norton, 1984.

Johnson, Allen, ed. *Dictionary of American Biography,* 20 vols. New York: Charles Scribner's and Sons, 1928–36.

Johnson, John J. *A Hemisphere Apart: The Foundations of United States Policy toward Latin America.* Baltimore: Johns Hopkins University Press, 1990.

Johnson, Paul. *A Shopkeeper's Millennium: Society and Revivals in Rochester, New York, 1815–1837.* New York: Hill and Wang, 1978.

Johnson, Ronald N. *The Federal Civil Service System and the Problem of Democracy: The Economics and Politics of Institutional Change.* Chicago: University of Chicago Press, 1994.

Jones, Dorothy V. *License for Empire: Colonialism by Treaty in Early America.* Chicago: University of Chicago Press, 1982.

Kaltman, Al. *Cigars, Whiskey, and Winning: Leadership Lessons from General Ulysses S. Grant.* Paramus, N.J.: Prentice Hall, 1998.

Kaplan, Amy, and Donald Pease, eds. *Cultures of United States Imperialism.* Durham: Duke University Press, 1993.

Kappler, Charles J., ed. *Indian Affairs: Laws and Treaties,* Vol. 2, *Treaties.* Washington, D.C.: Government Printing Office, 1904.

Keenan, Jerry. *The Great Sioux Uprising: Rebellion on the Plains, August-September, 1862.* Cambridge: Da Capo Press, 2003.

Keller, Robert. *American Protestantism and United States Indian Policy, 1869–1882.* Lincoln: University of Nebraska Press, 1983.

Kelly, Lawrence. *The Assault on Assimilation: John Collier and the Origins of Indian Policy Reform.* Albuquerque: University of New Mexico Press, 1983.

Kimmel, Michael. *Manhood in America: A Cultural History.* New York: Free Press, 1996.

Kinney, J. P. *A Continent Lost–A Civilization Won: Indian Land Tenure in America.* Baltimore: Johns Hopkins University Press, 1937.

Klein, Kerwin. *Frontiers of Historical Imagination: Narrating the European Conquest of Native America, 1890–1990.* Berkeley: University of California Press, 1997.

Kolko, Gabriel. *Railroads and Regulations, 1877–1916.* Princeton, N.J.: Princeton University Press, 1965.

———. *The Triumph of Conservatism: A Reinterpretation of American History, 1900–1916.* New York: Free Press, 1963.

Konkle, Maureen. *Writing Indian Nations: Native Intellectuals and the Politics of Historiography, 1827–1863.* Chapel Hill: University of North Carolina Press, 2004.

Kramer, Paul A. *The Blood of Government: Race, Empire, the United States, and the Philippines.* Chapel Hill: University of North Carolina Press, 2006.

Kreidberg, Marvin, and Merton Henry. *History of Military Mobilization in the United States Army, 1775–1945.* Washington, D.C.: U.S. Department of the Army, 1955.

Kugel, Rebecca. *To Be the Main Leaders of Our People: A History of Minnesota Ojibwe Politics, 1825–1898.* East Lansing: Michigan State University Press, 1998.

Kvasnicka, Robert M., and Herman J. Viola, eds. *The Commissioners of Indian Affairs, 1824–1977.* Lincoln: University of Nebraska Press, 1979.

LaFeber, Walter. *The New Empire: An Interpretation of American Expansion, 1860–1898*. Ithaca: Cornell University Press, 1963.

Lemire, Elise. *"Miscegenation": Making Race in America*. Philadelphia: University of Pennsylvania Press, 2002.

Lepore, Jill. *In the Name of War: King Phillip's War and the Origins of American Identity*. New York: Alfred A. Knopf, 1998.

Lewis, Bonnie Sue. *Creating Christian Indians: Native Clergy in the Presbyterian Church*. Norman: University of Oklahoma Press, 2003.

Liberty, Margot, ed. *American Indian Intellectuals*. St. Paul, Minn.: West, 1978.

Love, Eric L. *Race Over Empire: Racism and U.S. Imperialism, 1865–1900*. Chapel Hill: University of North Carolina Press, 2004.

Lowrite, Walter, ed. *American State Papers: Documents, Legislative and Executive, of the Congress of the United States, in Relation to Indian Affairs*. Vol. 1. Washington, D.C.: Duff Green, 1834.

Lynch-Brennan, Margaret. *The Irish Bridget: Irish Immigrant Women in Domestic Service in America, 1840–1930*. Syracuse: Syracuse University Press, 2009.

Maddox, Lucy. *Citizen Indians: Native American Intellectuals, Race, and Reform*. Ithaca: Cornell University Press, 2005.

Mangan, J. A., and James Walvin, eds. *Manliness and Morality: Middle-Class Masculinity in Britain and America, 1800–1940*. Manchester, U.K.: Manchester University Press, 1987.

Manley, Henry S. *The Treaty of Fort Stanwix, 1784*. Rome, N.Y.: Rome Sentinel, 1932.

Mardock, Robert. *The Reformers and the American Indian*. Columbia: University of Missouri Press, 1971.

Mark, Joan. *A Stranger in Her Native Land: Alice Fletcher and the American Indians*. Lincoln: University of Nebraska Press, 1988.

Martin, Ged. *Britain and the Origins of Canadian Confederation, 1837–1867*. Vancouver: University of British Columbia Press, 1995.

Mathes, Valcria Sherer, and Richard Lowitt. *The Standing Bear Controversy: Prelude to Indian Reform*. Urbana: University of Illinois Press, 2003.

McChristian, Douglas. *Fort Bowie, Arizona: Combat Post of the Southwest, 1858–1894*. Norman: University of Oklahoma Press, 2005.

McClintock, Anne. *Imperial Leather: Gender and Sexuality in the Colonial Contest*. New York: Routledge, 1995.

McConnell, Michael. *A Country Between: The Upper Ohio Valley and its Peoples, 1724–1774*. Lincoln: University of Nebraska Press, 1992.

McCurdy, Charles. *The Anti-Rent Era in New York Law and Politics, 1839–1865*. Chapel Hill: University of North Carolina Press, 2001.

McFeely, William S. *Grant: A Biography*. New York: Norton, 1981.

———. *Yankee Stepfather: General O. O. Howard and the Freemen*. New Haven: Yale University Press, 1968.

McGerr, Michael. *A Fierce Discontent: The Rise and Fall of the Progressive Movement in America, 1870–1920*. New York: Free Press, 2003.

McGillycuddy, Julia B. *McGillycuddy Agent: A Biography of Valentine T. McGillycuddy*. Stanford: Stanford University Press, 1940.

McLoughlin, William. *After the Trail: The Cherokees' Struggle for Sovereignty, 1839–1880*. Chapel Hill: University of North Carolina Press, 1994.

———. *Cherokee Renascence in the New Republic*. Princeton, N.J.: Princeton University Press, 1992.

McMurty, Larry. *The Colonel and Little Missie: Buffalo Bill, Annie Oakley, and the Beginnings of Superstardom in America*. New York: Simon and Schuster, 2005.

McPherson, James. *Battle Cry of Freedom: The Civil War Era*. New York: Ballantine Books, 1988.

Michaelsen, Scott. *The Limits of Multiculturalism: Interrogating the Origins of American Anthropology*. Minneapolis: University of Minnesota Press, 1999.

Miles, Tiya. *Ties That Bind: The Story of an Afro-Cherokee Family in Slavery and Freedom*. Berkeley: University of California Press, 2005.

Miller, Robert. *Native America, Discovered and Conquered: Thomas Jefferson, Lewis and Clark, and Manifest Destiny*. Westport, Conn.: Praeger, 2006.

Mills, C. Wright. *White Collar: The American Middle Classes*. New York: Oxford University Press, 1951.

Mills, Sara. *Discourses of Difference: An Analysis of Women's Travel Writing and Colonialism*. London: Routledge, 1991.

Milner, Clyde. *With Good Intentions: Quaker Work among the Pawnees, Otos, and Omahas in the 1870s*. Lincoln: University of Nebraska Press, 1982.

Moore, Christopher. *1867: How the Fathers Made a Deal*. Toronto: M&S, 1997.

Morgan, Lewis Henry. *The League of the Ho-De-No-Sau-Nee, or Iroquois*. New York: Mark H. Newman, 1851.

Moses, L. G. *Wild West Shows and the Images of American Indians, 1883–1933*. Albuquerque: University of New Mexico Press, 1996.

Moulton, Gary E. *John Ross, A Cherokee Chief*. Athens: University of Georgia Press, 1978.

Murdock, Eugene. *One Million Men: The Civil War Draft in the North*. Madison: State Historical Society of Wisconsin, 1971.

Namias, June, ed. *Six Weeks in the Sioux Tepees: A Narrative of Indian Captivity*. Norman: University of Oklahoma Press, 1997.

National Cyclopaedia of American Biography. 63 vols. New York: J. T. White, 1892–1984.

Nelson, William. *Almost a Territory: America's Attempt to Annex the Dominican Republic*. Newark: University of Delaware Press, 1990.

———. *The Roots of American Bureaucracy, 1830–1900*. Cambridge: Harvard University Press, 1982.

Nichols, David. *Lincoln and the Indians: Civil War Policy and Politics*. Columbia: University of Missouri Press, 1978.

Norgren, Jill. *The Cherokee Cases: Two Landmark Federal Decisions on the Fight for Sovereignty*. Norman: University of Oklahoma Press, 2004.

Novak, William. *The People's Welfare: Law and Regulation in Nineteenth-Century America*. Chapel Hill: University of North Carolina Press, 1995.

O'Brien, Greg. *Choctaws in a Revolutionary Age, 1750–1830*. Lincoln: University of Nebraska Press, 2002.

O'Brien, Jean M. *Dispossession by Degrees: Indian Land and Identity in Natick, Massachusetts, 1650–1790*. Lincoln: University of Nebraska Press, 1997.

Oehler, Chester. *The Great Sioux Uprising*. New York: Oxford University Press, 1959.

Olson, James C. *Red Cloud and the Sioux Problem*. Lincoln: University of Nebraska Press, 1965.

Orren, Karen, and Stephen Skowronek. *The Search for American Political Development*. New York: Cambridge University Press, 2004.

Osterhammel, Jürgen. *Colonialism: A Theoretical Overview*. Translated by Shelley L. Frisch. Princeton, N.J.: Markus Wiener, 1997.

Ostler, Jeffrey. *The Plains Sioux and U.S. Colonialism from Lewis and Clark to Wounded Knee*. New York: Cambridge University Press, 2004.

Otis, D. S. *The Dawes Act and the Allotment of Indian Lands*. 1934. Norman: University of Oklahoma Press, 1973.

Owens, Robert M. *Mr. Jefferson's Hammer: William Henry Harrison and the Origins of American Indian Policy*. Norman: University of Oklahoma Press, 2007.

Painter, Charles C. *The Dawes Land in Severalty Bill and Indian Emancipation*. Philadelphia: Indian Rights Association, 1887.

Pancoast, Henry. *Impressions of the Sioux Tribes in 1882, with Some First Principles in the Indian Question*. Philadelphia: Franklin Printing House, 1883.

———. *The Indian Before the Law*. Philadelphia: Indian Rights Association, 1884.

Paolino, Ernest. *The Foundations of American Empire: William Henry Seward and U.S. Foreign Policy*. Ithaca: Cornell University Press, 1973.

Parker, Arthur C. *The Life of General Ely S. Parker: Last Grand Sachem of the Iroquois and General Grant's Military Secretary*. Buffalo: Buffalo Historical Society, 1919.

Pearce, Roy Harvey. *Savagism and Civilization: A Study of the Indian and the American Mind*. Baltimore: Johns Hopkins University Press, 1967.

Perdue, Theda. *Cherokee Editor: The Writings of Elias Boudinot*. Knoxville: University of Tennessee Press, 1983.

———. *Cherokee Women: Gender and Culture Change, 1700–1835*. Lincoln: University of Nebraska Press, 1998.

———. *Slavery and the Evolution of Cherokee Society, 1540–1866*. Knoxville: University of Tennessee Press, 1979.

Perdue, Theda, and Michael Green, eds. *The Cherokee Removal: A Brief History with Documents*. Boston: Bedford/St. Martin's Press, 2005.

Philip, Kenneth R. *John Collier's Crusade for Indian Reform, 1920–1954*. Tucson: University of Arizona Press, 1977.

Phinney, Edward S. "Alfred B. Meacham: Promoter of Indian Reform." Ph.D. diss., University of Oregon, Eugene, 1963.

Pierson, Paul. *Politics in Time: History, Institutions, and Social Analysis*. Princeton, N.J.: Princeton University Press, 2004.

Plane, Ann M. *Colonial Intimacies: Indian Marriage in Early New England*. Ithaca: Cornell University Press, 2000.

Pollack, Eileen. *Woman Walking Ahead: In Search of Catherine Weldon and Sitting Bull*. Albuquerque: University of New Mexico Press, 2002.

Pommersheim, Frank. *Braid of Feathers: American Indian Law and Contemporary Tribal Life*. Berkeley: University of California Press, 1995.

Porter, Joy. *To Be Indian: The Life of Iroquois-Seneca Arthur Caswell Parker*. Norman: University of Oklahoma Press, 2001.

Pratt, Mary Louise. *Imperial Eyes: Travel Writing and Transculturation*. London: Routledge, 1992.

Priest, Loring Benson. *Uncle Sam's Stepchildren: The Reformation of United States Indian Policy, 1865–1887*. New Brunswick: Rutgers University Press, 1942.

Prucha, Francis P. *American Indian Policy in Crisis: Christian Reformers and the Indian, 1865–1890*. Norman: University of Oklahoma Press, 1976.

———. *American Indian Treaties: The History of a Political Anomaly*. Berkeley: University of California Press, 1994.

———. *The Great Father: The United States Government and the American Indians*. 2 vols. combined and unabridged. Lincoln: University of Nebraska Press, 1995.

———. *The Indian in American Society*. Berkeley: University of California Press, 1985.

———, ed. *Americanizing the American Indian: Writings by the "Friends of the Indian," 1880–1900*. Cambridge: Harvard University Press, 1973.

———. *Documents of United States Indian Policy*. Lincoln: University of Nebraska Press, 1990.

Rand, Jacki. *Kiowa Humanity and the Invasion of the State*. Lincoln: University of Nebraska Press, 2008.

Reddin, Paul. *Wild West Shows*. Urbana: University of Illinois Press, 1999.

Remini, Robert. *Andrew Jackson and His Indian Wars*. New York: Viking, 2001.

Resek, Carl. *Lewis Henry Morgan: American Scholar*. Chicago: University of Chicago Press, 1960.

Richardson, Heather Cox. *West from Appomattox: The Reconstruction of America after the Civil War*. New Haven: Yale University Press, 2007.

Richter, Daniel K. *The Ordeal of the Longhouse: The Peoples of the Iroquois League in the Era of European Colonization*. Chapel Hill: University of North Carolina Press, 1992.

Richter, Daniel K., and James Merrell, eds. *Beyond the Covenant Chain: The Iroquois and their Neighbors in Indian North America, 1600–1800*. Syracuse: Syracuse University Press, 1987.

Riis, Jacob. *The Making of an American*. 1901. New York: Macmillan, 1966.

Ritter, Gretchen. *Goldbugs and Greenbacks: The Antimonopoly Tradition and the Politics of Finance in America*. New York: Cambridge University Press, 1997.

Robertson, Lindsay G. *Conquest by Law: How the Discovery of America Dispossessed Indigenous Peoples of Their Lands*. New York: Oxford University Press, 2005.

Rodgers, Daniel. *Atlantic Crossings: Social Politics in a Progressive Age*. Cambridge: Harvard University Press, 1998.

Roediger, David. *Working toward Whiteness: How America's Immigrants Became White, The Strange Journey from Ellis Island to the Suburbs*. New York: Basic Books, 2005.

Rosen, Deborah. *American Indians and State Law: Sovereignty, Race, and Citizenship, 1790–1880*. Lincoln: University of Nebraska Press, 2007.

Rosen, Hannah. *Terror in the Heart of Freedom: Citizenship, Sexual Violence, and the Meaning of Race in the Postemancipation South*. Chapel Hill: University of North Carolina Press, 2009.

Rotundo, Anthony. *American Manhood: Transformations in Masculinity from the Revolution to the Modern Era*. New York: Basic Books, 1993.

Rushmore, Elsie. *The Indian Policy during Grant's Administration*. New York: Marion Press, 1914.

Ryan, Mary. *The Cradle of the Middle Class: The Family in Oneida County, New York, 1790–1865*. New York: Cambridge University Press, 1981.

Rydell, Robert. *All the World's a Fair: Visions of Empire at American International Expositions, 1876–1916*. Chicago: University of Chicago Press, 1984.

Sargent, Theodore. *The Life of Elaine Goodale Eastman*. Lincoln: University of Nebraska Press, 2005.

Satz, Ronald. *American Indian Policy in the Jacksonian Era*. Lincoln: University of Nebraska Press, 1975.

Saunt, Claudio. *A New Order of Things: Property, Power, and the Transformation of the Creek Indians, 1733–1815*. New York: Cambridge University Press, 1999.

Schultz, David A., and Robert Moranto. *The Politics of Civil Service Reform*. New York: P. Lang Press, 1998.

Schultz, Duane. *Over the Earth I Come: The Great Sioux Uprising of 1862*. New York: St. Martin's Press, 1992.

Scott, James C. *Seeing Like a State: How Certain Schemes to Improve the Human Condition Have Failed*. New Haven: Yale University Press, 1998.

Senier, Siobhan. *Voices of American Indian Assimilation and Resistance: Helen Hunt Jackson, Sarah Winnemucca, and Victoria Howard*. Norman: University of Oklahoma Press, 2001.

Sharpless, Rebecca. *Cooking in Other Women's Kitchens: Domestic Workers in the South, 1865–1960*. Chapel Hill: University of North Carolina Press, 2010.

Silva, Noenoe. *Aloha Betrayed: Native Hawaiian Resistance to American Colonialism*. Durham: Duke University Press, 2004.

Simpson, Brooks. *Let Us Have Peace: Ulysses S. Grant and the Politics of War and Reconstruction, 1861–1868*. Chapel Hill: University of North Carolina Press, 2001.

Skocpol, Theda. *Protecting Soldiers and Mothers: The Political Origins of Social Policy in the United States*. Cambridge: Belknap Press of Harvard University Press, 1992.

Skowronek, Stephen. *Building a New American State: The Expansion of National Administrative Capabilities, 1877–1920*. New York: Cambridge University Press, 1982.

Slattery, Charles. *Felix Reville Brunot*. New York: Green, 1907.

Smith, Andrea. *Conquest: Sexual Violence and American Indian Genocide*. Cambridge: South End Press, 2005.

Smith, Jean Edward. *Grant*. New York: Simon and Schuster, 2001.

———. *John Marshall: Definer of a Nation*. New York: Henry Holt, 1996.

Speroff, Leon. *Carlos Montezuma, M.D.: A Yavapai American Hero: The Life and Times of an American Indian, 1866–1923*. Portland: Arnica Press, 2004.

Starkey, Marion. *The Cherokee Nation*. North Dighton, Mass.: JG Press, 1995.

Stern, Bernhard. *Lewis Henry Morgan: Social Evolutionist*. Chicago: University of Chicago Press, 1931.

Stoler, Ann Laura, ed. *Carnal Knowledge and Imperial Power: Race and the Intimate in Colonial Rule*. Berkeley: University of California Press, 2002.

———. *Haunted by Empire: Geographies of Intimacy in North American History*. Durham: Duke University Press, 2006.

———. *Race and the Education of Desire: Foucault's "History of Sexuality" and the Colonial Order of Things*. Durham: Duke University Press, 1995.

Stover, John. *American Railroads*. Chicago: University of Chicago Press, 1961.

St. Pierre, Judith. "General O. O. Howard and Grant's Peace Policy." Ph.D. diss., University of North Carolina, Chapel Hill, 1990.

Street, Alfred B. *Frontenac, A Poem*. London: R. Bentley, 1849.

Strobel, Christoph. "Contested Grounds: The Transformation of the American Upper Ohio Valley and the South African Eastern Cape, 1770–1850." Ph.D. diss., University of Massachusetts at Amherst, 2005.

Stromquist, Shelton. *Reinventing "The People": The Progressive Movement and the Class Problem, and the Origins of Modern Liberalism*. Urbana: University of Illinois Press, 2005.

Strong, Nathaniel Thayer. *Appeal to the Christian Community on the Condition and Prospects of the New York Indians*. New York: E. B. Clayton, 1841.

Strong, Pauline T. *Captive Selves, Captivating Others: The Politics and Poetics of Colonial American Captivity Narratives*. Boulder, Colo.: Westview Press, 1999.

Stuart, George H. *The Life of George H. Stuart: Written by Himself*. Edited by Robert E. Thompson. Philadelphia: J. M. Stoddart, 1890.

Stuart, Paul. *The Indian Office: Growth and Development of an American Institution, 1865–1900*. Ann Arbor, Mich.: UMI Press, 1979.

Summerhill, Thomas. "The Farmer's Republic: Agrarian Protest and the Capitalist Transformation of Upstate New York, 1840–1900." Ph.D. diss., University of California, San Diego, 1993.

———. *Harvest of Dissent: Agrarianism in Nineteenth-Century New York*. Urbana: University of Illinois Press, 2005.

Summers, Mark. *The Era of Good Stealings*. New York: Oxford University Press, 1993.

———. *The Plundering Generation: Corruption and the Crisis of Union, 1849–1861*. New York: Oxford University Press, 1987.

Sutherland, Daniel E. *Americans and their Servants: Domestic Service and the United States from 1800 to 1920*. Baton Rouge: Louisiana State University Press, 1981.

Svaldi, David. *Sand Creek and the Rhetoric of Extermination: A Case Study in Indian-White Relations*. Lanham, Md.: University Press of America, 1989.

Swalzer, David. *A Friend among the Senecas: The Quaker Mission to Cornplanter's People*. Mechanicsburg, Pa.: Stackpole Books, 2000.

Taylor, Alan. *Liberty Men and Great Proprietors: The Revolutionary Settlement on the Maine Frontier, 1760–1820*. Chapel Hill: University of North Carolina Press, 1990.

———. *William Cooper's Town: Power and Persuasion on the Frontier of the Early American Republic*. New York: Alfred A. Knopf, 1995.

Thomas, Nicholas. *Colonialism's Culture: Anthropology, Travel, and Government*. Princeton, N.J.: Princeton University Press, 1994.

Tong, Benson. *Susan La Flesche Picotte, M.D.: Omaha Leader and Reformer*. Norman: University of Oklahoma Press, 1999.

Tooker, Elisabeth. *Lewis H. Morgan on Iroquois Material Culture*. Tucson: University of Arizona Press, 1994.

Topik, Steven. *Trade and Gunboats: The United States and Brazil in the Age of Empire*. Stanford: Stanford University Press, 1996.

Trachtenberg, Alan. *The Incorporation of America: Culture and Society in Gilded Age America*. New York: Hill and Wang, 1982.

Trautmann, Thomas. *Lewis Henry Morgan and the Invention of Kinship*. Berkeley: University of California Press, 1987.

Unger, Irwin. *The Greenback Era: A Social and Political History of American Finance, 1865–1879*. Princeton, N.J.: Princeton University Press, 1964.

Unger, Roberto Mangabeira. *False Necessity: Anti-Necessitarian Social Theory in the Service of Radical Democracy*. New York: Cambridge University Press, 1987.

Utley, Robert. *Frontier Regulars: The United States Army and the Indian, 1866–1891*. New York: Macmillan, 1974.

———. *The Indian Frontier of the American West, 1846–1890*. Albuquerque: University of New Mexico Press, 1984.

Van Hoeven, James W. "Salvation and Indian Removal: The Career Biography of Rev. John Freeman Schermerhorn, Indian Commissioner." Ph.D. diss., Vanderbilt University, 1972.

Vaughan, Frederick. *The Canadian Federalist Experiment: From Defiant Monarchy to Reluctant Republic*. Montreal: McGill-Queens University Press, 2003.

Wallace, Anthony F. C. *The Death and Rebirth of the Seneca*. New York: Alfred A. Knopf, 1969.

———. *The Long, Bitter Trail: Andrew Jackson and the Indians.* New York: Hill and Wang, 1993.

Waltmann, Henry George. "The Interior Department, War Department, and Indian Policy, 1865–1887." Ph.D. diss., University of Nebraska, 1962.

Wanken, Helen. "Woman's Sphere and Indian Reform: The Women's National Indian Association, 1879–1901." Ph.D. diss., Marquette University, 1981.

Warrior, Robert A. *The People and the Word: Reading Native Nonfiction.* Minneapolis: University of Minnesota Press, 2005.

Washburn, Wilcomb. *The Assault on Indian Tribalism: The General Allotment Law (Dawes Act) of 1887.* New York: Lippincott, 1975.

Webb, Theodore. *Impassioned Brothers: Ministers Resident to France and Paraguay.* Lanham, Md.: University Press of America, 2002.

Welke, Barbara. *Recasting American Liberty: Gender, Race, Law, and the Railroad Revolution, 1865–1920.* New York: Cambridge University Press, 2001.

Welsh, Herbert. *Address of Herbert Welsh, Corresponding Secretary of the Indian Rights Association, Delivered before the Mohonk Indian Conference, October 14th, 1886.* Philadelphia: Indian Rights Association, 1886.

———. *Four Weeks among Some of the Sioux Tribes of Dakota and Nebraska, Together with a Brief Consideration of the Indian Problem.* Germantown, Pa.: Horace F. McMann, 1882.

———. *Friendship that Asks for Pay.* Philadelphia: Indian Rights Association, 1887.

———. *The Indian Problem.* Philadelphia: Indian Rights Association, 1886.

———. *The Indian Rights Association.* Philadelphia: Indian Rights Association, 1884.

———. *A Sketch of the History of Civil Service Reform in England and in the United States.* Philadelphia: Indian Rights Association, 1889.

Welsh, William. *Indian Office: Wrongs Doing and Reforms Needed.* Philadelphia, 1874.

———. *Report of a Visit to the Sioux and Ponka Indians on the Missouri River, Made by William Welsh to the Secretary of the Interior.* Washington, D.C.: Government Printing Office, 1872.

———. *Reports to the Missionary Organizations of the Protestant Episcopal Church, and to the Secretary of the Interior, on Indian Civilization.* Philadelphia: McCalla and Stavely, 1870.

———. *Summing Up of Evidence before a Committee of the House of Representatives, Charged with the Investigation of Misconduct in the Indian Office.* Washington, D.C.: H. Polkinhorn, 1871.

———. *Taopi and His Friends; or, The Indians' Wrongs and Rights.* Philadelphia: Claxton, Remsen & Haffelfinger, 1869.

———, ed. *Journal of the Rev. S. D. Hinman, Missionary of the Santee Sioux Indians and Taopi, by Bishop Whipple.* Philadelphia: McCalla and Stavely, 1869.

West, Richard. *Satire on Stone: The Political Cartoons of Joseph Keppler.* Urbana: University of Illinois Press, 1988.

White, Geoffrey, and Lamont Lindstrom. *Chiefs Today: Traditional Pacific Leadership and the Postcolonial State.* Stanford: Stanford University Press, 1997.

White, Richard. *"It's Your Misfortune and None of My Own": A History of the American West.* Norman: University of Oklahoma Press, 1991.

———. *The Middle Ground: Indians, Empires, and Republics in the Great Lakes Region, 1650–1815.* New York: Cambridge University Press, 1991.

———. *Railroaded: The Transcontinentals and the Making of Modern America.* New York: Norton, 2011.

Whiteley, Peter. *Rethinking Hopi Ethnography.* Washington, D.C.: Smithsonian Institution Press, 1998.

Wiebe, Robert. *The Search for Order, 1877–1920*. New York: Hill and Wang, 1967.

Wiegman, Robyn. *American Anatomies: Theorizing Race and Gender*. Durham: Duke University Press, 1995.

Wilkins, David. *American Indian Sovereignty and the U.S. Supreme Court: The Masking of Justice*. Austin: University of Texas Press, 1997.

———. *Documents of Native American Political Development, 1500s to 1933*. New York: Oxford University Press, 2009.

Wilkins, David, and Tsianina Lomawaima. *Uneven Ground: American Indian Sovereignty and Federal*. Norman: University of Oklahoma Press, 2001.

Wilkins, Thurman. *Cherokee Tragedy: The Ridge Family and the Decimation of a People*. Norman: University of Oklahoma Press, 1986.

Wilkinson, Charles. *American Indians, Time, and the Law: Native Societies in a Modern Constitutional Democracy*. New Haven: Yale University Press, 1987.

Williams, Robert A., Jr. *The American Indian in Western Legal Thought: The Discourse of Conquest*. New York: Oxford University Press, 1990.

———. *Linking Arms Together: American Indian Treaty Visions of Law and Peace, 1600–1800*. New York: Oxford University Press, 1997.

Wilson, Raymond. *Ohiyesa: Charles Eastman, Santee Sioux*. Urbana: University of Illinois Press, 1983.

Wilson, Waziyatawin Angela, and Michael Yellow Bird, eds. *For Indigenous Eyes Only: A Decolonization Handbook*. Santa Fe, N.M.: School of American Research, 2005.

Wolf, Eric. *Envisioning Power: Ideologies of Dominance and Crisis*. Berkeley: University of California Press, 1999.

Wolfe, Patrick. *Settler Colonialism and the Transformation of Anthropology: The Politics and Poetics of an Ethnographic Event*. New York: Cassell, 1999.

Wooster, Robert. *The Military and United States Indian Policy, 1865–1903*. New Haven: Yale University Press, 1988.

———. *Nelson A. Miles and the Twilight of the Frontier Army*. Lincoln: University of Nebraska Press, 1993.

Wunder, John. *"Retained by the People": A History of American Indians and the Bill of Rights*. New York: Oxford University Press, 1994.

Wyckoff, William. *The Developer's Frontier: The Making of the Western New York Landscape*. New Haven: Yale University Press, 1988.

Young, Robert. *Colonial Desire: Hybridity in Theory, Culture, and Race*. New York: Routledge, 1995.

Zanjani, Sarah. *Sarah Winnemucca*. Lincoln: University of Nebraska Press, 2001.

Index

Garrett, Philip, 137

General Allotment Act of 1887. *See* Allotment Act of 1887

General Federation of Women's Clubs, 157

Genesee River Reservation, 32

Genocide, 81, 116

Georgia, 18–19, 33, 39, 41, 171 (n. 16)

Gila River Apache Indians, 81

Gilded Age, 10, 167 (n. 22)

Gillet, Ransom H., 33, 171 (n. 16)

Gorham, Nathaniel, 32

Governor Blacksnake, 32

Grant, Ulysses S., *58*, 95, 99; Indian affairs and, 62, 73–76, *74, 78*, 80, 89, 90–92, 97, 108, 110, 137, 149; investigation into Parker and, 94, 100, 101, 103, 106; Parker and, 1, 3, 57, 58, 59, 62, 67, 81, 89, 90, 180 (n. 6); peace policy and, 11, 59, 61, 112, 120, 180 (n. 6), 183 (n. 76)

Great Depression, 6, 12, 157, 158, 167 (n. 22)

Great Sioux Reservation, 123, 129, 135

Greenback Party, 119, 120, 188 (n. 16)

Gunter, T. M., 146

Hagan, William, 155

Handsome Lake, 32

Harlan, James, 60

Harlan Bill, 60

Harney, William S., 59–60, 68, *68*, 71

Harper's Weekly, *74, 115, 117*, 148

Harring, Sidney, 24

Hauptman, Laurence, 33, 34, 172 (n. 23)

Hayes administration, 115

Heavy Runner, Chief, 79

Henderson, John B., 67

Hideous System, A (IRA), 149

Holland Land Company, 32

Holman, William S., 129

Hooker, Charles, 146

Hoopa Valley Reservation, 24, 77

Houston, H. H., 137

Howard, Oliver O., 56–57

How to Grow Rich (Bland), 119

Indian affairs: agricultural development and, 45, 84, 123, 146, 150, 186–87 (n. 2); Christian "civilizing" and, 90, 95, 96–97, 98, 99, 104, 105, 139, 183 (n. 72), 187 (n. 6), 187–88 (n. 10); Civil War ending and, 20–21, 52–53, 55, 56, 57, 98, 169 (n. 28), 177 (n. 3); criminal law and, 23, 24, 26, 32; genocide and, 81, 116; massacres, 55, 61, 76, 79–80, 107, 149; medicinal traditions, 118; railroads and, 121, 127, 137, 140–41; Reconstruction and, 3, 11, 21, 51–53, 87, 160–61; starvation, 51, 54, 81–82, 84, 94, 102–3, 138; "the vanishing Indian," 14, 28, 168 (n. 4); white businessmen and, 91, 98, 137, 140, 193 (n. 27). *See also* Allotment Act of 1887; Allotment policy; Assimilation; Office of Indian Affairs; Treaties; U.S. colonialism; U.S. Congress; U.S. Indian policy; U.S. Supreme Court

Indian Appropriation Bills: 1862, 60; 1868, 77; 1869, 73, 82, 92; 1870, 82, 101, 105; 1871, 25–26, 84, 87; 1885, 24

Indian citizenship, 89, 115, *115*, 139–40, 150, 192 (n. 9)

Indian Citizenship Act of 1924, 158–59, 196 (n. 6)

Indian New Deal, 12, 159

"Indian problem," 3, 14–15, 125, 140, 182 (n. 53)

Indian Removal Act of 1830, 18, 19

Indian Reorganization Act of 1934, 159

Indian Rights Association (IRA), 17, 129, 192 (n. 14); allotment and, 116, 133, 134, 137, 138, 140, 142, 143, 149–50, 151–53; assimilation and, 113, 114, 116, 122, 137, 138, 139, 156; education and, 137, 138–39, 141; Indian citizenship and, 139–40; lobbying and, 131, 134, 137, 138, 143, 152, 163; media campaign, 138, 141–45, 152, 163, 193 (n. 32), 194 (nn. 34, 44, 46), 195 (n. 57); membership of, 132, 191 (n. 85); National Indian Defense Association (NIDA) and, 12, 124, 126, 128, 131, 133, 134–35, 140–43, 155; reform agenda of, 114, 116, 122, 134–35, 137–45, 147–50, 155, 156, 160, 191 (nn. 1–3), 193 (n. 27). *See also* Bland, Thomas A.; Welsh, Herbert

"Indian Ring," 102, 107, 108

Indian Service. *See* Office of Indian Affairs

Indian's Hope Association, 135

Indian sovereignty, 7, 121, 126, 130, 170 (n. 54), 196 (n. 6); contradictions in, 14–15, 86; defined, 21; Tonawanda Seneca and, 30, 32, 48, 50; U.S. Congress assault

Morris, Robert, 32

Nast, Thomas, *115, 117*
Nation, 107, 110
National Civil Service Reform League
  (NCSRL), 148
National Indian Defense Association
  (NIDA), 124–33, 159, 163, 189 (n. 44);
  allotment and, 113, 114, 116, 126–27,
  130–31, 132–33, 142, 143–44, 146,
  151–54; education and, 127, 132, 139;
  founding of, 113, 124–25; Indian members
  of, 130–32; Indian Rights Association
  (IRA) and, 12, 124, 126, 128, 131, 133,
  134–35, 140–43, 155; reform arguments,
  12, 113, 114, 123, 125–26, 139, 145–47,
  155, 161
Native American tribal groups: Apache, 81,
  82, 107; Arapaho, 55, 68, *68*, 82; Bannock,
  68; Brule, 61; Caddo, 142; Cayuga, 48;
  Cheyenne, 55, 61, 68; Chickasaw, 20,
  61, 63, 126; Choctaw, 20, 33, 61, 63, 89,
  126; Comanche, 68, 131; Creek, 16, 20,
  126, 131; Crow, 68; Dakota, 54–55, 141;
  Delaware, 16, 27, 33, 126–27; Iroquois, 13,
  14, 30–34, 37, 39, 171 (n. 4); Kiowa, 27, 68,
  131, 142; Klamath, 112, 120, 121; Lakota,
  59–60, 61, 68, 122, 123, 124, 128–29, 130;
  Modoc, 112, 120, 121, 188 (n. 24); Navajo,
  68, 81; Osage, 17; Paiute, 144; Papago,
  107; Peoria, 131; Piankeshaw, 18; Piegan
  Indians, 79–80; Ponca, 121, 143; Pueblo,
  157; Quapaw, 133; Seminole, 83, 126;
  Shawnee, 27, 31; Shoshone, 68; Sioux, 24,
  54, 55, 123, 128, 130, 135; Wyandot, 27, 85.
  See also Cherokee Nation; Seneca Indians;
  Tonawanda Seneca
Navajo Indians, 68, 81
Nebraska, 61, 105, 135
New Government Party, 46, 48
New Mexico, 81, 157
New York Constitution of 1821, 35, 39, 44
New York Herald, 100
New York Post, 144
New York State, 3, 116, 187 (n. 6); after
  American Revolution, 31–32; reservations
  of, 32–33, 45–49, 171 (n. 10); Seneca
  Indian treaty ceding land in, 32–33, 171
  (n. 13); tenant farmers of, 41–43, 174

(n. 59); "the vanishing Indian" of, 13–14,
  28, 168 (n. 4); Tonawanda Seneca and, 1,
  23, 29–30, 35, 39–44, 45–50, 57, 157
New York Sun, 144
New York Times, 55–56, 103
New York Tribune, 56, 142
Nicholas, Mark A., 45
North Pacific Railroad, 97

Office of Indian Affairs (OIA): allotment and,
  108–9, 111, 131, 134, 152–53, 187 (n. 6);
  Board of Indian Commissioners (BIC)
  and, 73, 75, 92, 99, 108, 131, 132, 149; civil
  service reform and, 116, 129, 147–49, 195
  (nn. 56, 62); Civil War and, 52–53, 55,
  56, 58, 177 (n. 3); Commissioner Parker's
  bureaucratic reforms in, 9, 72, 76–79, 80,
  90–93, 108–9, 111; Commissioner Parker's
  Indian policy reforms in, 3–5, 8–9, 30,
  72, 75, 81–83, 88, 89–90, 94, 95, 98, 110,
  161–62; Commissioner Parker's removal
  from, 100–107, 184 (n. 20), 185 (n. 34),
  186 (n. 59); corruption in, 63, 64, 75, 76,
  78, 82, 90, 97, 99, 100, 134, 147, 149, 177
  (n. 3); development of, 10, 153, 156–57,
  167 (n. 21), 175 (n. 77); in late nineteenth
  century, 10, 116, 129, 144–45, 153, 155,
  163; Okmulgee Council and, 89, 99–100;
  oversight of, 63, 90–93, 108–9, 182–83
  (n. 70), 183 (n. 72); peace commissions,
  1860s, 52, 59–66, 67–72, 80–81, 178 (n. 41);
  possible transfer to War Department and,
  63, 65–67, 71–72, 78–79, 80, 108, 121, 162,
  180 (n. 7); starving Indians and, 81–82,
  102–3; Tonawanda Seneca and, 34–35, 45;
  treaties and, 20, 80, 84–90
Ogden, David, 32
Ogden, Thomas L., 32, 33
Ogden Land Company: resolving treaty
  dispute with Tonawanda Seneca, 44, 45, 49,
  57; Seneca Indian treaties ceding land and,
  32–38, 40–41, 42–44, 52, 172–73 (n. 33),
  173 (n. 45), 174–75 (n. 64); Tonawanda
  Seneca and, 9, 10–11, 29–30, 156, 161, 162
Oglala Lakota Indians, 61, 122, 123, 124, 130
Oil Spring Reservation, 33
Okmulgee Council, 89, 99–100
Old Chiefs Party, 46, 48
Old Winnebago Reservation, 140

Oman, Henry, Jr., 77
Oregon, 53, 112, 120
Orren, Karen, 6
Osage Nation, 17
Ostler, Jeffrey, 122, 123

Paine, N. E., 43
Painter, C. C., 131, 132, 137–38, 141, 143, 144, 149–50, 152, 155
Paiute Indians, 144
Pancoast, Henry, 135, 137, 139, 192 (n. 9)
Panic of 1837, 34, 42
Papago Indians, 107
Parker, Arthur C., 38
Parker, Elizabeth, 13, 28, 167–68 (n. 1)
Parker, Ely S., 4, 28; allotment and, 89, 158; appointment as Commissioner of Indian Affairs, 73, 75, 179 (n. 4); assimilation and, 3–4, 52, 65, 70–71, 97, 112, 161–62; charges of corruption against, 82, 94, 95, 97, 100–107, 149; Civil War service and, 1, 3, 20, 52, 57–58, 165 (n. 1), 178 (n. 27); early life, 13–14, 83, 167–68 (n. 1); peace commissions, 1860s, 56, 59–72, 76, 93, 94, 178 (n. 41), 181 (n. 25); reforms developed during early Reconstruction, 51–53, 58–72, 80–81, 83, 125, 159, 160–61; Tonawanda Seneca governance and, 44–50, 52, 57; Tonawanda Seneca resistance and New York allies, 39–41, 44, 173–74 (n. 49); Tonawanda Seneca resistance campaign and, 11, 29–30, 34–36, 37–41, 52, 59, 156, 157, 162, 167 (n. 18), 172 (n. 23), 173 (nn. 38–45); treaties and, 3, 17, 51–52, 64, 72, 80, 84–90, 161–62, 182 (n. 53). *See also* Board of Indian Commissioners; Grant, Ulysses S.; Office of Indian Affairs; U.S. Department of the Interior
Parker, Newton, 29
Parker, Nicholson, 36, 37
Parker, William, 38, 45, 46
Patents in fee, 126, 128, 132, 157
Peabody, Elizabeth P., 144
Peace commissions of 1860s, 9, 56, 59–72, 73, 76, 80–81, 93, 94, 120, 178 (n. 41), 180 (n. 6); Peace Commission of 1867, 61–63, 84, 178 (n. 30), 181 (n. 25); Peace Commission of 1868, 52, 61–62, 67–72, 68, 70, 82, 84, 181 (n. 25). *See also* Fort

Philip Kearney; Fort Smith
Pendleton Act of 1883, 147, 195 (n. 56)
People's Party Shot and Shell (Bland), 120
Peoria Indians, 131
Phelps, Oliver, 32
Piankeshaw Nation, 18
Pickering, Timothy, 31
Piegan Indians, 79–80
Pierce, Franklin, 43
Pine Ridge Reservation, 122, 123–24, 129, 142
Pitchlynn, Peter, 89
Plea for the Indians, A (Beeson), 53
Plenary power, 22, 23, 48, 154
Plumb, Preston, 151
Polk, James K., 23, 26, 41
Ponca Nation, 121, 143
Pope, John, 54
Populist Party, 120
Porter, Pleasant, 131
Postcolonial thought, 6, 7
Potawatomi Nation, 17, 27
Pratt, Richard Henry, 117, 141, 193 (n. 32)
Problem of Indian Administration, The, 156–57
Progressive Era, 10, 150, 167 (n. 22)
Prucha, Francis, 55, 75–76, 155, 158
Pueblo Indians, 157

Quakers, 59, 90, 91, 137, 141; Office of Indian Affairs (OIA) and, 76, 77, 79; Seneca Indians and, 32, 33–34, 46, 48
Quapaw Indians, 133
Quick Bear, 123

Racism, 104, 106, 185 (n. 44), 193 (n. 27)
Railroads, 97, 119, 120, 121, 127, 137, 140–41
Rand, Jacki, 7, 27
Reconstruction, 97, 163; early idealism of, 1–2, 10, 56–57, 75, 98–99, 110; education and, 82–83; federal government expansion during, 8, 57, 98, 167 (n. 17); Indian affairs and, 3, 11, 21, 51–53, 87, 160–61; Parker's reforms developed during, 51–53, 58–72, 80–81, 83, 125, 159, 160–61; U.S. War Department and, 66–67
Red Cloud, Chief, 122, 123, 124, 129, 130, 142
Red Cloud agency, 108